STAND IN FAITH

GILGAL DEVOTIONALS

Nathalie Nérée, Ph.D.

BALBOA
PRESS
A DIVISION OF HAY HOUSE

Copyright © 2016 Nathalie Nérée, Ph.D.

All rights reserved. No part of this book may be used or reproduced by any means, graphic, electronic, or mechanical, including photocopying, recording, taping or by any information storage retrieval system without the written permission of the author except in the case of brief quotations embodied in critical articles and reviews.

Scripture quotations marked NLT are taken from the Holy Bible, New Living Translation, copyright © 1996, 2004, 2007. Used by permission of Tyndale House Publishers, Inc. Carol Stream, Illinois 60188. All rights reserved.

Balboa Press books may be ordered through booksellers or by contacting:

Balboa Press
A Division of Hay House
1663 Liberty Drive
Bloomington, IN 47403
www.balboapress.com
1 (877) 407-4847

Because of the dynamic nature of the Internet, any web addresses or links contained in this book may have changed since publication and may no longer be valid. The views expressed in this work are solely those of the author and do not necessarily reflect the views of the publisher, and the publisher hereby disclaims any responsibility for them.

The author of this book does not dispense medical advice or prescribe the use of any technique as a form of treatment for physical, emotional, or medical problems without the advice of a physician, either directly or indirectly. The intent of the author is only to offer information of a general nature to help you in your quest for emotional and spiritual well-being. In the event you use any of the information in this book for yourself, which is your constitutional right, the author and the publisher assume no responsibility for your actions.

Any people depicted in stock imagery provided by Thinkstock are models, and such images are being used for illustrative purposes only.
Certain stock imagery © Thinkstock.

Print information available on the last page.

ISBN: 978-1-5043-6217-7 (sc)
ISBN: 978-1-5043-6218-4 (hc)
ISBN: 978-1-5043-6239-9 (e)

Library of Congress Control Number: 2016911343

Balboa Press rev. date: 08/05/2016

Pour toi, Papi, je t'aime.

INTRODUCTION

What started off as a small fellowship of seven women has grown into this book. In the fall of 2012, a girlfriend of mine contacted me wanting to do a forty-day abundance program that included positive affirmations. We, along with five other friends, started exchanging daily emails. After completing the abundance program, I suggested we continued our fellowship by reading *The Purpose Driven Life*. We spent forty days savoring Rick Warren's teachings. That led to my next suggestion of sharing daily entries from Mark Nepo's *The Book of Awakening*. The journey went on well into the summer of 2013. After several books and many forty-day journeys, the emails became a burden. Life got in the way, my girlfriend was planning her wedding, and I was too scared to lead the fellowship alone.

So time passed. The more time passed, the more the absence of daily encouragement pressed on my soul. I needed to write daily as my means of comfort, writing kept me sane and empowered me; writing was my means of seeking God. The fear of putting myself out there kept me from writing. What if I ran out of books to read? What if I changed and no longer believed the things I wrote? What if my new age beliefs changed to old doctrines? Thoughts of uncertainty and fear fluttered my mind. So the days went on and my soul continued to cry out for expression, for truth and for encouragement.

I can remember it clearly, February 2014, I prayed and asked God for a sign. I needed a sign to know whether I should make the commitment to write daily devotionals and lead the fellowship alone. The fear quickly crept in. What if I run out of things to write? What if no one reads my emails? What if I make a fool of myself? What if I just can't keep up? How long was I going to be able to write daily? The fear rushed in. I kept praying for a sign. "A sign, God! Just give me a sign!" Within the next seven days, I received four emails from four different individuals telling me how much they missed reading my daily messages. One friend begged for me to resume writing and said her days were so much better when she read my emails. The sign was clear. It was time to write again.

But what book would I select? If I was going to do this daily I needed a solid book, it couldn't be one I was into today and rejected tomorrow. I sought advice from my dad; he suggested the Bible, specifically the New Testament. Again, fear crept in. What if I insulted someone? What about the summer I spent training with Dr. Brian Weiss, shouldn't I write about that experience?

Should I select his book, *Many Lives, Many Masters*, which radically changed me? What about his influence on my spiritual growth? Would he and his wife, Carole Weiss, my Omega Mom, welcome my writing? Their teaching and guidance had been pivotal in my spiritual growth. Would I gain their approval? Confusion quickly settled and fear paralyzed me. I continued to pray, this time praying about which book to select. I prayed and prayed, but nothing came to mind except my dad's suggestion. So, I settled for the Bible.

In April 2014, I embarked on the Gilgal Devotionals journey. I would love to say that I was writing the emails to serve my friends and family, but the truth is I was writing them to serve myself. I wrote them to hold myself accountable for being in the Word daily. I wrote words that I needed to read. I wrote messages that I needed to hear and I wrote about God's love and grace to convince myself. In the process I encouraged and brought hope to others. Every day I woke up in the early hours of the day to read and write. The first months I was paralyzed by fear on a daily basis. I was afraid of running out of things to write. I was afraid of not interpreting the Word correctly. I was afraid of others' opinions and feared they would think I was a fluke. Thankfully, I made one commitment to myself and that was to be authentic and real, so everyday I woke up, pushed through the fear, and wrote about those things I needed to read. When I was going through times of uncertainty, I wrote about His plans for my life; when I was going through times of loss and regret, I sought His Word in regards to repentance and forgiveness; when I felt alone, I wrote about Him always being with me; when I was in a financial bind, I wrote about Him being my provider; when I was scared, I wrote about how He didn't give me a spirit of fear, but of power, love, and self control. I wrote about whatever I was going through, and somehow others were able relate. And what started as a small circle of individuals receiving my daily emails grew into hundreds and has now evolved into this collection.

So, why the name "Gilgal Devotionals"?

While I was growing up, my grandfather had a small vacation home in the mountains of Haiti, at the entrance hung a decal engraved "Gilgal." The word stayed with me. Over twenty years later, in the midst of finding myself, my voice, and my path, "Gilgal" resurfaced in my life. Through TD Jakes's teachings, I learned the meaning of Gilgal and suddenly understood my grandfather so much better. I understood why my grandfather turned to Gilgal for rest and rejuvenation, for stillness and strength.

Today, through Gilgal Devotionals, I continue to do the work of my grandfather, Baptist Pastor Luc R. Nérée, who was a student of the Word, a teacher of the gospel, and the Lord's faithful servant. My grandfather made it his life's work to educate and serve and did so through his humanitarian work and his weekly evangelical writings and radio programs.

Gilgal Devotionals have provided a platform for me to serve others with my most precious gift of written words. I pray that through the entries of this book you may find the hope you need to push through, and I pray that the words may strengthen your faith and remind you of God's unconditional love for you. Lastly, I pray that you too may *Stand in Faith* everyday of your life!

Love,

Nathalie

Stand in Faith
Gilgal Devotionals

KINGDOM

"... Seek first His kingdom and His righteousness, and all these things will be added to you." Matthew 6:33

Today, rather than chanting your needs to God, seek first His kingdom! Your heavenly Father already knows all your needs (Matthew 6:31) and as you seek Him, all your needs will be met. That's a promise!

The Greek word for "seek" has many translations, including "to worship," "to want," "to endeavor," "to pursue," and "to require." In simple language, to seek the kingdom of Heaven is to be concerned about and all about the kingdom. Could it be that instead of seeking that which you want, you should seek God? Could it be that rather than chasing dreams, you should chase God?

Instead of running after the man, chasing more money, seeking more connections, looking for more hookups, is it possible that all those things will come to you if you seek the Kingdom first? Even better, when you seek God first, He blesses you with no strings attached! (Proverbs 10:22) When you seek God first, the blessings will come chasing you!

Seeking the Kingdom means to view everything through your spiritual lenses. Seeking the Kingdom requires your highest thought, your complete focus on something much bigger than you. Seeking the Kingdom means to focus on spirit rather than flesh, on spiritual wealth rather than earthly goods, on love rather than anger, on peace rather than division.

God promises that as you seek Him, His Kingdom, and His righteousness, you will find your heart's deepest desires. So today, stop seeking your heart's desires at His expense, instead, seek Him. Don't settle for less than the Kingdom. Don't settle for dust when you can have a kingdom that is unshakeable. As you seek and find the Kingdom, you will be "like a tree planted by streams of water, which yields its fruit in season and whose leave does not wither, whatever you do will prosper." (Psalm 1:3)

Seek His Kingdom and prosper!

My Prayer for You Today:
Father, with a pure heart today we seek you. Lord, be in all the details of our lives. We need you. Father, thank you for the realization that the world can't fill us, only you can. Today we seek more of you. Be with us. We love you and praise you. Amen.

FAITH

"Faith…the evidence of things not seen." Hebrews 11:1

Farmers are the best examples of faith-people. They bury and plant seeds and wait faithfully and expectantly to reap their crops. Today, let us be like farmers as we bury and plant our hopes and dreams in God and wait faithfully and expectantly, knowing that they will come to pass.

God takes us from faith to faith as we grow spiritually. Looking back at your life, you can identify situations when you believed God for the unseen. He took you from faith for getting through school to faith for landing your first job. He took you from faith for a spouse to faith for saving your marriage. He took you from faith for losing weight to faith for healing the lump in your breast. Over and over, God has taken you from faith to faith.

Today is no different. Have faith! Have confidence in things not seen. Your faith is not in the situation, but rather in your God who has shown you His loyalty. He is the same yesterday, today, and forever. (Hebrews 13:8) He was faithful before and He will continue to be faithful.

Today, call those things that are not as though they are! (Romans 4:17) Call yourself the boss; call yourself a mother, a wife, an attorney, a doctor, a writer, a chef, a survivor, an actor, a retiree. Whatever dream you decide to bury in Him, call yourself it as though you are! He is faithful and has already declared you victorious.

My Prayer for You Today:
Father, you said that if we have faith as small as a mustard seed we could move mountains. Today we thank you for taking us from faith to faith as you grow us spiritually. Thank you for the journey, which has not been easy, though your love has made it worthy. Today, Lord, we call those things that are not as though they are in Jesus's name, knowing that you have already answered. We love you and praise you. Amen.

THANK AND PRAY

"I do not cease to give thanks for you, making mention of you in my prayers." Ephesians 1:16

In His letters to the gentiles, the Apostle Paul wrote about the importance of giving thanks and praying for one another. We are in this together! We need to pray for one another!

You have so much to be thankful for. Today thank Him. Thank Him for your journey. Thank Him for everything you have been through that shaped you into who you are, thank Him for always providing and protecting, always loving and forgiving, always giving and saving.

Beyond thanking Him for His goodness and grace, thank Him for the people in your life today. Say a prayer for a random someone: the lady in front of you at the Starbucks line, the clerk at the movie theatre, the people of your city, your neighbor. We are all journeying through life and we all need prayers. Let us pray for one another.

Today, give thanks and mention someone in your prayers. Pray that God covers that person with His love and His grace. Pray that God fulfills His purpose in their life and that He uses them to bless others.

Give thanks and pray!

My Prayer for You Today:
Lord, today we pray for those battling a tougher journey than us. We pray for the people in our cities. We pray for the oppressed and abused. Lord, let your presence be known in their lives. Father, we thank you that you are always in control, that in the midst of chaos and confusion, there you are; in the midst of joy and happiness, there you are. We surrender all to you and find peace in knowing that your love never ends. We praise you and love you. Amen.

HAVE YOUR BEING IN HIM

"In God I move and breathe and have my being." Acts 17:28

Today may you be filled with Him and be in awe of His greatness!

My hope for you today is that wherever you are right now, you may be aware of His presence in you. May you take a deep breath and realize that He is always with you and that though the world may seem out of control, you are safely wrapped in His love and grace.

Today may you breathe a little easier, smile a little wider, sing a little louder, dance a little harder, and rest a little deeper knowing that God is in control. Wherever you are, there He is. Whatever you do, God is there with you. Relax. Breathe. Smile.

In case you forget: God lives in you. Move, breathe and have your being in Him!

My Prayer for You Today:
Father, we surrender our day to you. Let everything we do be done in you and through you. We pray for our neighbors who are being abused and mistreated. Do something, Father. We surrender this world to you. So many things do not make sense to us, but we trust that you are a God who restores and saves. Do something! We surrender all in Jesus's precious and holy name. Amen.

GRATITUDE

"A live dog is better off than a dead lion." Ecclesiastes 9:4

Today, be grateful for what you have!

You may not have the job of your dream, but you have a job! You may not be at your ideal weight, but you can work towards it. You may not have the perfect spouse, but you have a companion. Be grateful. Your kids may be unruly, but you have kids. Your mother may get on your nerves, but be thankful she is around to annoy you. Rather than focusing on what you do not have, spend time thanking God for what you do have.

God wants you to be grateful. As you learn to appreciate and take care of what you have, He will bless you with more, He will enlarge your territory, (1 Chronicles 4:10) He will give you blessings you will not have enough room to store. (Malachi 3:10) But before any of this can happen, you must develop an attitude of gratitude.

Today, wherever you are, with whomever, doing whatever, take a minute to thank God for bringing you this far. Thank Him for the journey. Thank Him for providing. Thank Him for blessing you with exactly what you needed: the exact pain you needed to grow, the exact friends and dysfunctional family you needed to mature, the exact amount of challenges, the perfect amount of success to continue to seek Him. Thank Him for always giving exactly what you needed.

Be grateful for everything!

My Prayer for You Today:
Father today we want to thank you for everything, for every smile and every tear, for every blessing in disguise, for every heartache and every mountain, we want to thank you for being with us every step of the way, thank you for disguising your love as helpful friends and supportive family members. Thank you for growing us spiritually in order for us to be dependent on you. Today we stand on your blessings and thank you from the bottom of our hearts. We love you and praise you. Amen.

WORRIES AND CARES

"Give all your worries and cares to God, for he cares about you." 1 Peter 5:7

God cares about you and will take on your burdens. Give them all to Him!

When you try solving your own problems, you worry and stress because your vision and plans are limited. God never intended for you to go through life alone. You are too small and too limited. You need to rely on Him, whose grandeur is inexplicable, whose ways are bigger than your ways, whose thoughts are higher than your thoughts (Isaiah 55:8) and whose strength is made perfect in weakness. (2 Corinthians 9:12)

Today, whether you are worried about cash or health, children or parents, family or work, cast all your worries on Him. He can take care of it all while you rest in His peace. Jesus was the perfect example of sleeping through storms. Winds and waves didn't disturb His rest—He slept amidst a storm. Similarly, today find rest amidst your heartaches; cast all your worries on Him knowing that with one word He can calm any storm.

God loves you and cares about you. Stop worrying. Stop contemplating. Stop overthinking. Everything will be just fine. You have a savior who sleeps through storms, who walks on water, and who loves you beyond words. Relax. Enjoy your day and rest in His everlasting love.

My Prayer for You Today:
Father, you continue to amaze us. Your inexplicable love and unimaginable grace bring so much peace to us. Lord, today we cast all our worries to you—our families, our health, careers, finances, dreams, frustrations—everything is at your altar. Fill us with your peace. We thank you for your love. We praise you for your greatness. We pray all this in Jesus's precious and holy name. Amen.

FRIENDS

"As iron sharpens iron, so one man sharpens another." Proverbs 27:18

Your intimate circle influences your spiritual life.

If your friends do not sharpen you, get new friends! You become like those who surround you. You are called to love and accept all, not to hang out and be intimate with all. Choose your inner circle wisely.

God values relationships. "It is not good for man to be alone." (Genesis 2:18) God wants you to experience life in fellowship and community. Yet you need to be cautious about who influences your life. "Bad company ruins good morals;" (1 Corinthians 15:33) "make no friendship with a man given to anger, or go with a hot-tempered man." (Proverbs 22:24)

Today, choose your friends wisely. Surround yourself with those who love and celebrate you; spend time with those who sharpen and encourage you; invest in those who build and support you; walk with those who are on the same spiritual journey as you; laugh with those who value your smile; love those who ignite the spirit of God in you!

My Prayer for You Today:
Father, today we thank you for friends who have grown into family. We thank you for surrounding us with God-loving people. We thank you for loving us through our friends. Today we ask for extra blessings upon our friends, we ask for extra miracles and extra healing. We pray that as you bless us with amazing friends, we in turn can be faithful and loving friends to others. We praise you and love you. Amen.

FINAL SAY

"Make your motions and cast your votes, but God has the final say."
Proverbs 16:33

God has the final say! He alone has the final say!

It is not what your friends say, not what your parents say, not what society says, it is what God says! It does not matter what the situation looks like, it does not matter who lied or betrayed you, God has the final say.

Today, do not shed another tear over what others say, trust God and His promises for your life. Don't waste another breath on proving your point. You may lose friends, but do not lose sleep. He alone has the final say.

You are exactly where you should be; your intentions are good, your spirit is well, you are loved by and important to so many, and most importantly you are loved by and important to God. God has the final say in every area of your life and His say is always positive, it always brings peace and joy, it always mends and heals, it always loves and soothes, it always prevails.

Relax, God has the final say!

My Prayer for You Today:
Father, thank you that you have the final say. Thank you that you always have the perfect plan for our lives. Today we cast all our worries on you and we trust you to take care of us like you have always done. We surrender all to you and praise you for continuous blessings. Thank you that your final say places us above and not below, thank you that your final say declares us the head and not the tail. We thank you and love you. Amen.

TODAY

"If you wait for the perfect conditions, you will never get anything done."
Ecclesiastes 11:4

Today is the day! Whatever you have been putting off, get it done today!

Stop saying, "When I win the lottery I will donate to charity," give what you can today. You won't be any happier with a new job, new house, new car, or new spouse—if you are miserable now, you will be miserable then. Your happiness is directly related to your relationship with God!

"This is the day the Lord has made…" (Psalm 118:24) Today is the day to do what you have been putting off. Stop waiting for the perfect conditions; take action now! "Do not despise small beginnings." (Zechariah 4:10) Do what you can today. Save one dollar, write one sentence, read one page, do five sit ups, eat one less spoonful, breathe one deep breath, say one less word, give one extra hug.

God has never called the qualified; do not wait to be rich, to be healthy, to be happy, to be strong, to be tall, to be old, to be spiritual, to be anything. God will qualify you through the journey! Do it now. Do it today! Trust God to take you from step to step, from amateur to expert, from bottom to top, from tail to head, from doubt to faith.

Take a leap of faith now!

My Prayer for You Today:
Father, forgive us for always wanting perfect conditions. Lord, we know that your time is perfect and your ways are perfect. Fill us with courage, strength, and faith to take the first step in your name. We lift up our dreams and aspirations to you. We lift our hearts to you. Guide us, Lord. Be with us, Jesus. We praise you and love you. Amen.

ABOVE

"Set your minds on things above." Colossians 3:2

How different would your life be if you set your mind on things above?

Instead of fretting over traffic, use that time to pray; instead of being impatient with your kids, be grateful for their presence; instead of complaining about what you do not have, notice God's hand as always being your lending hand. Look for God in the mundane and everyday; set your mind on things above. Set your mind on God.

Today, set your mind on things above! Look at the bright side of things. Look at the God side of things. Dream big. Have hope. Smile. Laugh. Encourage people. Send a love text. Send an email to wish an old friend a great week. Buy lunch for your coworker. Call your mother.

As you set your mind on things above, you will be amazed at how you will experience His love.

Be blessed!

My Prayer for You Today:
Father, today we choose to set our minds on you. We choose to experience your love and your grace as we encourage and love others. We surrender our week to you. Show yourself to us this week. Be with us as we move, breathe, and have our being in you. We pray all this in Jesus's holy name. Amen.

SMILE AND FAVOR

"They did not conquer by their own strength and skill, but by your might power and because you smiled upon them and favored them." Psalm 44:3

God smiles at you and favors you!

Take a few minutes to let it soak in: God, your God, your Creator, smiles at you and favors you! He thinks the world of you. As you move through your day and do the silly quirks that only you do, as you laugh at yourself and hang out with your friends and family, He is looking at you and smiling. He is so proud of you.

Friend, you are a conqueror because His love and favor are upon you. You are a beautiful soul, because He lives in you. God delights in you!

Today, do not try to do or be anything. He loves you as you are. He has been with you through your journey and smiles at how far you have come. He has seen the loving person you are becoming, He knows how much you have grown spiritually and how you seek to better yourself. He knows your heart and your good intentions. All those things make Him smile. God is so proud of you!

Smile, He is smiling at you right now!

My Prayer for You Today:
Father, we are so humbled by your favor and love. Thank you, Lord, that you smile upon us. Thank you that our individual quirks and ways are blessings from you. Today we just want to take a moment to praise you and thank you for your love. We are in awe of your grace and are amazed by your unconditional love. We thank you and love you. Amen

OBLIGATION TO LOVE

"Owe nothing to anyone—except for your obligation to love one another." Romans 13:8

You are obligated to love people!

In the days of controversies: debates over same-sex marriages, transgenders, abortions, terrorists, Republicans, Democrats, riots, police brutality, etc… we still have an obligation to love one another. Unfortunately, our disagreements have often led to the belief that it's okay to hate and belittle, to deny and abuse, to curse and crucify.

Today, whether you stand on the right or the left, you have an obligation to love. Whether you agree with someone's opinion or not, you have an obligation to love. So, in the midst of your disagreements and despite your harsh critiques, you are called to love others.

"God so loved the world that He gave…" (John 3:16) So today, love the world enough to give them space for their opinions despite your disagreement, give your neighbor space to live without your brutality, give yourself, your love, your time, your resources, despite the recipient's opinion. Love, it is your obligation!

My Prayer for You Today:
Lord, we surrender our homes, our cities, our country, our world to you. Lord, you know the mean and cruel things happening and we believe that you can change them. Today, Father, we stand only on your word, we stand solely on your love. Give us the courage to love those who are different than us and to serve those we despise. Father, thank you for your love which inspires us to love. We surrender all to you and take our obligation seriously today in Jesus's name. Amen.

TRUST

"For I know the one in whom I trust." 2 Timothy 1:12

Life's troubles have a way of blinding us. When faced with challenges, we tend to panic and quickly forget God and His magnitude. We start to believe the lies—the reports, the statistics, the trends—while forgetting that the One whom we serve needs no report. He follows no trend and is not limited by human resources. Life's giants do not intimidate or scare Him. Today, let us remember the One in whom we trust: the Giant of giants, the God of gods, the Alpha and Omega, the Creator of Heaven and Earth.

You are a child of God. Trust Him. Trust in the One who sleeps through storms, the same One who with one word can hush the wind, the One who walks on water and can turn water to wine, the One whose name can move mountains, whose blood can change history, the One who "even the wind and the waves obey." (Matthew 8:27)

Today, don't trust the chaos, don't trust the trends, trust Him! Speak to the giants in your life and let them know who is in charge. Your God is in charge! He can change any situation suddenly; He can heal anything surely. Trust Him. Don't get distracted by the storms of life—keep your eyes on the One who can calm any storm.

My Prayer for You Today:
Lord, we trust in you. Today we choose to keep our eyes on you despite our scary situations. We trust in your love, we believe in your power, and we know that with one word you can calm any storm. Father, speak today! Speak a word into our lives and let your peace fill us. We trust you and love you. Amen.

RELAX

"I do not give like the world gives." John 14:27

Breathe; what God has for you is for you!

God doesn't give like the world gives. He doesn't praise you one day and crucify you the next. He would not give you the land and take it back. He does not give scarcely. God is abundant and will bless you according to His riches and His abundance. (Philippians 4:19)

God wants you to know that you can enjoy the ride. Stop worrying about losing, stop playing the negative "what-ifs" in your head. God is your supplier and He gives abundantly. He will continue to provide. He will grant your heart's deepest desires and will bless you with better than you can imagine. He will not tease you with your dreams and take them away. He loves you too much for that. He will not give you more than you can handle; He knows exactly what you want and want you need. Trust Him.

Today, "Do not let your hearts be troubled and do not be afraid." (John 14:27) You are exactly where you should be. Trust Him. Your wildest dreams, your deepest desires are all yours and He will not take them from you. Rest in His love. Enjoy the journey. Breathe. Smile. Relax.

My Prayer for You Today:
Father, thank you that you give abundantly and according to your riches. Help us today to relax, to breathe, and to enjoy the journey as you continue to bless us. Lord, take away all fears of loss and help us to find rest in the certainty of your love. We love you and pray all this in Jesus's name. Amen.

VICTORY

"You have already won the victory…because He who is in you is greater than he who is in the world." 1 John 4:4

With God in you, the victory is yours!

Do not doubt in the dark what God has shown you clearly in the light. Situation after situation He has shown you His faithfulness; time after time His love has been evident to you; years after years He has revealed His great plans for you, and nothing has changed now. Trust Him!

"God is greater and He knows everything." (1 John 3:20) Your victory has already been declared. You cannot fail. Trust Him. Today, in the midst of your heaviness, in the middle of your uncertainty, among your worries and fears, anchor yourself to the One who has shown you over and over that He is with you and will never leave you. As you focus on Him, He will direct your path. Relax, breathe, and trust Him!

He who is in you is greater than he who is in the world! Your situation, your worries, your heartaches are miniscule compared to His magnitude. He knows the beginning and the end. He has already declared you victorious.

My Prayer for You Today:
Father, soothe our hearts. You know our worries, our uncertainties and our troubles. Take over, Lord. Today we take your yoke and find rest in you. We thank you that you are bigger than anything we are facing, thank you that you have already declared our victory. Be with us today as we walk in faith and in trust in Jesus's name. Amen.

DO GOOD

"Trust in the Lord and do good." Psalm 37:3

Trust Him and do good!

Whether you're praying for rain or for sunshine, trust Him and His timing. Continue to do your best and leave everything else in His hands. You are at the edge of your breakthrough—do not give up now. Trust Him and He will give you the desires of your heart.

God's timing is perfect. It is not always our timing, but it is the best timing. You can trust Him. He has taken you this far. He knows your deepest desires and you must trust Him to bring them to pass. Trust Him, He has your best interest at heart and He delights in you.

Today, trust Him and do good. Smile. Be good. See the good in others. Do not let your heart be troubled. Enjoy your day. Laugh. Relax. He is in control and will bless you with the desires of your heart.

My Prayer for You Today:
Father, today we trust you. Help us to keep our eyes on you as we wait expectantly. Lord, fill us with courage to do good. We trust your timing and trust your love. Thank you that you have already answered. We praise you for your greatness. Be with us today. We pray all this in Jesus's name. Amen.

FAITH

"Make every effort to add to your faith." 2 Peter 1:5

Your faith is your responsibility!

So many times in the Bible, we read stories of Jesus performing miracles based on an individual's faith; the paralytic, the woman who bled for 12 years, the blind man who gained his sight—those miracles were results of their individual faith. Jesus said on different occasions "your faith has saved you," (Luke 7:50) "your faith has healed you," (Matthew 9:22) "your faith has made you well," (Luke 17:19) and when he healed the paralytic, the Bible said "[Jesus] seeing their faith…"(Mark 2:5) performed the miracle.

Could it be that your lack of faith is holding back your miracle? You cannot keep praying about it and speaking doubt. You can't believe God for a healing but talk about the lack of cure for your condition. You can't pray for provision and continue to talk about never getting out of debt. Seeing is not believing, believing is seeing!

Today, make every effort to add to your faith. Convince yourself that His Word about you is the truth. Keep repeating His Word until you believe it. When a negative thought arises, shut it out with His promises. Say scriptures out loud. Remember and think about all the times He showed up in your life. Think about the miracles He's performed for others. If He answered prayers before, He will answer again. He doesn't change. Believe in Him. Trust His Word. He is faithful. He is a God who delivers, who answers prayers and who has you in the palms of His hands!

Have faith!

My Prayer for You Today:
Father, today we build our faith based on who you are and on your Word. Lord, help us, take captive every thought and make it obedient to Christ. Today we choose to build our faith, waiting expectantly on your promises. We trust you. We are so grateful for your love and loyalty to us. You are so amazing. We love you and praise you in Jesus's name. Amen.

WORDS

"Let everything you say be good and helpful, so that your words will be an encouragement to those who hear them." Ephesians 4:29

Your words have power; use them to build and to encourage!

If you are a God-person, a Christian, a Jesus-person, a spiritual person, a loving person, whatever you want to call it, you cannot and should not use your tongue loosely. You have a responsibility to choose your words intentionally. If you are a God-person you do not get to curse others, to hold grudges, to diminish and gossip, to be nasty and mean; you do not have the freedom to use words to cut others down.

Use your words to encourage and love. The Bible tells us that "death and life are in the power of the tongue" (Proverbs 18:21) and that "by your words you will be acquitted, and by your words you will be condemned." (Matthew 12:37) Words have power! Use them carefully.

Today, choose your words wisely. Think before you speak! Let everything you say be in accordance with Him who you love and Him who strengthens you. Let your interactions with others leave them better than you found them. Let your words encourage and build, let your words empower and soothe, let your words be in alignment to His Word.

My Prayer for You Today:
Father, take hold of our tongues. Lord, too often we say things we regret and hurt those we love. Forgive us. Take hold of our tongues and let our words be in accordance with your Word. Lord, you know our hearts and our intentions. We surrender all to you. We thank you for your love and give you praise. We pray all this in Jesus's name. Amen.

CANNOT GO BACK

"I have opened my mouth unto the Lord, and I cannot go back." Judges 11:35

How many times have you asked God for something and promised to get your life together or go to church, only for you to break that promise? For many of us, this is a constant battle. Today, let us open our mouths onto God and commit to never go back!

You've begged to get the job and promised never to complain again; prayed for provision while promising to tithe; prayed for the test to be negative and promised to cease your sexual activities; prayed to win the case and promised to never deceive anyone again; prayed for healing and promised to go to church regularly... only to break the promises over and over and over again.

Thankfully God's mercy is new everyday. (Lamentations 3:23) Thankfully He is not only a God of second chances, but He is a God of thousands and thousands of chances. He understands our weaknesses and forgives our trespasses. He loves us regardless of our empty promises and He will continue to bless us despite our shortcomings.

Today, let us be men and women of Christ-like character. Make a decision to not only talk the talk but to walk the walk. The Bible tells us "faith without works is dead." (James 2:14) Let us do what we say we will do, let us commit long after the feeling passes, let us open our mouths and commit our lives to Him and never go back!

My Prayer for You Today:
Lord, today we stand together as we open our mouths to you and surrender our hearts and lives to you. Father, you know our shortcomings, you know our weaknesses, help us, fill us with courage and strength to stick to our commitments. We can only do it through you. Thank you that your mercy is new everyday, thank you that you love us anyway. We praise you for your faithfulness; we love you for your greatness. Amen.

HIS VOICE

"Whether you turn to the right or to the left, your ears will hear a voice behind you, saying, 'This is the way; walk in it.'" Isaiah 30:21

God is always with you, leading the way. Are you listening?

In the midst of your intuition, at the core of your gut feeling, there holds God's still voice leading the way. Unfortunately many of us let our friends' voices or society's norms drown out His voice only to find ourselves lost and in despair. Whether you are struggling to go right or left, to take the job or not, to move or not, to marry or not, to divorce or not, to say yes or no, whatever it is you are wrestling with, He is there to lead the way.

Before you make a choice, seek Him; in the midst of a decision, seek Him; after making a commitment, seek Him. Always seek Him! God loves us so much that He gives us access to Him in stillness. Spend time in His presence as you seek for answers. Shut out the world and open your heart to His voice.

Today, remember: "The mind of man plans his way, but the Lord directs his steps." (Proverbs 16:9) Seek Him and He will show you the way. Whatever is weighing on your mind, pray about it right now!

My Prayer for You Today:
Father, today we surrender our indecisiveness to you. You know our struggles, you know what we wrestle with, whether to stay or go, whether to push or give up, whether to call one more time or not. Lord, you know better than we do. Lead us, guide our steps, we need you. Help us to shut out the world and open our ears and hearts to you. Thank you that it is already done. Amen.

SPEAK IN LOVE

"Speak the truth in love." Ephesians 4:15

Before you blow up, speak in love!

Too often we speak out of emotions. We speak out of anger, pain and fears, yet we are called to speak the truth in love. We tend to overlook intentions; we get blinded by our feelings and justify cutting our neighbors with our words. We defend our truth, deny other's truth while the ultimate truth remains unspoken.

Today, speak the truth in love. Let His truth be the basis of your discussion. Let His love be in the midst of your arguments. Friend, life is too short to hold on to grudges, relationships are too valuable to be broken by resentment, your peace and joy are too important to be disturbed by anger. Let it go and speak in love.

The Apostle Paul says, "Speak the truth in love, growing in every way more and more like Christ." (Ephesians 4:15) Today let this be your goal: speak in love more like Christ!

My Prayer for You Today:
Father, too often we are muted by our anger and our past. Today, help us to let go, forgive and move on while speaking the truth in love. Be in our conversations, Lord, open our hearts to see those who hurt us the way you see them. Be in the mist of our discussions; be in our speaking and in our words. Today we pray for courage to have hard conversations, courage to be vulnerable, and courage to forgive. We surrender our relationships to you; restore them in Jesus's name. Amen.

RESTORE DOUBLE

"I will restore double to you." Zechariah 9:12

Take heart, God will restore double to you!

All of us have felt the pain of betrayal. You sacrificed for friends only for them to leave you. You put your neck out for your neighbor, only for him to cut you. You gave your best, only to be told it was not good enough. The truth is: there are blessings in disappointments, soul-discoveries in betrayal, and rewards in sacrifices.

God will restore double to you. God has declared you the head, not the tail. (Deuteronomy 28:12) God sees your heart. He knows how much you have sacrificed. He has heard your cries and your helpless prayers. He knows how much you want it. Trust Him, He will restore double to you.

Today, keep the faith. Keep a good attitude. Keep up the good work. It is between you and Him. Do not be distracted by the world, let everything you do be done for Him. Whether you are defending a case as an attorney or welcoming customers as an office secretary, do it for His glory because true rewards and abundant life only come from Him.

He will restore double to you!

My Prayers for You Today:
Father, thank you that you promised to restore double to us. Lord, for all our unnoticed efforts, for all the work we have done that is overlooked, for all our good intentions that were misunderstood, we turn to you. You know our hearts. Thank you that true rewards only come from you. We dedicate our days and our work to you in Jesus's name. Amen.

PROSPER

"He shall be like a tree planted by the rivers of water, that brings forth its fruit in its season, whose leaf also shall not wither; and whatever he does shall prosper." Psalm 1:3

When you trust God and commit your ways to Him, you will prosper at everything you do.

If today you are feeling weary and uncertain, this is your reminder that your success is guaranteed. Your leaves shall not wither, and your fruits are certain. It does not matter what things look like today, you have a God who is faithful and who loves you. Breathe. You shall prosper!

In the midst of your uncertainty, in the middle of your stress and chaos, know that you are anchored to the One who never changes. Jesus reminded us to "remain in [him], as [he] also [remains] in you. No branch can bear fruit by itself; it must remain in the vine. Neither can you bear fruit unless you remain in [him]." (John 15:4)

Today, remain in Him and prosper!

My Prayer for You Today:
Father, be with us today as we seek to remain in you. Lord, you know our hearts, you know our struggles. We surrender our day and our lives to you. Fill us with courage and enthusiasm, renew us, Lord, we need you. We pray all this in Jesus's name. Amen.

MOTHERS

"She is clothed with strength and dignity... She opens her mouth in wisdom, and the teaching of kindness is on her tongue... Her children rise up and bless her, her husband also, and he praises her, saying: "Many daughters have done noble things, but you surpass them all." Proverbs 31:25-29

Mothers are a gift from God. Today let us be grateful for the women in our lives who have taught us wisdom, who have shared their kindness and love and have exemplified God's love.

Whether you have had a child grow in your womb or in your heart, whether you have raised children from birth or have influenced others for a short period of time, today God and the world celebrates you. God has used you to bless, mold, shape, and love His children. He entrusted them in your care, and for that you are blessed.

For all you have done as a mom, an aunt, a friend, a sister, a cousin, a confidant, a listening ear, God celebrates you. "You surpass them all" in your love, your kindness, your generosity, your wisdom, and your strength. His favor is upon you for mothering His children.

God bless you!

My Prayer For You Today:
Father, thank you that you have loved us through women. You have placed strong women in our lives as mothers, aunts, sisters, and friends and today we are so thankful for each and everyone of them. We thank you, Father, and ask you to bless them in all areas of their lives. We pray all this in Jesus's name. Amen.

FATHERS

"So he returned home to his father. And while he was still a long way off, his father saw him coming. Filled with love and compassion, he ran to his son, embraced him and kissed him." Luke 15:20

The Bible is filled with stories of incredible fathers, in Luke 15:20, we read the parable of the lost son who returned home to a welcoming and loving father. The son rejected his father's instruction, yet when he returned home his father welcomed him with open arms.

Similarly, God is always there to welcome us home. It does not matter what you did in the past, or how often you rejected Him; God's love for you allows Him to welcome you home over and over again. His arms remain open to you. Today, whether you felt the love of an earthly father, or suffered the pain of his absence, know that you have a Heavenly Father who delights in you and is in awe of you.

Rejoice, your Heavenly Father loves you and welcomes you with open arms.

My Prayer for You Today:
Lord, today we thank you for earthly fathers. Lord, we thank you for your fatherly love for us. Thank you for your love and your grace. Thank you, Lord, that you continue to welcome us home regardless of our shortcomings. We are amazed by your unconditional love. We love you and praise you. Amen.

TRUST

"Blessed is the man who trusts in you." Psalm 84:12

When the going gets tough, the tough trust Him! Today, trust God!

Trust is not a natural response; when life throws curveballs at us our natural response is to panic and worry. When your situation is spinning out of control and you are stressed at work, overwhelmed at home, frustrated with your significant other, and angry at the world, it is difficult to imagine that there is a God who you can trust. It is even harder to fathom that there is a God who is in complete control and who is for you!

Trust God one day at a time, one moment at a time. He is in control. When life seems unbearable and uncontrollable, He is still on the throne. When you are feeling tired and wearing, He still has you in the palms of His hands. Trust Him. It is impossible to understand all the events of your life because His thoughts are higher and His ways are higher. (Isaiah 55:8) One thing is certain: you can trust Him.

Today, in the midst of your storm, trust Him! He is able to calm any storm. He is able to change any situation. Relax. Breathe. Pray and trust Him.

My Prayer for You Today:
Father, you know our individual situations. Show up today in our lives. Lord, help us to keep our eyes on you as our world is spinning out of control. We anchor our lives and our hearts to you knowing that you are loyal, you are loving, and you will never leave nor forsake us. Today, have your way in our lives. We love you and praise you. Amen.

BEAUTY

"He will give a crown of beauty for ashes…" Isaiah 61:3

Smile, God will give you beauty for ashes, blessings for your tears, success for all your failures, prosperity for all the lack you have experienced, a strong marriage for all the sacrifices you made, a solid foundation for all the times you stood on shaken ground. He will give you a crown of beauty!

God looks at the heart. (1 Samuel 16:7) He knows your intentions; He knows your heart and will reward you. Keep being true to yourself, keep doing your best, keep taking the risk to love and forgive, keep putting one foot in front of the other. In due time, God will bless you with the desires of your heart.

Today, remember that God will give you a crown of beauty. He will reward all your sacrifices. He will bless you abundantly. He has great plans for you. Breathe. Relax. Smile. His crown of love, grace, peace, joy, and glory is upon you!

My Prayer for You Today:
Father, thank you that you see our hearts. Thank you, Lord, that you will give us beauty for ashes, blessings for all the times things didn't workout, success for our failures. We thank you that you are so loving and so loyal. Today we rest in your love and in your grace. We love you and praise you. Amen.

SUCCESS

"The God of heaven will give you success." Nehemiah 2:20

God will give you success!

Success is your birthright. As a child of God, success is your destiny, success is your DNA. Your success is a gift from God. Do not worry about the naysayers, do not lose sleep over those who curse you. Your success is solely in His hands. Continue to do your part. You do not have to agree with everything others say, you certainly do not have to downplay your greatness to stroke someone else's ego; do your part with character and truth and leave to rest to God.

"All the promises of God in Him are yes and amen." (2 Corinthians 1:20) God promises you success and He always keeps His promises. Your success is certain, guaranteed, irrevocable, a must, and absolute. Keep your eyes on Him. His promises do not have an expiration date. You cannot mess up His plans. Be certain that the God of Heaven will give you success.

Today, if you needed a sign to relax, this is it. If you needed an affirmation that your success is assured, let this devotional be a reminder. God will give you success!

My Prayer for You Today:
Father, thank you that success is a gift from you. Thank you, Lord, that our coming and going are in your hands. We do not know what the future holds, but we know you, the One who holds the future and we are so thankful that you are for us. Thank you for your love. Thank you that every promise will manifest in our lives in Jesus's precious and holy name. We love you and praise you. Amen.

PRAY

"God has surely listened and has heard my prayer." Psalm 18:6

Today, like David, let this be your testimony: God has listened to you and has heard and answered your prayer.

God surely listens and hears your prayers. Tell Him your deepest desires; cast your worries upon Him because He cares for you. (1 Peter 5:7) Nothing is too big for Him to handle. In the midst of your financial problems, the death in your family, your infertility challenges, the growth of your business, all of it, pray and be assured that He listens. Over and over you will experience God's blessings and love through answered prayers. If He answered your prayers then, He definitely will answer them again.

Today, be encouraged. Thank Him already for answered prayers. Pour out your complaints to Him. Tell Him your trouble. (Psalm 142:2) He listens and hears you. And be certain that God will make you the head, not the tail (Deuteronomy 28:13); He will keep you from backsliding (Jeremiah 3:22); He will give you success (Nehemiah 2:20) and He will give you the desires of your heart. (Psalm 37:4)

Pray without ceasing. God hears your prayers and will answer you. Keep praying!

My Prayer for You Today:
Father, thank you that you are so loving that you give us the ability and opportunity to come to you in prayer and you listen. Thank you for listening to us. Lord, you know our deepest desires, let them be fulfilled in your divine time and at your will. We thank you that your thoughts are higher than ours and we trust you with everything. Have your way in our lives today and everyday in Jesus's name. Amen.

STRENGTH

"Those who trust in the Lord will renew their strength." Isaiah 40:31

He who began the good work in you will carry it on to completion. (Philippians 1:6) Let your strength be renewed in Him!

Trust God as you seek for strength to push one more time, to face one more day, as you go through one more procedure, and as you experience one more loss. Trust God and renew your strength as you bite your tongue one more time, as you try again, as you love again, as you give up yourself again, as you commit to another project. Let your strength be renewed in Him.

God will remain loyal to you and to your dreams. Trust Him to answer your prayers. Trust God to bless you and open the floodgates of heaven upon you. Trust God to work things out in your favor. Let your strength be renewed, as you are certain that God will do what He promises and that He will answer your prayers.

Trust in God and be strengthened!

My Prayer For You Today:
Lord, thank you that in you, our strength is renewed. Thank you, Father that our faith allows us to have the strength to hold on, to hang on, to persist, and to persevere. Thank you, Lord, that our strength comes from you. Lord, we thank you today for miracles and answered prayers. We thank you for our lives and we trust you. Everything is in your hands. Amen.

SOMETHING NEW

"Do not call to mind the former things or ponder things of the past. Behold, I will do something new." Isaiah 43:19

God is up to something in your life. He is working on something new, behold!

Look around, your breakthrough is happening right now. You have prayed long enough, sought Him continuously, and He has answered. Your mind keeps thinking of the past and pondering on your missteps, but God is making something new. All along He has been preparing you for this moment.

He is making something new! It may look the same, but it is not. The conversation seems familiar, but it is opening the right door; you are in the same position at work, but with a new purpose; same relationship, but with a new destiny. Behold, He is making something new! With Him in you, the new creation has come! (2 Corinthians 5:17)

Today, pay attention, God is making something new. Things will feel different. Be thankful. You are different, better, smarter, more suited, your breakthrough is here! If you were praying for a sign, here it is: God has answered, He is making something new! Smile.

My Prayer for You Today:
Father, thank you that you are making something new. We are so thankful, so excited to see your blessings manifested in our lives. Thank you, Lord, that you have prepared us for this moment. We praise you for your love, we thank you for your grace. We love you, Lord. Amen.

JESUS

"Let us fix our eyes on Jesus, the author and perfecter of our faith…"
Hebrews 12:2

Fix your eyes on Jesus!

The more I know Him, the more amazed I am at Jesus. Friend, let us not put anyone on a pedestal but Him. Jesus is the greatest example we have. Whatever you are going through, fix your eyes on Him. In your quest to be a better husband, a better wife, a better mother, friend, entrepreneur—look to Him. You will find all the answers in Him, in His character, in His example, in His love. Fix your eyes on Him!

Today, know that Jesus is the answer. He came so we could have life abundantly. He walked the earth to show us that we will all be tempted, all accused even when we are doing right, but he reassured: "take heart I have overcome the world." (John 16:33) So today, take heart, your savior, your friend, your Lord, your teacher has overcome the world and with Him you will too.

Fix your eyes on Jesus and be amazed!

My Prayer for You Today:
Father, thank you for your love. Thank you, Jesus, that you are the greatest example of love. Today, help us to keep our eyes on you. Remind us to look to you and not the world. Fill us with strength as we overcome and soar in Jesus's name. Amen.

BE STILL

"Be still and know that I am God." Psalm 46:10

Be still!

In our quest for success and purpose we tend to get agitated and stressed, forgetting that He is God. When you remember that your life is in His hands, and realize that your plans are miniscule compared to His grandeur, you will breathe a little easier. Your life is but a speck compared to His power. Be still and know that He is God.

God can work it out. He can work anything out. Relax! Wait on Him in confident trust. Be still. Nothing is impossible to Him. (Matthew 19:26) He is at work right now in your life. Relax. Remember the time you stressed over school, remember when you worried about paying your bills, remember when you thought you would never make it through—He was there all along and worked things out. If He did it then, He will do it again.

Today, be still. Breathe. Relax. Whenever you start worrying, remind yourself that He is in control and He is for you. Be still and know that He is God. He is God! Nothing scares Him. Nothing can catch Him off guard, and nothing can make Him skip a beat. Relax.

God is working in your life. No need to overthink nor overstress, you can go through your day confident that He is God and in complete control. Be still...

My Prayer for You Today:
Father, thank you that you are God. Lord, our visions often get blurred by our circumstances, but today we are reminded that you are God and nothing is impossible for you. Lord, we surrender our lives to you. Thank you that you know our deepest desires and you answer our most sacred prayers. We praise you and love you. Amen.

KEEP THE FAITH

"I have fought the good fight, I have finished the race, I have kept the faith." 2 Timothy 4:7

You have come too far to quit now.

Like Paul, let us fight the good fight and finish what God has given us. Whether it is your marriage or your job, your exercise plan or your book, your business or your relationship—do not quit! God has purpose and meaning for everything He has given you. You cannot quit when time gets hard, you cannot give up when your relationship is challenging, you cannot throw in the towel because things are difficult. Keep the faith and finish!

Friend, "fight the good fight of faith." (1 Timothy 6:12) Whatever you do, keep the faith. If you lose your way, keep the faith. If you lose the job, keep the faith. If you bury your parents, keep the faith. If you lose your spouse, keep the faith! Whatever you do, keep the faith. You have come too far; God has shown you too much to lose faith now.

Today, whether you are believing God for a house or a spouse, for health or wealth, whether you have been praying a month or ten years, keep the faith! Finish the course. Do not quit on your dreams; do not give up on your prayers. Our God is faithful.

My Prayer for You Today:
Father, today we pray for the grace to endure. Help us, Lord, to keep the faith as we trust you to keep your promises. Today, Father, help us to commit, give us the hope needed and the trust needed to resist the temptation to quit. We surrender all to you, Lord, and like Paul, we will finish the race in Jesus's name. Amen.

SMALL BEGINNINGS

"Despise not the day of small beginnings." Zechariah 4:10

God is taking you from blessing to blessing, from small to big. Be encouraged!

Everyone starts somewhere. No one starts at the top of the mountain. Stop comparing yourself to others; you cannot expect to have overnight what they built in years. Keep pushing on, keep doing your best. It does not matter if your bank account is small today, it does not matter if you can only walk half a mile today, it does not matter if you only have ten clients today; where you are today is only the beginning. The oak tree was once a small acorn!

God is working on great things for you and through you. "Whoever can be trusted with very little can also be trusted with much." (Luke 16:10) Do your best with what you have now no matter how small it may seem. Show God that you can be trusted with little so that He can entrust you with more. As you go from faith to faith, from blessing to blessing, God is going to enlarge your territory. He will give you more than you can imagine because He knows He can trust you.

Today, do not despise small beginnings!

My Prayer for You Today:
Father, thank you for small beginnings. Help us to be diligent and committed workers with little so that you may entrust us with more. We surrender all things to you. We trust you with our lives. We are honored by your love and humbled by your grace. We love you and praise you in Jesus's name. Amen.

PLANS

"I know the plans I have for you," declares the Lord, "plans to prosper you and not to harm you, plans to give you hope and a future." Jeremiah 29:11

God has great plans for you!

If you ever doubt what God is doing in your life, consult this scripture. If it does not fit in the categories of prosperity, hope, and future, then it is not in God's plans for you. Stop worrying about something bad happening, stop fearing loss, do not lose sleep over your future—He promises that you will prosper, that you will be full of hope and have a great future.

Today, as you reflect on your plans and wonder about His plans, analyze all plans against this rubric: prosperity, hope, and future. Those are God's promises for your life. He has plans to prosper you, to grow you, and to give you hope and an abundant life.

In the midst of your everyday struggle, do not lose sight of His plans. God is for you and His plans for you are amazing. Trust Him!

My Prayer for You Today:
Father, thank you that you have great plans for us. Lord, today we rebuke all thoughts of loss and fear, all ideas that our future could be anything but great. Today we open our lives and our hearts to your plans, have your way with us. We trust you and love you. Amen.

LIFE TO THE FULL

"The thief comes only to steal and kill and destroy; I have come that they may have life, and have it to the full." John 10:10

Jesus did not come so that you could live a mediocre life. He did not sacrifice this much for you to live paycheck to paycheck, pill to pill. He did not shed his blood so you could cry yourself to sleep at night. He came so you could live life abundantly, to the full, spilling over.

Beware of thieves: the people, habits, thoughts that steal your joy, remind you of your mistakes, tell you mediocrity is your fate. Beware of the miserable people who are looking for company. Be careful of those things and thoughts that destroy and steal your hope. Thankfully, God is bigger than any thief, stronger than any addiction, more powerful than any family pattern.

Today, claim what is rightfully yours: an abundant life, full of purpose and peace, overflowing with joy and love. He came so you can have life to the full. Have it today!

My Prayer for You Today:
Father, we know that we are living below what you intended for us. Today we ask that you uproot anyone and anything that keeps us shackled to fear and mediocrity. We open our hearts and our lives to abundance. Let the blessings flow abundantly on our health, families, finances, relationships, and careers. We surrender all to you in Jesus's name. Amen.

EVERLASTING GOD

"**Have you never heard? Have you never understood? The Lord is the everlasting God, the Creator of all the earth. He never grows weak or weary. No one can measure the depths of his understanding.**" Isaiah 40:28

God is not tired of you.

You have played the same song, prayed the same prayers, broke up with the same person, made the same promises, yet God is not tired of you. He is not bored with you, not disgusted by your dysfunction, and not annoyed by your empty promises. He doesn't grow weary or weak.

His greatness no one can fathom. (Psalm 145:3) God is amazing. He is great. He is ever lasting and He is the Creator of all. He formed you. (Jeremiah 1:5) He will provide for you. He is always focused on you. Your situation does not scare Him and He is not tired of working out your problems. Thankfully, God never grows weak. He cannot be overthrown. He cannot lose.

Today, be encouraged—God knows you and loves you. He has great plans for you. (Jeremiah 29:11) He is always working in your life whether you perceive it or not. Today He is making new things for your life. Be encouraged. Be hopeful; our everlasting God is powerful and loving and blessing you right now!

My Prayer for You Today:
Lord, your power and strength bring us the hope we need to keep going on. Today, though we may feel defeated, we know you can never be defeated, though we may feel tired, we are grateful that you are never weak. Lord, thank you that your plans are higher than our plans and your thoughts higher than our thoughts. Today we fix our eyes on you and ask that you lead us faith by faith. We pray all this in Jesus's precious and holy name. Amen.

BEHIND THE CURTAIN

"We have this hope as an anchor for the soul, firm and secure. It enters the inner sanctuary behind the curtain." Hebrews 6:19

God is behind the curtain of your life, orchestrating everything for your good. You can enjoy center stage!

Your hope in God keeps you firm and secure. When you trust Him, it does not matter what your life looks like on the outside—behind the curtains God is calling all the shots. Like a play, people will come in and out of your life, scene after scene will add variance to your story, but the Author remains the same. God, the Author of your life remains the same and in control.

"The Author and Perfecter of faith" (Hebrews 12:2) is behind the curtains orchestrating your life. You can stand firm and secure knowing that He is in control. Your hope is in Him. Your life is in His hand. You can breathe now.

Today, no matter what is going on in your life, remember that He is behind the curtain. Anchor yourself to Him and find His peace, which surpasses all understanding, and may He guard your heart and mind. (Philippians 4:7)

My Prayer for You Today
Father, thank you that you are behind the curtains, calling all the shots. Lord, thank you that you are orchestrating life in our favor. We thank you for that. Today we anchor our soul, mind, and body to the hope we have in you. Guard us from unbelief, and keep us from doubting. We surrender all to you in Jesus's name. Amen.

YOU WILL NOT DROWN

"When you go through deep waters and great trouble, I will be with you. When you go through rivers of difficulty, you will not drown!"
Isaiah 43:2

You may be neck deep today, but you will not drown!

When your lifeguard walks on water, when your God is able to still the wind, even when you walk through the valley of the shadow of death, He promises to be with you. (Psalm 23:4) You can relax. Breathe. God will see you through. He didn't bring you this far to leave you.

In the midst of rivers of difficulty, let God shape your character and strengthen your faith. His power is made perfect in your weakness. (2 Corinthians 12:10) He will never leave you. (Deuteronomy 31:6) He is the same God on your best day and on your most difficult day. He doesn't change and His love will never cease.

Today, be encouraged—you will not drown!

My Prayer for You Today:
Father, thank you that in the midst of difficulty you are there. Thank you that you are the same loving God on the mountaintop as you are in the valley. Today we cling to you, to your promises, to your love as we pray and hope for better days. Thank you for your loyalty. We pray all this in Jesus's precious and holy name. Amen.

DO NOT WAVER

"He did not waver through unbelief regarding the promise of God, but was strengthened in his faith and gave glory to God." Romans 4:20

Abraham's faith was amazing. Like him, let us stand on God's promises, not wavering through unbelief.

God has a way of testing our faith through the situations we face. He often asks us to do unimaginable things, yet He promises to be with us as we walk through the valley of the shadow of death. (Psalm 23:4) God did not ask you to take the job, have the family or build the business knowing you would not face trials and tribulations. He called you to it so that through the journey your faith would be strengthened. Depend on Him every step of the way.

Today, have faith like Abraham who was "fully convinced that God is able to do what He promised." (Romans 4:21) Do not waver through unbelief but rather give glory to God, assured that His promises will come to pass. What God promises, God does! Trust Him. Let your faith be strengthened as you wait expectantly for His promises to manifest in your life. Do not waver in unbelief. You have a God who keeps His promises!

My Prayer for You Today:
Father, thank you that you keep your promises. Today we will not waver, we will not doubt, we will not lose hope as we wait expectantly on you and your promises. Father, if you said it, it has to come true. Thank you for your loyalty, thank you for your grace, we praise you for your love in Jesus's name. Amen.

LOVE

"Do everything with love." 1 Corinthians 16:14

Do everything with God!

Over the years, I have learned to substitute the word "love" with the word "God" because God is love. When you do everything with God, everything prospers. The ground you stand on with Him becomes holy ground. The work you do with Him becomes miraculous work. His Word spoken through you becomes prophetic word.

Take God out of the box. He is in everything and knows everything. Include Him in all your being and in all your activities. When you do everything with God, you are sure to be doing everything with love, with your best foot forward, your best effort and your truest self.

Today, whether you decide to spend your day in bed or run a marathon, do it with Him. Whether you decide to go out to lunch with friends or stay home with family, do it with love—do it with Him. Whatever you do today, do it with Him and watch His love overflow.

My Prayers for You Today:
Lord, thank you that you are everything and you are in everything. Father, today we invite you into all aspects of our lives. Lord, thank you that whatever we include you in will prosper, thank you that as soon as your presence is recognized everything becomes holy. Thank you, Father, that you are love. Be with us today as we do everything with love and with you. We pray all this in Jesus's name. Amen.

REAP

"I sent you to reap that for which you did not labor." John 4:38

Great news: God will give you blessings you did not work for!

In the natural world, you get what you work for and you reap what you sow. Thankfully we have a supernatural God who takes pleasure in blessing us in supernatural ways. God will bless you in ways that do not make sense. It does not make sense that the accident did not kill you, it does not make sense that your finances are increasing, and it does not make sense that your family is soaring.

God gives underserving grace, unexplainable promotions, and unmerited blessings. Continue to do your best, placing one foot in front of another, and God will send you to reap that which you did not labor. God sees your heart, He knows your struggles, and will reward you with a harvest you did not sow. God will bless the righteous and cover him with favor like a shield. (Psalm 5:12)

Today, keep the faith. Keep doing your best. Keep believing. Keep giving. Keep praising. Keep rejoicing. Keep hoping. Keep praying. Nothing goes unnoticed. God will open floodgates of blessings unto your life. He will bless you in ways you could never imagine.

You will reap according to His riches!

My Prayer for You Today:
Father, thank you for undeserving blessings and unwarranted grace. We are so excited about your blessings. You amaze us. Thank you for promotions, thank you for increase, thank you for better, thank you for breakthroughs. We praise you and love you and are so thankful to you. Amen.

FAITH

"Faith is the substance of things hoped for, the evidence of things not seen." Hebrews 11:1

Faith it 'till you make it!

God has placed dreams and aspirations in you, have faith that His promises will come to pass. Do not let others crowd your vision. Do not let others talk you out of your dreams. They cannot see your dreams because they are not theirs. You, on the other hand, must continue to believe and hope for "things not seen."

Faith is the substance of things hoped for, the evidence of things not seen. You must continue to pray and push for what God placed in your heart. You have not seen the miracle yet but know it is on its way. You have not landed the job yet, but God has already answered.

Today, do not mope around faithless, be reminded that God is at work in your life even if you do not see it. He is the Great Puppeteer. He is working behind the scene. God is for you. He knows the desires of your heart and He promises to grant them as you continue to seek Him first.

Be strengthened in faith, God is at work!

My Prayer for You Today:
Father, you know the deepest desires of our hearts. Today we focus on things not seen because you are a God who answers prayers. Thank you, Lord, that all your promises will come to pass. We surrender our day to you, and keep our eyes on you, Lord. We praise you and love you. Amen.

GOD LOVES YOU

"Let the message about Christ, in all its richness, fill your lives."
Colossians 3:16

Jesus is the greatest love story ever written. Today, let the richness of His love fill your life.

"By this we know what love is: Jesus Christ laid down his life for us." (1 John 3:16) There is no greater love than to give one's life for another. Love always requires sacrifice, and Jesus made the ultimate sacrifice. He loves you that much!

Today, let the richness of His love, the richness of His sacrifice, the richness of His teachings fill your life. Let it remind you of how precious and valuable you are. Let it encourage you to love and sacrifice for those you love. Let His love be your light.

GOD LOVES YOU!

My Prayer for You Today:
Father, thank you for the greatest love story. Thank you that we are your righteousness through Jesus's sacrifice. Thank you Lord for your love that is indescribable and unconditional. Today, let your love fill us, let our lives be soaked in the deepness and richness of your love and grace. You continue to amaze us. We love you and praise you. Amen.

WORDS

"Death and life are in the power of the tongue." Proverbs 18:21

Choose your words carefully and let them bring life.

Your words have the power to heal, to bring hope, to inspire, and to build. Speak positive words over your life. Complaining has not worked thus far for you, so stop! You cannot keep talking about how horrible you have it and expect your life to be wonderful. You cannot keep cursing your relationships and expect them to thrive. You cannot keep calling your son a terror and expect him to behave like an angel. Speak that what you want.

Words have creative power; use them to create the life you desire. Let your words speak of your faith. Use your words to testify of God's love and grace. Speak His Word.

Today change your words. Declare that you are blessed and highly favored. You are healthy and wealthy. You are a success and everything you touch prospers. Speak what you want! No, you are not broke; God is your provider. No, you are not tired; He is your strength. No, you are not confused; He gives you wisdom, power, and understanding. Speak it!

My Prayer for You Today:
Father, let everything we say today bring glory to you. Help us to choose our words carefully and let our words speak of our faith in you. Thank you for the creative power of words. You amaze us, Lord. Today we choose to believe and speak your Word. We praise you with our words and praise you with our lives. We love you. Amen.

TODAY REJOICE

"This is the day the Lord has made. We will rejoice and be glad in it."
Psalm 118:24

Today, let us rejoice.

Though things may look dark, desperate and dead, we have a God who can change things, who can resurrect situations, who brought Jesus from the dead. My guess is that Jesus's followers must have felt terrible on the day of his crucifixion; to watch their Lord die a shameful death must have shaken their faith to the core. But thank God for this sacrifice and thank God that His death was reversible.

Today, let us rejoice and be glad as we continue to be amazed and changed by what happened two thousand years ago on Calvary. He died so that we could live. (2 Corinthians 5:15) He died so that we could have eternal life. (John 3:16) "He himself bore our sins in his body on the cross so that we might die to sins and live for righteousness." (1 Peter 2:24)

Be inspired: what seems like death is getting ready to resurrect. What was a terrible day for followers became the greatest day of hope. God will do the same in your life. He will restore and resurrect the situation you have been praying about.

Rejoice!

My Prayer for You Today:
Father, you amaze us. Thank you that Jesus died on the cross for us. Thank you that you loved us so much, Lord, that you gave your son. Thank you, Father, for the cross. Today we place our crosses at your altar knowing that you are the God of resurrection and restoration. We praise you today. Amen.

ASK BIG

"According to your faith, let it be done to you." Matthew 9:29

Friend, your life is a direct reflection of your faith. According to your faith, let it be done!

The Bible tells us: "you have not because you do not ask God." (James 4:2) Too often, our limited faith keeps us from asking and praying for big things. We want to believe God for things that make sense but His grandeur and magnitude will never make sense to us. Muster enough faith to ask for crazy, big, out-of-this-world miracles.

There's nothing impossible for God (Luke 1:38). There isn't a miracle too big, a task too enormous, a situation too destroyed for God. Have faith in the One who is insuperable and the One who can do exceedingly above and beyond. Have faith enough to pray according to His ability. Have faith to ask according to His opulence.

Today, pray big! Ask for a double portion, a double miracle. Pray for your wildest dream and more. Your God is big enough to restore your marriage, to break addictions, to soar your business, to give you the life of your dreams. Your God is big enough for all of it. Believe it! Rank up your faith, pray big, think big, and ask big. God will amaze you!

My Prayer for You Today:
Father, today rather than asking according to our faith, we ask according to your ability. Amaze us, Lord. You know the desires of each and everyone of us. Lord, we bind those desires on earth and ask you to do the same. Father, we ask for double blessings, crazy miracles, unimaginable breakthroughs. We pray for exceedingly above and beyond blessings, we pray for things we can't even fathom and we know that you will answer. We thank you in advance. We love you. Amen.

WISDOM AND STATURE

"Jesus grew in wisdom and stature and in favor with God and with people." Luke 2:52

As you walk through your spiritual journey, I pray that like Jesus you may increase in wisdom and stature and in favor with God.

When you are living according to His Word and through Him, don't be surprised when all of a sudden doors open for you and everything you touch prospers. As you grow in Him, you'll learn to depend on His wisdom and not your own. You will be comfortable standing in faith. You will be able to walk by faith, not by sight. You will learn to pray first and act second.

Today, know that your wisdom and stature comes from the Omniscient One. The more you seek Him, the more wise you become and the more His favor will invade all areas of your life. Today, if things don't make sense, if you need guidance, if you need favor—seek Him. "If you need wisdom, ask our generous God, and he will give it to you." (James 1:5)

Turn to Him and grow in wisdom and stature.

My Prayer for You Today:
Lord, there are so many things we do not understand. Father, today we pray for wisdom. Help us. Guide us. Enlighten us, Lord. You know the beginning from the end. Today we come to you as we seek to grow in wisdom and in stature. Lord, wrap us in your love and in your favor, fill us with your wisdom and your strength. We give all the glory to you in Jesus's precious and holy name. Amen.

GIVE

"I do not give like the world gives." John 14:27

Today we ought to thank God that He doesn't give like the world gives. In a world where paybacks, revenge, scratch-my-back-and-I'll-scratch-yours, and you-don't-get-anything-for-frees are the norms, it's difficult to understand that God's grace, love, peace, and blessings are given freely and without having to earn them.

Friend, you don't have to scratch God's back to get His favor, it's already all over your life. You don't have to earn His love; Jesus Christ paid the price in full. You certainly don't have to worry about doing anything to warrant His blessings, it brings Him great pleasure to bless you. God doesn't give like the world gives.

When you know God, you can relax into your blessings. You don't have to worry about losing your spot; you don't have to fear tomorrow. You don't have to worry about God taking everything away. He doesn't give like the world gives! God gives abundantly. He gives with no expectations. He gives because that is His character. He gives because He is God! He gives when we don't deserve it. God gives and doesn't take it back. He gives because that's who He is. "God so loved the world that He gave..." (John 3:16)

Today, do not be troubled, enjoy His blessings, and let His giving inspire you to give.

My Prayer for You Today:
Father, thank you that giving is part of who you are. Thank you, Father, that though we do not deserve it, you gave your son and you continue to give abundantly. Thank you that everything is paid for. Thank you that we do nothing to deserve your love and your grace yet you bless us with them. We thank you for your giving. We praise you for your awesomeness. We love you. Amen.

STOP THE CHASE

"Surely goodness and mercy shall follow me all the days of my life."
Psalm 23:6

Did you know that God will hunt you down to bless you?

You don't have to chase your blessings, you certainly don't have to chase a man, surely you do not have to chase others' approval, or chase clients and fans; God's mercy and goodness will follow you. When you know who is in control of your life, when you live according to His will, you can sit back and watch His blessings pour over you with little effort.

Friend, it pleases God to bless you. His love, His blessings, His grace, His mercy will follow you. All of a sudden things will fall effortlessly into place, you will get breaks you didn't work for and promotions you didn't pursue. You will meet people who will build you up. You will gain favor with God and men. When you dwell in the shelter of the almighty (Psalm 23:6) you will be amazed at how much God blesses you.

Today, stop the chase. His goodness and mercy shall follow you. Find your dwelling in God. Move, breathe and have your being in Him (Acts 17:28). His favor is over your life. Dwell in His love.

My Prayer for You Today:
Father, you amaze us. Thank you that your goodness and mercy follow us. Today we cease all chases, we break the habit of chasing friends, chasing success, chasing favor and we relax in your love and in your grace. Lord, we thank you that as we seek you, you will grant us the desires of our hearts. Thank you for you love. Thank you for your mercy. Thank you, Father, for everything. We love you and praise you. Amen.

CHARACTER

"Tribulation brings perseverance; and perseverance, proven character; and proven character, hope…" Romans 5:4

Your trouble hasn't been in vain!

Your trials and tribulations haven't been random, nor have they been in vain. They were building your character all along. You are not who you used to be. Look back—that frail, uncertain, weak person no longer exists. You have been through too much to remain the same. No longer naïve, no longer needing others' approval, no longer deceiving, God has radically changed your character. Be thankful!

God is in the character-building business. He is more concerned about your character than your circumstances. As you change inwardly, your circumstances will also change. What used to bring you stress, now gets you on your knees trusting Him. You used to spend time proving yourself by your degrees and accomplishments, now you can relax knowing that your identity is in Him. The challenges you feared now are embraced as they strengthen your faith and trust in Him and build your character.

Today, give yourself a pat on the back; you have come so far. Thank Him for radically changing you, and your character. You are well. You have grown so much. God is pleased with you. Your character reflects His love and your trust in Him. Smile!

My Prayer for You Today:
Father, thank you for radical change. Thank you, Lord, for changing our characters to reflect our authentic self. Lord, we know we're not where we should be but we are so thankful for progress in you. Thank you, Father, that you have changed our characters; the journey hasn't been easy, yet it hasn't been in vain. Thank you. We are excited about how you will continue to change us. We praise you for blessings. We thank you for your love in Jesus's precious and holy name we pray. Amen.

NOT OFFENDED

"Blessed is the one who is not offended by me." Matthew 11:6

Has God ever offended you? You may be quick to answer no, but I'm here to confess that I have felt offended by God. Have you ever prayed for something diligently, only to see God bless someone else with it? Ever needed something desperately and watch your neighbor take for granted the very thing you needed? How about when you've prayed for the winning lottery ticket and you end up winning not the grand prize, but $5. I am among those who have felt offended by God. If you're anything like me, you've yelled out several times "Come on God, you've got to be kidding me!"

Jesus told His disciples "blessed is the one who is not offended by me." While Jesus was performing miracles, His own cousin John the Baptist was in prison waiting to be beheaded. John the Baptist must have felt offended. Are you offended by what God is doing for others while you wait on Him? Being offended by God is equivalent to losing faith. You've prayed so much and your unanswered prayers have left your faith dead and dry. Take heart. When God blesses those who betray you, when He delivers those who trapped you, and answers the prayers of your enemies, are you able to still trust Him?

Today, don't be offended by God's grace. Don't be offended by His delayed responses. Don't let the blessings of others rob you of your faith. He has you in the palms of His hands. Keep the faith. If He answered the prayers of others, He will surely answer yours.

Today take no offense. Keep the faith. Keep praying. Trust Him!

My Prayer for You Today:
Father, today we thank you for blessing those around us. Thank you, Lord, that your love for them gives us hope of your love for us. Thank you, Father, that you bless the just and the unjust, thank you that none of us are deserving of your love and grace but you love us anyway. Today we surrender all unanswered prayers to you, Lord, and we trust that if you've answered others' prayers you surely will answer ours. We trust you with our lives, we depend on you for our needs, we lean on you for everything. We praise you, Lord, and give you glory in Jesus's name. Amen.

THE DOOR IS OPEN

"I have opened a door for you that no one can close." Revelations 3:8

What God has for you is for you! Nothing He sets aside for you can be taken from you. Relax.

You don't have to chase it, you don't have to lose sleep over it, it's not going to happen on your time, it will not happen by your might, but when God opens a door for you, no one can close it! God's favor is all over your life. Relax and soak it in.

God wants you to know that the door has been opened for you. He opened the floodgates of heaven on all areas of your life: your health, your marriage, your children, your family, your career, your business, even your car. He leaves nothing untouched and nothing unblessed. You can kiss your worries goodbye and start praising. The door is open!

Today, don't envy your neighbor; his piece of the pie will never take away from yours. Rejoice! Give thanks! Your door is open. Take a step!

My Prayer for you today:
Father, thank you for opened doors. Lord, we pray for discernment and wisdom to know when you have opened a door. Father, guide our steps, lead us step-by-step. Today we praise you and give you all the glory for open doors. Thank you for your love. Thank you, Lord, for your favor. We know we don't deserve it but we are so thankful that you love us. Thank you. Thank you. Thank you. Amen.

PEACE

"For God is not the author of confusion but of peace." 1 Corinthians 14:33

Friend, God's peace and love, which surpass all understanding, resides in you. Confusion and chaos cannot exist where He is because He is a God of order and peace.

All of us will experience a time when we feel confused, out of control, and lacking peace. Though our circumstances may make us feel this way, God is never confused. He knows the beginning from the end. He has plans to prosper us and give us a future. God is never looking at us scratching His head and wondering what to do next. He is God, He knows!

If you are facing a stressful situation or feeling confused, if you are in need of direction or experiencing chaos, know that your exterior can be shaken, yet you can still hold on to His peace, which resides in you. His peace allows you to stand firm. His peace reminds you that no matter what comes your way, you can handle anything because you can do all things through Him. (Philippians 4:13) His peace allows you to declare like David, "I will not be shaken." (Acts 2:25)

Today, in the midst of stress and confusion, know that God is the author of peace. Today, while your world is spinning out of control, anchor your heart to the One who never changes. Today, chaos and noise may knock at your door, but let His peace reside in your heart.

My Prayer for You Today:
Lord, thank you that you are the author of peace. Though we do not understand our circumstances, we trust you, Lord. Father, come now and fill us with your peace and your love. Help us to stand firm in faith knowing that you have great plans for us. We surrender all to you; it's not by our might but by your power. We praise you and love you. Amen.

I WILL HELP YOU

"For I am the Lord, your God, who takes hold of your right hand and says to you, "Do not fear: I will help you." Isaiah 41:13

Whatever you are facing today, God wants you to know that He will help you.

When the rug has been pulled from under you, when chaos invades your house, when you suddenly have no control, do not fear; God will help you! Now you must learn to let go. Let go of loved ones, of possessions, of control, of expectations.

Friend, God took hold of your right hand and won't ever let it go. Rest in Him. Know that whatever is happening today, He is your help. He is your strength. God is your light. Hang on to Him. God is the same yesterday, today and forever. (Hebrews 13:8) If He took care of you before, He will do it again. The same God who raised Jesus Christ from the dead, will raise you from your circumstances. Hang on!

Today, in the midst of your difficulty, do not fear. God will help you. With His help you are sure to be a victor, you are certain to soar, assured to be a conqueror, guaranteed to be stronger than before. Do not fear; God will help you!

My Prayer for You Today:
Lord, you know the details of all our lives. You know the mountains we are facing, and we thank you that no mountain is too big or too much for you. Today we put our trust in you, Lord, assured that you will deliver us, you will strengthen us, and certain that our help comes only from you. Hold on to our right hand, Father, and lead us one step at a time. We thank you already for deliverance. We praise you for strength. We give all the glory to you in Jesus's name. Amen.

LOVE

"Let love be your highest goal." 1 Corinthians 14:1

Let love be the goal. God has shown you, despite your shortcomings, that love is His goal. Today, like Him, love above all.

Relationships will always have drama, family will always be demanding, and friends will constantly disagree. People will disappoint you, but love them anyway. Jesus Christ was betrayed and unjustly accused, yet His love is the greatest love story ever told. He was crucified, yet His love changed the world.

Let your love change your family. Let love enlarge your circle. Let love light up your city. Let love be your highest aim. Overlook the actions of others and love them anyway. Overlook your own faults and love yourself anyway. After all, if God loves you so much, you ought to follow His example.

Today, love, love, love!

My Prayer for You Today:
Father, thank you for the greatest love story in Jesus Christ. Thank you, Father, that your highest goal is and always has been love. Thank you for your love that saves. Thank you for your love that heals. Thank you, Father, that though we don't deserve your love, you love us anyway. We praise you. Help us today to follow your example and to love. We give all the glory to you in Jesus's name. Amen.

WORTHY

"Look at the birds of the air: they neither sow nor reap nor gather into barns, and yet your heavenly father feeds them. Are you not of more value than they?" Matthew 6:26

Today, let nature remind you of God's sovereignty. Let it show you how much the Creator takes care of His creations.

You are valuable to God. You are not random nor unclaimed, not unnoticed nor unidentified. God knows you. He knows your name. He knows the number of hairs on your head. (Luke 12:7) You are valuable to him. And if God cares about you, God will take care of you. That is His nature. Friend, nothing is happening by chance. God is not random. He is a God of order. Your life is unfolding as it should in His hand.

God wants you to remember your worth. Remember that you are valuable to Him. Remember that it's not by your work but by His love. Remember that nothing you do can separate you from Him. (Romans 8:38) Remember that as a child of the King of kings you are royalty, you inherited the Kingdom, you have value and are valuable to Him.

You are worthy!

My Prayer for You Today:
Father, thank you that your love makes us worthy. Thank you, Father, that you always take care of us. Help us today to remember our worth in you. Lord, we surrender our lives to you. Bless us in unimaginable ways. Fill us with your love and wrap us in your grace. We give all the glory to you in Jesus's name. Amen.

FAITH AND ENDURANCE

"Follow the example of those who will inherit God's promises because of their faith and endurance." Hebrew 6:12

Faith and patience will reward you with God's promises. Today, keep the faith and be patient.

The testing of your faith produces patience. (James 1:3) You have been praying for a breakthrough, praying for answers, waiting on a miracle. Today, keep on praying and do not lose faith. Pray without ceasing. (1 Thessalonians 5:17) Knock and keep on knocking! Ask and keep on asking! Seek and keep on seeking!

Do not become spiritually dull, defeated, and tired. God has already answered. Your miracle, your request will come at the perfect time. Keep on praying faithfully. Pray with expectation. Believe that He has answered you. God is growing your seed of patience. It will happen. His promises are *yes* and *amen*. (2 Corinthians 1:20) They will come to pass. Keep the faith.

Today, follow the example of those who will inherit God's promises. Be faithful and patient. His blessings are without repentance. (Romans 11:29) Keep praying. Keep knocking. Keep seeking. God has great things in store for you.

My Prayer for You Today:
Father, today fill us with faith and patience. We know that you answer prayers, Lord, but sometimes we feel impatient. Forgive us. Today we ask that you answer now. Give us a sign today, Lord. Speak to us. Thank you for your favor and grace. We love you and pray all this in Jesus's precious and holy name. Amen.

WALK BY FAITH

"For we walk by faith, not by sight." 2 Corinthians 5:7

Walking by faith is not for the faint of hearts. For those of us blessed enough to trust Him, we've had nights where our fears kept us up. We spent nights wondering how things were going to turn out, and played out every possible situation in our heads. We experienced times when we didn't see the end nor believed there was a light at the end of the tunnel, but God in His omniscient power, and in His unconditional love made a way.

Friend, like a blind man, walking by faith requires a cane. A cane of hope, a cane of trust, a cane anchored in the One who knows it all and knows best. Walking by faith requires you to take a step not knowing what will come next. But like a blind man who relies on his cane, rely on your cane, your God, who always leads and clears the way one solid and secure step at a time.

Today, whether you are facing a health crisis, a financial crisis, a challenge in your relationship, or you are in a season of abundance and joy, know that God is your cane as you walk blindly by faith. Be certain that God is for you. Let Him guide your step. Don't be too prideful to get on your knees. Seek the One who knows it all and the One who loves you most. Today, God wants you to know He's still there.

Walk by faith!

My Prayer for You Today:
Father, hold on a little tighter to your children. We need you, Lord. Help us to feel, experience, and know your presence in a deep way. Father, today we pray for peace, although we are like blind men on this journey. Lord, we put all our hope and trust in you knowing that you are for us. Father, come now, fill us with your peace. We surrender all to you—worries, doubts, tribulations, headaches, heartaches, diseases, relationships, business challenges, financial strains; everything is at your altar. We cast all our worries on you because you care for us. Thank you. We praise you. Amen.

PASS THE TEST

"Perseverance must finish its work so that you may be mature and complete, not lacking anything." James 1:4

God is more concerned about your character than your circumstance. Who are you becoming?

You've struggled with the same issues year after year, complained about the same people over and over, had to learn the same lessons day after day. Is it possible that God is testing you and shaping you? God is building your character. He is loyal and persistent.

Today, lay down your ego and pass the test! God is shaping you to stand firm in the midst of trouble. He is teaching you to turn the other cheek. Your Father is building your character. God wants you to bless those who curse you, to serve those who betray you, to forgive those who hurt you, and to love those who lie to you. Jesus did it for you on a much higher scale, now it's your turn!

God will finish the work He started in you. He loves you too much to leave you bitter and dishonest. He cares too much to watch you gossip day after day. He thinks the world of you and can't see you living in mediocrity. He is determined to make you mature and complete, not lacking anything. Today, pass the test!

My Prayer for You Today:
Father, thank you for your loyalty and perseverance. Lord, thank you that you are building our characters. Father, the journey is not always easy but we thank you that you are always there and always working for our good. Today, give us strength to pass the test, to shut our mouths when we want to curse, to close our ears to anything that dishonors you. Help us Lord to be patient and loving no matter the circumstance. We love you, Lord, and thank you for your love. Amen.

THINK OF HIM

"Whatever is true, whatever is noble, whatever is right, whatever is pure, whatever is lovely, whatever is admirable—if anything is excellent or praiseworthy—think about such things." Philippians 4:8

If your thoughts are bringing you stress and worry, change them.

It's amazing how in a split second we can go from feeling amazing to total panic all because of the crazy thoughts in our heads. You feel a slight pain in your arm, then you suddenly think: "it's broken... no it's cancer... *omg* they're going to cut my arm off". Similarly, you get in an argument with your spouse and start thinking one senseless thought after another. Stop letting crazy thoughts control you.

The Apostle Paul clearly described what to think about, he said to think of those things that are true, noble, right, pure, lovely, admirable, excellent, and praise worthy. Think of God things! Think of the way He loves you. The way He is orchestrating life in your favor. Think of the miracles He already performed in your life and the miracles He will perform in your life. Think of the dreams He will make come true. Think of the way He continues to bless you and your family. Think of the prayers He's answered.

Friend, today take captive every thought and align it with the Word of God. Your mind plays tricks on you but His Word is true and lights the way. You may think it's risky, but His Word tells you to trust. When you are scared and think of quitting, His Word says "Fear Not". When your mind says you'll be embarrassed if you fail, His Word says that when you look to Him, you shall never be ashamed. (Psalm 34:5) When your mind says you have to fight, His Word says He will go before you and fight for you. (Isaiah 52:12) When your mind says you are alone, His Word says He will never leave you nor forsake you. (Deuteronomy 31:6)

Think of His Word. Think of Him!

My Prayer for You Today:
Father, take captive every thought. When we think of depleting thoughts, fill us with your Word, which brings life and hope. Father, help us today to hold on to what you say about us, help us to meditate on your word, let it seep out of every pore of our being. Today we think of you, Lord, your everlasting love, your grace, your loyalty, and we trust you. We love you, Father. Amen.

VISION

"Where there is no vision the people perish." Proverbs 29:18

Take a risk, dream a dream, have a vision for your life.

Too often our dreams scare us, our vision is blurred by fear and insecurity. Will I really build my business? Does the ideal spouse really exist? Will I ever get out of debt? Am I ever going to afford a house? We let our fears blind us from God's power. Your role is not to know the "how" but to know the "who," the One who will answer your prayers and clear your vision.

Today, have a vision for your life. Pray. Involve God in every detail. He has big plans for you. Let His plans be your vision. Take a risk. When fear says no, let your faith whisper yes. If you don't take the risk, you forfeit the miracle. Step out in faith. You've always wanted the business; take a step towards it today. You've dreamed of being an author; write a few lines today. You want to get out of debt; make an extra payment today.

Envision your life today the way God sees you. Dream big and pray hard. Have faith, if you can envision it, He can grant it. Nothing is impossible to Him and it brings Him great pleasure to bless you. Whether you are trying to lose weight or wanting to buy a house, envision it, let Him in every detail. God can move mountains.

My Prayer for You Today:
Father, today help us to have faith-based vision. Lord, let our vision be filled with you. Lord, remind us today of your grandeur, your magnitude, your love, and your grace. Forgive us for living by fear rather than by faith. Take over, be in every detail of our lives, be in our coming and going, we surrender all to you in Jesus's precious name. Amen.

SEASONS

"For everything there is a season, a time for every activity under heaven."
Ecclesiastes 3:1

There is a season for everything. Enjoy your current season!

Friend, God wants you to complete the test. He wants you to learn from the journey. He wants you to keep on keeping on! In all seasons there is beauty and something to be thankful for. In your hardest season, seek Him. In the darkest hour look for His light. We complain about winter and miss out on the beauty of snow. We moan about spring and overlook the beauty of blooming flowers. We whimper about the hot summer days, never being grateful for the rays of the sun. We complain about the fall leaves and miss out on the change of colors. Similar to nature's seasons, our lives have seasons and rather than focusing on the beauty of every season, we complain about the smallest things.

In every season of your life, God places people and circumstances filled with beauty to awe you. Find beauty in your season. God colors every season with new awareness, new friendships and new growth. Are you missing out on the beauty of your season? In your season of singlehood, find the beauty and peace of being committed to God. In your season of transitions, find the lessons of God's grace. In your season of preparation and during your time in school, enjoy the journey. Whatever the season, there are hidden blessings and countless lessons.

Today, whatever your season, find beauty in it and thank God. All seasons end but His love lasts forever. If you're going through a tough season, remember that this too shall pass. Though the grass withers and the flowers all die, God endures forever. (Isaiah 40:8)

God's love reigns in all seasons. He loves you, now and always.

My Prayer for You Today:
Father, today we pray for strength and eyes to see your beauty and your love in every season. We pray for discernment and faith to know your love. We thank you for seasons; we thank you for beauty in every season. We thank you for preparation and restoration. We praise you, Father. We love you Lord. Amen.

IMITATE GOD

"Imitate God, therefore, in everything you do because you are his dear children." Ephesians 5:1

In a world where we all strive to be individuals, today be an imitator. Be a copycat. Imitate God in everything!

Early in life we spend time trying to be what the world wants us to be. We imitate our friends, we copy what celebrities do, we start dating someone and pick up all their habits and mannerisms, and the list goes on. Then as we mature we spend time trying to do things our way. We break the norm. We strive to be individuals. We often do so in all the wrong ways, full of ego and lacking humility. And the game continues, defining ourselves based on perceptions and vanity. Friend, the only one to imitate is God. Just as children follow the example of their parents, follow the example of your Creator.

The Bible tells us to: "be perfect, as your heavenly Father is perfect." (Matthew 5:48) "Be merciful, just as your Father is merciful." (Luke 6:36) "Be kind and compassionate to one another, forgiving each other, just as in Christ God forgave you." (Ephesians 4:32) "Become blameless and pure, children of God without fault."(Philippians 2:15)

Today, imitate God. Follow His example. Imitate Him in the way you treat others and yourself. Imitate God by being gracious, by giving and forgiving. Imitate God by being fearless and powerful, full of God-confidence and strength. Imitate God. You are safe with Him. You stand on the Rock. Imitate God by being true. Imitate God by speaking those things that are not as though they are. (Romans 4:17) When you imitate God you will be amazed at how you too can move mountains, you too can speak life, you too can love and be loved beyond your imagination.

Today, as a child of God, imitate Him!

My Prayer for You Today:
Father, thank you that you are the best example for us. Lord, help us today to imitate you. We are your children, help us to respond how you respond, to act how you act and to love how you love. Lord, fill us with your confidence and your strength. Be with us today as we speak life, as we move mountains, as we stand strong on your Word. We love you and pray all this in Jesus's precious and holy name. Amen.

PEOPLE OF LIGHT

"Live as people of light! For this light within you produces only what is good and right and true." Ephesians 5:8-9

Live as people of light!

If your life is full of lies, schemes and deceits, you are not living authentically. If your life is full of worry and wrongdoing, fears and anxiety, you are not in touch with the light within you. Get in touch with who you really are—a person of light! You hold in you the everlasting, omniscient, all powerful, true, right, and good light of the world. Greater is He that is in you! (1 John 4:4) Live as such; live as people of light.

God has declared you the salt of the earth. (Matthew 5:13) He called you to be fishers of men. (Matthew 4:19) He named you the head, not the tail. (Deuteronomy 28:13) And destined you as a person of light. Are you living up to your status? Are you defining yourself based on God's definition?

Today, live as people of light. Whatever is true, noble, right, pure, lovely, admirable, praise worthy, and excellent, think and do those things. (Philippians 4:8) God can only produce what is good, right, and true. Let Him shine through you. Today, remember who you are. You a person of light! Walk into work and let your attitude, your service, your care, your faith, and your love shine. Let everyone who comes in contact with you today feel and know His light.

My Prayer for You Today:
Father, thank you that you have declared us people of light. Thank you that as your children we hold your light inside of us. Lord, break all barriers today, break walls of shyness and fear, break shackles of worry and dismay, and let your light shine through us. Father, let everyone who comes in contact with us today know that you are God. We love you. We praise you. Amen.

SACRIFICE OF PRAISE

"Through Jesus, therefore, let us continually offer to God a sacrifice of praise—the fruit of lips that openly profess his name." Hebrews 13:15

Wherever you stand today, make the sacrifice of praise.

When life gets too stressful to praise and you are frustrated with God, praise Him anyway. When what you worried about actually happened and you are down and out, push beyond your own strength and praise Him anyway. Friend, there are times saying "thank you" to God just doesn't make sense, but thank Him anyway. Combat stress with praise and worship. Combat doubt and fear with praise and worship. Combat disappointment and detours with gratitude.

Today, let your lips profess His name. God is not asking you to sacrifice your dreams or your hopes, He just wants your praise. He doesn't want you to sacrifice your faith, He wants a sacrifice of praise when you don't understand. He wants you to lift His name in the midst of your storm. He wants you to worship and trust Him when you are down and out. He wants your trust in the midst of your confusion. Let the fruit of your lips profess His name.

Tomorrow's success is developed in today's stress. Praise Him through your stress. Speak things that are not as though they were (Romans 4:17). Worship and praise Him through your stress. Speak life over your life. Place His promises above your problem. Today, while you are in the pit, offer Him a sacrifice of praise.

My Prayer for You Today:
Father, today we praise you and profess your name. We don't understand our situations, we are frustrated and depressed, but Lord, we trust you. Father, we lift up your name. If it weren't for you, we wouldn't have made it this far. Thank you for your love. Thank you, Lord, for your grace. Thank you for your loyalty. We praise you. You are amazing. We love you, Lord. Amen.

SELF-CONTROL

"A person without self control is like a city with broken-down walls."
Proverbs 25:28

Today God wants you to know that your lack of self-control is destroying your blessings. Practice self-control!

You have prayed for better days, wished for a brighter future, longed for a solid marriage, yet you lack self-control in your temper, insecurities, fears, and bad habits. You have been talking about your failing health, yet you lose all self-control in a bag of chips. Your lack of self-control is killing your dreams. You have to bring some structure into your life in order to receive and enjoy all that God has in store for you. No bad habit, no fear, no insecurity is bigger than the One who lives in you. Tap into His power in order to bring control in your life.

"Better a patient person than a warrior." (Proverbs 16:32) Today, be patient with others and with yourself. Practice self-control by being slow to anger and quick to forgive. Practice self-control by being disciplined. Practice self-control by shutting your mouth and ears to gossip and opening your heart to His Word. Practice self-control in all areas of your life by focusing on God. Feed your spiritual needs rather than your flesh's desires.

Today, open your heart to God's blessings by being someone of character with great self-control. Your destiny is worth the structure. Your life is worth the change. And your future depends on it. God has great things in store for you. Let Him know you are ready by being disciplined and displaying self-control.

My Prayer for You Today:
Father, you know our weaknesses and our shortcomings, help us today to practice self-control in all areas of our lives. Lord, speak to us as we can often feel discouraged and overwhelmed. We thank you that no addiction, no bad habit, no fear is greater than you. Take over, Lord. We surrender our lives to you. Amen.

FOR ME

"This I know, that God is for me." Psalm 56:9

David's words in this Psalm are so powerful. In spite of the enemy's attacks, he declares: "this I know, that God is for me."

Like David, faithfully and firmly declare this statement. Are you able to stare at your physical illness, and say, "this I know, that God is for me"? Can you face your financial distress, and yell out, "this I know, that God is for me"? Can you stare at your family drama, your frustration at work and your uncommitted boyfriend and say, "this I know, that God is for me"?

Friend, God is for you. Whatever happened in your past—the pain, the neglect, the disappointment—and whatever is happening now, God will use to build you. Everything will be used to strengthen you. He will make all things work together for your good. (Romans 8:28) He is for you. God is for you!!!!

Today, let this sink in the depth of your spirit. Whatever you are facing, remind yourself that God is for you. A single situation may disappoint you, and you may be inconvenienced by a delay, but when you know that God is for you, everything is a blessing, and every situation will be received with a grateful heart. Change your perspective; see His loving hands in everything. He is for you!

Know this for sure: God is for you!!!!

My Prayer for You Today:
Father, thank you that you are for us. Lord, when we think and meditate on those words we are so amazed, so humbled at your love and your consideration. Thank you, Father. Lord, thank you that everything is moving along according to your plans. Help us to see delays as blessings, to see disappointments as benedictions. We trust you, Lord. We praise you, Father. We pray all this in Jesus's precious name. Amen.

DREAM BIG

"Ask me and I will make the nations your inheritance, the ends of the earth your possession." Psalm 2:8

"I am the Lord, the God of all mankind. Is anything too hard for me?" Jeremiah 32:27

Today God wants you to ask and dream BIG.

If you walked into a high-end store and were told you could have whatever you wanted, I pray you wouldn't be the person who would timidly pick up the free napkin with the brand's logo. Your timidity and small prayers do not impress God. He dares you to dream big and to ask for the impossible. Do it! Ask and pray according to His ability, not your lack of faith. In need of transportation, would you ask God for a bus pass or a Rolls Royce? He certainly can provide either one, the choice is yours to ask. Ask!

God is able to provide exceedingly more than we ask, according to His power. (Ephesians 3:20) Is anything too hard for Him? God provides according to your faith. He is able to subside your physical pain and completely heal your body. He is able to pay your monthly bills and clear out all your debt. He is able to provide you with the small business you want and multiply it to a multi-million dollar company. Whatever it is, God is able! Nothing is impossible to Him. (Matthew 19:26) Are miracles hard for God to perform? Ask and find out!

Today, have faith. Ask and it will be given to you. (Matthew 7:7) Dream BIG, pray BIG, and believe BIG. You serve a BIG God. Asking for anything less is an insult. If God answered others' big prayers and big dreams, why wouldn't He answer yours? The same God who blessed Abraham will bless you. The same God who brought Oprah from poverty and neglect to a successful billionaire will bless you. The same God who healed Wayne Dyer can heal you. Ask Big, pray Big, and have faith in your BIG God.

My Prayer for You Today:
Lord, today we dare to ask BIG. Father, multiply our finances, bless our homes, heal our bodies, restore our relationships. Lord, breathe purpose into our lives, leave no area untouched. Father, we believe in you, we believe in your abilities and we know that your purpose for us is to live an abundant life. Today we open ourselves to abundance in all areas of our lives. We love you, Lord. We praise you. We thank you for hearing our prayers and answering. In Jesus's precious and holy name we pray. Amen.

PRAYER AND SUPPLICATION

"Be anxious for nothing, but in everything by prayer and supplication, with thanksgiving, let your requests be made known to God."
Philippians 4:6

Pray, request, and thank God for everything.

Today, whatever your need, pray, request, and thank God as you let Him know your desires. Whether you are believing God for healing or for a new car, for restoration in your business or healed relationships with your family, for financial blessings or guidance in your marriage, whatever it may be, take your requests to Him by prayer, with supplication and thanksgiving.

Over and over Jesus reminds, "Fear not," "Do not worry," and "Be not afraid". If God can create the Heavens and the Earth out of nothing, He can take care of your situation. "Be anxious for nothing." (Philippians 4:6) When you remember how powerful and omniscient God is, and you believe in His love and loyalty for you, you are able to stand firm, with bills piling up and challenges increasing by the minute, and say like Paul "None of these things move me."(Acts 20:24)

Today, whatever you face, by prayer and supplication, with thanksgiving bring your requests to God. He will answer. He is faithful. He is the true provider. He loves you and it pleases Him to bless you. Do not worry. He holds you safely in His hands. Relax.

My Prayer for You Today:
Father, here we are in prayer bringing our needs to you. You know our requests, Lord, you know the desires of our hearts, we thank you already for answering. We praise you, Lord, for being loyal. Lord, we agree right now collectively on the requests as we place them all on your altar. Answer, Lord, in Jesus's name. Amen.

STEPS

"The heart of man plans his way, but the Lord establishes his steps."
Proverbs 16:9

God orders your steps. Trust Him.

If things are not according to your plans, if what you hoped for is not what happened, trust the Master's plan! He leaves nothing to chance. He has plans to prosper you and to give you hope, plans to give you a future better than you could ever imagine. (Jeremiah 29:11) He knows exactly how to alter your plans in order to bring you to your highest self. He knows how to orchestrate circumstances to give you your best life and fulfill His purpose through you. Breathe. Trust Him.

Friend, if God knows even the number of hairs on your head, (Luke 12:7) how much more does He know? Trust Him. In the midst of making plans, remember that He establishes your steps. When things are not going as planned, remember the Master's plan is the master plan. Relax. Enjoy the process. Breathe. Let go. He is in total control.

Today, let God establish your steps.

My Prayer for You Today:
Lord, thank you that in the midst of our plans, you order our steps. Thank you, Father, that you know better than we do and your plans far surpass our plans. Help us today to let go of our plans and to trust you. Lead us, guide us and be with us. We thank you. We trust you. We surrender all to you. Have your way. We pray all this in Jesus's precious name. Amen.

BREATHE

"In God I move and breathe and have my being" Acts 17:28

Your being is in Him. Move, breathe, and be in Him!

Do not let chaos and foolishness overtake you. Life's pettiness has a way of consuming us. Decide today to be filled by His love. You are wrapped in His grace, strengthened by His light. Everything you do, every breath you take, can be done in God.

Today, remind yourself that you move, breathe, and have your being in Him. Relax. Be at peace. Take a deep breath. Experience joy that only His presence brings. Let His love seep out of all your pores. Love people. Enjoy your life. Smile. Laugh. Wherever God is, there is hope, love, and peace.

Move, breathe, and have your being in Him. Breathe hope, love, and peace. Breathe God.

My Prayer for You Today:
Father, today we move, breathe, and have our being in you. Be with us today as we love one another. Fill us today with your peace and your love and allow us to enjoy every minute of this day with profound joy. Lord, thank you that you are so awesome. Thank you, Father, that you love us so much. We love you. We praise you. We give you all the glory in Jesus's name. Amen

ACCLAIM HIM

"Blessed are those who have learned to acclaim you." Psalm 89:15

In everything, praise God!

You've made it this far because of Him. Acclaim God! Your business, your marriage, finishing school, your health, all of it has been a manifestation of His love for you. Praise Him. Things should have fell apart, but they didn't. The accident could have killed you, but it didn't. Your rough childhood could have doomed you, but it didn't. His grace and His favor were always upon you. Today, acknowledge Him.

Blessed are those who have learned to applaud God in all circumstances. When you know God is for you, whatever is happening in your life is another opportunity to bring Him praise. In doing so, God will multiply your blessings. God will reward your faith in Him. He delights in your trust.

Today, praise, shout, and thank Him for all He has done. You are blessed. He has saved you. He loves you. You are a victor and a conqueror by His grace. Praise Him because He has never stopped blessing you!

My Prayers for You Today:
Father, today we praise and acclaim you for all the days of our lives. Lord, we know that if it weren't for you we wouldn't be here. Thank you for being loyal to your words. Thank you for always being with us. Your faithfulness and love amaze us. Thank you, Father, that you are so good. Today we shout your name. We give you all the glory. Thank you. Thank you. Thank you. Amen.

TGIF

"Their sins and lawless acts I will remember no more." Hebrews 10:18

TGIF: Thank God I'm Forgiven!

Friend, you no longer have to be a slave of your missteps. You are no longer a prisoner of your wrong doings. We have all fallen short, we have all done and said things that were hurtful and mean but today, thank God, we do not have to keep beating ourselves up. We do not have to live with guilt and shame, because we have been forgiven! God chose to forget our shortcomings.

Your past doesn't make you a bad person; your God has redeemed you. He has set you free. He has forgiven you and has forgotten your mean words. He no longer remembers your conniving ways and the lies you've told. He removed your transgressions. (Psalm 103:12) God delights in you and shows mercy to you. (Micah 7:18)

Today, do not let old thoughts, or old friends remind you of what you have done. As soon as the thought comes up say: "thank God I'm forgiven!" His love and favor is upon you. Let His mercy and grace inspire you to forgive others. God sees you with eyes of love, forgiveness, and grace.

God loves you and has forgiven you!

My Prayer for You Today:
Father, thank you that despite our wrongdoings you love us. Thank you that you have forgiven us and we are no longer slaves of our past and prisoners of our anger. Thank you, Father. Help us today to forgive those who have hurt us. Let your love seep in us so that just like you we can look at our neighbors with eyes of mercy and grace. Lord, you are awesome and we praise you today. Amen.

LEAN ON HIM

"Lean on, trust in, and be confident in the Lord with all your heart and mind and do not rely on your own insight or understanding." Proverbs 3:5

Our understanding is so limited. God's thoughts and His ways are higher than our thoughts and our ways. (Isaiah 55:9) Thus it is pointless for us to rely on our own understanding. Trust Him and lean on Him. God has a way of making everything work together for our good. (Romans 8:28) What is hurting you today may well be a blessing in disguise. Trust Him.

Friend, be confident in God. Our thoughts are limited, our understanding is impartial, but God knows it all and is omniscient and powerful. Lean on Him. He has promised to be with us and allows us to cast our worries on Him. Today, do just that. Cast your worries on Him because He cares for you. (1 Peter 5:7)

Stop trying to understand your circumstances. Stop trying to make sense of chaos. Let your struggle build your faith and increase your confidence in God. You will never fully know why it is happening to you. The cards you are dealt do not make sense, but God would never let you be put to shame. (Psalm 34:5) Like the great puppeteer, He is orchestrating life in your favor.

Breathe. Lean on and Trust Him. He is loyal!

My Prayer for You Today:
Father, there is so much we do not understand. Today we lean only on you. Be with us and work through us as we walk through valleys of life. Lord, strengthen us and uphold us as we cast our worries on you. Fill us with courage, Father, we thank you that you make everything work together for our good. We trust you even when we don't understand. We praise you even when our voices shake. We love you. Amen.

EXTINGUISH

"Take up the shield of faith, with which you can extinguish all the flaming arrows of the evil one." Ephesians 6:16

You have the power to extinguish all that is not from God.

Your burden is not too heavy, your stress is not too much and your challenge is not too high. You have the ability to extinguish all worries, all doubt, all fear, all struggles through your faith in God. A fireman is never afraid of flames because he trusts in the power of his hose. Likewise, you too—unshaken and unmoved by life—you trust in the power of your God. You have faith in your "hose," in your God, knowing that you can extinguish all flames!

God will not let you be tempted more than you can handle. He is faithful. (1 Corinthians 10:13) He loves you too much to let you be consumed by the flames of life. You have all the power in you. With God nothing is impossible. (Matthew 19:26) Have faith. Speak to the flames in your life. With power and faith declare all flames extinguished!

Today, with your faith, extinguish the flames! With your faith, move mountains! With your God, live abundantly. God has declared you the head, not the tail. He called you the salt of the earth. Use your power, use your faith, and extinguish!

My Prayer for You Today:
Father, you amaze us. Thank you that our faith is in you. It's not by our ability but by your might. Lord, today we extinguish all flames in our lives, we break all holds of misery, of poverty, of sadness, of depression, of stress and envy, of addiction and corruption, we extinguish all that is not from you and declare ourselves free and victors in Jesus's precious and holy name. Amen.

UNWAVERING FAITH

"In hope against hope he believed…without becoming weak in faith… with respect to the promise of God, he did not waver in unbelief…"
Romans 4:19

The story of Abraham beautifully illustrates a man's radical and unwavering faith. Like Abraham, do not waver in unbelief but trust that God's promises will come to pass.

Friend, never doubt in the dark what God has shown you clearly in the light. God has shown you over and over that He answers prayers. You know that He can make things change suddenly. Remember that He will never leave you, nor will he forsake you. Today, when faced with another challenge, do not fall in doubt. Now is the time to exercise your faith, now is the time to stand firm in His promises. Refuse to waver in unbelief. If He's done it before, He will do it again.

"Why do you have such little faith? If God cares so wonderfully for wildflowers that are here today and thrown into the fire tomorrow, he will certainly care for you." (Matthew 6:30) In hope against hope, believe! Without becoming weak in faith, trust Him!

Today, make a commitment to *stand in faith*. Decide today that no matter what, you will believe blindly, radically, and forcefully in the promises of God. Make up your mind and decide that no matter what things look like now, you will believe in God. Commit to prayer. Pray without ceasing. Do not waver in doubt. Believe.

Faith is a choice. Today, choose faith!

My Prayer For You Today:
Father, you know our hearts, you know our worries and stresses, and forgive us, Lord, that too often we doubt, that while we wait on your promises we tend to be poisoned with unbelief. Father, today we rebuke all doubt, and choose to stand boldly in faith, proclaiming that we live by faith, not by sight. Lord, we trust you. Father, we believe in you. We surrender our lives and our hearts to you. Have your way. We love you. Amen.

PRAY

"Pray continually." 1 Thessalonians 5:17

Prayer doesn't happen at a specific time, but it happens continuously. Be in constant communication with the One who loves you most. Today, pray continually.

Get in the habit of talking to God. In every moment, involve Him. Acknowledge His presence through simple short prayers. Before you answer a phone call, you may say, "Lord be in this conversation, speak through me and for me." While meeting with a difficult client take one deep breath and ask, "Father take over." In the midst of enjoying great company whisper to God, "Thank you!" Whatever you do, wherever you are, take the opportunity to pray.

Today, pray continually. Pray without ceasing. God is always with you and always available to you. Prayer is your powerline—use it! As you focus on praying, your thoughts will be less on the world and more on the One who loves you and who created the world.

Be Blessed. Pray.

My Prayer for You Today:
Father, today we pray for more: more blessings, more peace, more joy, more health, more abundance, more excitement, more meaningful relationships, more you! Fill us, Lord, with your grace and your love. We need you. In a time where our lives are dry, Father, only you can replenish us. Move in us and through us now. We love you and pray in Jesus's name. Amen.

REMARKABLE SECRETS

"Ask me and I will tell you remarkable secrets you do not know about things to come." Jeremiah 33:3

If you ever wonder where things are going in your life, ask God. He will answer in ways only you will understand. You will suddenly get an idea, someone will say something that will strike you, or you will run into an old friend. Whatever it is, keep your heart and your mind open. God will tell you remarkable secrets about things to come.

Today, spend time asking God in prayer about things to come. The Bible tells us to "Ask and you shall receive; seek and you shall find." (Matthew 7:7) Ask and seek Him about things to come. Don't spend time worrying about the future; ask Him!

If you are wondering about God's wonderful plan for your life, ask Him. He knows!

My Prayer for you:
Father, reveal your secrets about wonderful things to come in our lives. Give us clues, give us a glimpse. Tell us, Lord! Today we ask in Jesus's name to guide our steps. We need you. We love you and praise you. Amen!

SHINE

"You will shine like stars in the sky." Philippians 2:15

This is your destiny: to shine like stars in the sky.

The Apostle Paul said it long before Rihanna wrote the song *"Shine Bright Like a Diamond."* Friend, you are not meant to live a dull, boring life. As a child of God you are meant to shine like stars. You are the salt of the earth. (Matthew 5:13) You are the light of the world. (Matthew 5:14) You are not just anybody; you are a shining star!

Understand your role and your importance here on earth. God's favor is upon you to do His work. His love fills you in order for you to love others. His son served you so you can serve your neighbor. Put aside selfish ways and stop grumbling. Let the Kingdom of God that is within you shine through you.

Shine! Let your goal today be to put a smile on five people's faces. Shine! Tell someone you love and appreciate them. Shine! Do a random act of kindness. Shine! Pray for someone through a text message. Shine!

Today, do what you do best: shine!

My Prayer for You Today:
Father, help us to shine today. Use us to serve others, to put a smile in someone's face today. Lord, thank you that you use ordinary people to do your work here on earth. Today we are at your service. Show us how to help and serve others. Fill us with your light and your love. We love you, Lord. We praise you. Amen.

BE AT PEACE

"A heart at peace gives life to the body, but envy rots the bones."
Proverbs 14:30

Be at peace with yourself.

Stop looking at others. Stop competing with your neighbor. Comparison robs you of your peace and envy rots the bones. Look to Him. If you were supposed to have their life, their job, their spouse, you would have it. Since you don't, it's not yours! Move on. Stop resenting people. There's no need to envy their success. Stop assuming that their lives are better than yours. Stop putting others on a pedestal. Put God on the throne of your life where He belongs.

Because you know God, you can be at peace with your life and yourself. You can love your journey and be grateful for how far you've come. Don't waste time envying others, look to God. Keep your eyes on Him; with Him you can move mountains. With Him you can grow your business. With Him you can improve your relationships. With God you can find the partner you seek. With God you can finish school and build the career of your dreams. Trust in His promises. Seek His attention. Praise Him for His love.

Today, be at peace knowing that God is for you! Be at peace assured that others' blessings will never diminish yours. Be certain that God is abundant and will meet all your needs according to His riches. (Philippians 4:19) Let others' success and happiness increase your joy and deepen your peace, assured that if God did it for them, He will certainly do it for you too!

My Prayer for You Today:
Father, thank you that you are abundant. Thank you for blessing our neighbors with success, health, joy, and the desires of their hearts. Thank you that just like you did it for them, you will do it for us. Thank you, Lord, for your love and grace. Today help us to keep our eyes on you and our hearts at peace. We love you and praise you. Amen.

GOD ANSWERS

"Before they call I will answer. While they are still talking about their needs, I will go ahead and answer their prayers!" Isaiah 65:24

Before you even utter a word, God knows your needs and He will answer.

Before you can yell out *help,* God sends out His army of angels to your rescue. Before you reach the end of your rope, He already has a plan. Before you are in too deep, He will answer. Before you even pray about your issue, He will answer your prayer! Trust Him. He already knows.

Friend, God knows the beginning and the end. He knows what you are going through and has already answered. His word is true and if He says He will answer, He will answer! It's impossible for Him to lie. Relax. Breathe. If He knows the number of hairs on your head, (Luke 12:7) how much more does He know? He knows about your sickness. He knows the challenges in your relationship. He knows about your late bills and your unruly children. He knows! He knows it all and the great news is, He has already answered!

Before you can pray about it, God has already answered! Today, just thank Him. Yell out, "Thank you!" He has already answered. Thank Him for answering the prayers you have yet prayed. Thank Him for meeting the needs you are oblivious to; praise Him for being so amazingly great.

My Prayer for You Today:
Lord, thank you that even before we pray, you answer. You continue to amaze us. You are so awesome. Help us to remember that you know all things and that you love us. Help us to see your love and your hand in everything. We thank you for answered prayers, we thank you for dreams come true, we thank you for deliverance, and we thank you for healing. We love you and praise you. Amen.

RENEWED STRENGTH

"Those who trust in the Lord will renew their strength." Isaiah 40:31

Your trust in God will give you new strength.

To some of us a new day with the same challenges and the same routine is simply unbearable. But when you trust God with where you are, you can conquer your day faithfully, with enthusiasm and strength. He is working things out in your favor even if you don't see it. He is moving mountains for you and making new things in your life.

The Bible tells us, "Do not lose heart. Though outwardly we are wasting away, [inwardly] we are being renewed day by day." (2 Corinthians 4:16) God is renewing your strength. You can go another day at that boring job; God will give you strength. You can deal with another angry customer. You can put up with yet another unruly student. You can listen to the ranting of a difficult client. God is renewing your strength. You can do it through Him and with Him.

Today, trust God with where you are. He has you in the palms of His hands. Let your faith in Him, and your confidence in His love renew your strength. You are exactly where you are supposed to be.

Trust Him and be renewed.

My Prayer for You Today:
Father, we trust you. Fill us with new strength today, with new enthusiasm and courage to go on with the same routines. We need you, Lord. Though we may feel discouraged and tired, we trust you and believe your promises. Fill us now. Be with us. We need you. We surrender today to you. Reveal yourself and give us insight on the new things you are doing in our lives. We love you, Lord. We praise you, Father. Amen.

STAND FIRM

"Believe in the Lord your God, and you will be able to stand firm." 2 Chronicles 20:20

Believing in God alone allows you to stand firm. Wow!

Regardless of what you are going through, you are able to stand firm. Today keep calm and prevail. Stop lying to yourself by saying, "I'll never make it through," "This is too much," or "I can't take it anymore." Yes, you will make it. No, it isn't too much. Yes, you can take it! With God you are stronger than you think. With Him you stand taller than you can imagine and you can do all things.

Like a deeply rooted tree still standing, enduring seasons of drought and rain, you too, deeply rooted in God, will stand firm through the seasons of your life. Anchored to the One who strengthens you, you will never be uprooted. Like the Apostle Paul, you will learn how to be content with whatever you have. Like him, you will know how to live on almost nothing or with everything. You will learn the secret of living in every situation, whether it is with a full stomach or empty, with plenty or little, for you can do all things through Him who strengthens you. (Philippians 4: 11-13)

Today, stand firm! Stand in faith. Stand firm knowing that this too shall pass. Stand firm knowing that nothing under His control is ever out of control. Stand firm assured that God is at work in your life. Stand firm.

My Prayer for You Today:
Father, thank you that today we are able to stand firm because of you. Thank you, Lord, for strengthening us and building us. We surrender all to you. You know the deepest desires of our hearts, Father, let it be your will to grant them. Move in our lives today; we need you. Thank you, Father, for everything. We love you and praise you. Amen.

SMILE

"Do all things without grumbling or disputing… as lights in the world."
Philippians 2:14-15

I bet you didn't know that the sun doesn't grumble because it has to shine! You too are called to be and do without grumbling. You too are called to shine as lights in the world.

We all have things we don't like to do, responsibilities and commitments we would rather live without, yet fulfilling them with a poor attitude only makes them harder to bear. Grumbling and disputing, pouting and shouting, bitching and complaining do not reflect who you are. You are the light of the world! (Matthew 5:14)

Today, enjoy the most boring tasks. Be thankful for your least favorite commitment. Praise and worship. Serve and love. Don't go through your day hiding your light behind a bad attitude; like the sun, shine, because that's what you are meant to do!

God declared you the light of the world. Smile and shine!

My Prayer for You Today:
Father, forgive our poor attitudes. Help us today to face our day with a grateful heart. When we are tempted to grumble, remind us of your love. When we are tempted to complain, remind us of our blessings. Thank you, Father, that we are the light of the world doing your work. We are so grateful and so thankful for this privilege. We love you. We praise you. Amen.

KNOW

"Be still and know…" Psalm 146:10

Today, know these things:

Know that God is for you. Know that your life is in His hands. Know that He works things out for your good. Know that He will never leave you nor forsake you. Know that no matter how dark things seem, He shines. Know that what He says about you is true. Know that He loves you. Know that you could never do anything so bad that He would abandon you. Know that His grace is new everyday. Know that He forgave you for everything already. Know that you don't have to work for His love, He gives it to you freely. Know that just being you is enough for Him. Know that you are fearfully and marvelously made. Know that what you are worried about, He already worked out. Know that He is God and nothing is impossible to Him.

When you know these things for sure, nothing can shake you. No circumstance can convince you otherwise. Today, know that He is for you. And if God is for you, you are in great shape!

Be still and know that He is God!

My Prayer for You Today:
Father, help us to know in the depth of our souls the truth of who you are and the depth of your love for us. Help us, Father, to find comfort in this knowing, to find hope in this knowledge and build our faith on your promises. Be with us today as we face our day boldly in the truth of who you are and in your love and grace. We love you. Thank you. Amen.

NEW THING

"Do not call to mind the former things…for I am about to do something new. See, I have already begun! Do you not see it?" Isaiah 43:18-19

Are you aware that God is doing something new in your life? Can you perceive it in the midst of your worry?

Forget the past, forget what didn't work out, God is for you and He is making something new in your life. Look deeper! Your week may not be going as planned, your conversation may not have gone the way you had wish, but guess what? All that doesn't matter because things are exactly as they should be. God is making new things in your life. God is for you!

The old has gone, the new is here. (2 Corinthians 5:17) God is laying the foundation for your blessings. He is doing something new in your life. Trust Him. Stop focusing on the past. Do you not see your future in His hands? Today, look deeper. He is shaping you and preparing for new things. He is strengthening you and sharpening you for greater things. His work for you and in you has already begun. Trust Him.

My Prayer for You Today:
Father, thank you that you are for us. Thank you, Lord, that whatever is happening, it is happening in our favor. Forgive us for not trusting you enough. Thank you for the new things you are doing in our lives. Thank you for new blessings. Thank you for amazing breakthroughs. We love you and praise you! Amen.

PREPARE AND EQUIP

"All scripture is inspired by God ... God uses it to prepare and equip his people to do every good work." 2 Timothy 3:16-17

The Word of God prepares us to do good work.

If you listen to your family and friends, their advice will change like the seasons. If you listen to the news, you'll never know what the heck to do. Even if you listen to yourself, you may find yourself in a bind. Listen to God. His word is a lamp at your feet. (Psalm 119:105) God is the same yesterday, today, and forever. (Hebrews 13:8) He doesn't change. Let His Word prepare and equip you!

Whatever you are facing today, find your answer in Him. Confused and lost, dig in His Word for guidance and strength. God gave us His Word as our daily bread. When life knocks you down, use your best resource: His Word.

His Word will never return null and void. (Isaiah 55:11) It will accomplish His desires and purpose. Hang on to His Word. Today, you don't have to recite a bunch of scriptures, you don't have to memorize the Bible, but know that there's power in His Word. It will equip and prepare you as you step out in faith.

You are prepared and equipped by God, now go out and do great work!

My Prayer for You Today:
Father, thank you that your Word never returns null and void. Thank you, Lord, that you have given us your Word as guidance and strength to prepare and equip us. Thank you, Father, that with you we can do all things. Be with us today as we do your work. We love you and praise you. Amen.

REST

"It is useless for you to work so hard from early morning until late at night…for God gives rest to his loved ones." Psalm 127:2

For all the times you felt unproductive and lazy, know that rest is a gift from God.

In our fast-paced society, we can feel pressured to always be doing something. We are so busy we can hardly find time to breathe. When we listen to the world, a calendar may reflect our worth, the emptier our calendar, the more unworthy we think of ourselves. We run around restless, thinking God will be impressed by our business. God is not impressed with our lack of sleep and tiredness. He is certainly not impressed with how irritated we are when we are fatigued and overworked.

Rest. Relax. Chill out. Life is about balance. Work hard, play hard, and rest hard too. Work hard, pray even harder, and rest even more. Allow God to bless you with physical and spiritual rest. Rest in faith knowing that things happen not by your effort, but by His grace. Rest in His love knowing that you are always taken care of. Rest in His grace assured that your worthiness is in Him, not in the world's standards.

Today, slow down. Rest. Sleep a little longer. If you don't make it the gym today, you are not a bad person. If you leave the laundry in the dryer another day, it doesn't make you a lazy wife. God gives rest to his loved ones. He loves you, rest in Him.

My Prayer for You Today:
Father, thank you that you give rest to those you love. Thank you that we are among those you love. Father, today break all shackles of guilt from us that keeps us going without rest. Fill us with your love and grace and allow us to rest in you knowing that we are already worthy and we are already perfectly loved and accepted by you. Thank you, Lord. Amen.

WATER

"One who waters will himself be watered." Proverbs 11:25

You reap what you sow!

Water is a vital source of life. In the concrete world, water brings life and hydrates. Similarly, in the spiritual realm, we are called to bring life and hydrate our neighbors through relationships. Who are you watering today?

Today, build someone up. Water someone in your life; in doing so, you too will be watered. Give that which you seek to receive. Love. Listen. Be patient. Be kind. Water those you love. Let them know how much you appreciate and love them. Surprise them!

As you water those around you, know that God will water you. God will fill you with His love and grace. He will provide for all your needs. He has declared you the salt of the earth. Go out and water!

My Prayer for You Today:
Father, help us today to water those we come in contact with. Help us to be bold enough to love the unlovable, to serve the ungrateful, and to keep watering with a cheerful and servant heart. Thank you, Father, that you promised that as we water, we will be watered. We thank you for your love that fills us, thank you for your grace that protects us, thank you for your light that shines in us. We praise you and love you. Amen.

FAITH IT

"We live by faith, not by sight." 2 Corinthians 5:7

Living by faith is not for the faint of heart. Today, faith it 'till you make it!

Faith is the confidence in what we hope for, and the certainty in what we do not see. (Hebrews 1:11) It is being able to see your deliverance while you're still dealing with the storm. It is knowing without a doubt that God's promises will come to pass in your life. Faith allows you to wake up day after day in the cold and punch in to that dead-end job certain that in due time God will bless you with better.

Friend, faith will make you do some crazy things. Jesus taught us that, according to our faith, it will be done. (Matthew 9:29) And he assured that a mustard seed of faith can move mountains. (Matthew 17:20) Today, when things don't make sense, hang on to your faith. When it's dark and you have no clue where life is taking you, hold on to your faith in the One who has taken you this far. When your children are hurting and your family is falling apart, have faith that God is still in control. When your marriage is in ruins and your job is useless and your reputation is on the line, hang on to God. Have faith. He is with you in the storm. Live by faith assured that your God will never leave you nor forsake you. He makes all things work together for your good.

Walk by faith.

My Prayer for You Today:
Father, because of you we live by faith not by sight. Lord, in the midst of darkness, shine your light on us. We need your direction and guidance. You know the mountains we face. Today, we declare ourselves overcomers in Jesus's name. Thank you for building our faith. We trust in only you. We praise you and love. Amen.

DECREASE

"He must increase, but I must decrease." John 3:30

Here's the secret to a better life: increase God and decrease yourself.

What you focus on grows. Unfortunately, we tend to focus on our problems, our needs, our wants, and our desires. We focus on what annoys us and what drives us crazy at the expense of the things and individuals we ought to be grateful for. We constantly talk about the things that irritate us. Today, rather than focusing on what is wrong, focus on the One who is right.

Focus on God and watch Him increase in your life. Meditate on His Word. Be in constant communication with Him. Pray and practice obedience. Increase your focus on Him and decreasing the focus on you.

Today, focus on that which you wish to increase. Do not overlook your blessings while talking about your problems. Do not neglect your loved ones while focusing on your enemies. And do not decrease your God while talking about yourself. What you focus on grows. Focus on God!

As you increase God, He will take you to new heights!

My Prayer for You Today:
Father, today we lay ourselves down so you can rise up. We decrease in order for you to increase. Today we choose to keep our focus on you, who is the true healer, the true deliverer, and the true provider. Come into our lives and reveal yourself; take us to new heights so that we will know it was only done because of you. We praise you and love you. Amen.

SCALE

"With my God I can scale a wall." Psalm 18:29

Your faith in God makes you confident. With God you are victorious. Wall after wall, mountains after mountains, God will equip you every step of the way and will be with you as you overcome every circumstance. With Him you can scale a wall.

Friend, with God you can scale a financial wall. With Him you can overcome a health wall. With your Creator you can conquer a career wall. Whatever it is, with God you can scale it! We are called to walk by faith, not by sight. (2 Corinthians 5:7) God will guide you step by step and you will be amazed.

Today, have God-confidence. You can scale whatever comes your way. Relax into your day knowing that your time is in His hands. He loves you and will never leave you or forsake you. You can do anything with Him. Be confident!

My Prayer for You Today:
Father, with you we are confident that we can overcome anything. Thank you that it's not by our strength but by your might. Thank you for always being with us. Today we trust you, Father. Break every ounce of fear and worry and fill us with your love. We love you. Amen.

GENEROSITY

"A generous person will prosper; whoever refreshes others will be refreshed." Proverbs 11:25

The generous will prosper!

Today, give in order to prosper. Refresh to be refreshed. Generosity is a lifestyle. It is not limited to your finances. Are you generous with your time and your attention? Are you generous with your words and encouragement? Are you generous with your resources? A generous person will prosper, so today be generous!

"Remember this: whoever sows sparingly will also reap sparingly, and whoever sows generously will also reap generously." (2 Corinthians 9:6) It's simple: give that which you want to receive. Refresh others and you will be refreshed. Build others with your words and your attention and you too will be built. Love others and you too will be loved.

Today, in your search for success, remember that your generosity is linked to your prosperity. Give yourself. Share your advice. Tell your story. Give a hand. Smile. Be patient. Understand. Encourage. Sow hope. Pray for someone. Send a friendly text.

Generosity is the language of love. Today, speak love!

My Prayer for You Today:
Father, thank you that you are the perfect example of generosity. Lord, thank you that your grace and your love are abundant. Be with us today as we move and breathe in you and show your generosity in everything we do. We love you, Lord. We lift everything to you. Thank you. Amen.

TRUE HEART

"Let us draw near with a true heart in full assurance of faith." Hebrews 10:19

Draw near to God with a true heart, full of faith. God is waiting!

Friend, too often our own thoughts of unworthiness and guilt keep us from drawing closer to God. We let our past keep us from Him. We convince ourselves that because of the abortion, the divorce, or the affair God is angry. For this, we stay away from Him. Well, today I have good news: despite it all, God wants you to draw close to Him.

Be assured that nothing can separate you from God's love! (Romans 8:38) Your past can't separate you from Him, and neither can your future mistakes. Relax in His love. Be assured that "if we confess our sins, he is faithful and just and will forgive us." (1 John 1:9) Let go of the past. God has already forgiven you. He chose to forget your past. Right now, today, you have a clean slate. Embrace it!

So, draw near to Him with a true heart full of gratitude and faith. Understand that God loves you and is smiling at you. He delights in you and has forgiven you. Nothing will ever separate you from His love. Stop punishing yourself. Stop replaying your mistakes. Today, throw away the guilt. God has forgiven you. He loves you right now. He loves you completely and unconditionally. Draw near to God through prayer and stillness with a true heart that delights in Him. Stand on your unwavering faith in His goodness and mercy. He loves you! He really, really, really loves you!

Smile!

My Prayer for You Today:
Father, today we draw near to you with a true heart. We seek your presence, Lord, with our hearts open and true. We are so grateful for your love and your grace. Your love amazes us. Thank you that you are faithful and you forgive us. We are in awe of you, Lord. Thank you. Today we pray for our brothers and sisters, who are crippled by guilt. Free them, Lord, with your love in Jesus's name. Amen.

SALVATION AND RIGHTEOUSNESS

"He has dressed me with the clothing of salvation and draped me in a robe of righteousness." Isaiah 61:10

God has made you blameless. You can relax now!

We have all done things we regret. We have all said things we wish we could take back. Great news, today you can stop beating yourself up. Nothing you do or say will change the past; release yourself from the shackles of shame holding you hostage. Let go of anger and wishing things were different. God has clothed you with His redemption. He has wrapped you in His grace. Let it go!

God is your strength and your defense. He has become your salvation. (Isaiah 12:2) You are set free. You have been made right. His salvation and righteousness are upon you. You are well taken care of.

Today, move through your day with the awareness of His righteousness. When you are tempted to feel and think like a victim, remember that God uses every experience to shape you. When you are angry and frustrated with yourself, remember His righteousness covers you and has taken every past mistake into consideration. Today, move, breathe, and have your being in Him.

His grace and His love are upon you. You are going to be just fine!

My Prayer for You Today:
Father, today we thank you for your grace and love that have made us righteous. We know we don't deserve it but we are so thankful. Help us today to break free from criticism and self-judgment and empower us to shine in your love and through your presence. Thank you that we are your righteousness through Jesus. We praise you. Amen.

GOOD OLD DAYS

"Don't long for the good old days." Ecclesiastes 7:10

Don't get stuck in the past. Your coming days will be brighter than your former days.

Friend, God is working now just like He worked in the good old days. When we focus on the past, we focus on maintaining old ways rather than creating and developing new ideas! We reminisce about the past while letting the present slip away. Instead of working on your marriage right now, you are sad thinking about how great things used to be. Rather than budgeting your money now, you cry over the stocks you lost. Don't long for the good old days, live today!

God tells us, "Behold, I will do something new." (Isaiah 43:19) God is constantly creating something better in our lives. God says He is the potter and we are the clay. (Isaiah 64:8) He is shaping and molding us for new things, for better things, for extraordinary things.

Today, don't let your throwback hold you back. Don't hold on to His past manifestations while overlooking His present revelations. God is making something new in your life. If He blessed you then, He will bless you again. Your latter days will be better than your former days. He will do something new in your life. Forget about the good old days, look to the amazing, miracle-filled, blessed days ahead.

My Prayer for You Today:
Lord, thank you that you are doing new things in our lives. Thank you that our good old days do not compare to what you have in store for us. We are so excited, so ready to be surprised by you, Father. Lord, reveal yourself to us so that we no longer hold on to old manifestations but that we see and experience your current work here and now. Amaze us, Lord, in Jesus's name we pray. Amen.

PRUNING

"I am the true vine, and my Father is the gardener. He cuts off every branch of mine that doesn't produce fruit, and He prunes the branches that do bear fruit so they will produce even more fruit." John 15:1-2

God is pruning you for more!

Today, don't mistake God's pruning for God's punishment. Gardeners cut branches in order for them to grow stronger. Similarly, a great hairstylist cuts and trims ends regularly in order for your hair to grow stronger and healthier. God is pruning you in order to be stronger. Stop crying over cut-off branches! Stop chasing those individuals God pruned out of your life. It is for your good!

Friend, your responsibility is to remain in Him. Remain faithful and prayerful. Remain committed and trust Him. Trusting God includes trusting His pruning. Psalm 92:14 ensures that you "will still bear fruit in old age, and will stay fresh and green." As long as you remain in Him, you will prosper, you will succeed, and you will bear fruit.

Today, remember God is pruning you, not punishing you! Trust Him. He loves you. If He takes away something from your life, it is to grow you stronger and better. Let it go and trust Him.

My prayer for You Today:
Father, thank you that you are the great gardener. Thank you for pruning us as painful as it may feel, we know it's because you love us and you have called us to bear more fruit. Today, help us to remain in you in prayer and to trust you. We need you. We love you and praise you. Amen.

SHINE

"You are the light of the world. A city built on a hill cannot be hidden."
Matthew 5:14

This is your identity: you are the light of the world! Wow!!!

Light shines, it heals, it exposes, it drowns out darkness, it enlightens, and it brings hope by illuminating the way. You are the light of the world. You too shine, you heal, you drown out darkness, you enlighten, and you bring hope! There's a reason why others look to you—you are a city built on a hill. You cannot be hidden. Others admire you and seek out your example and help. This is your identity. Don't you realize it?

Today, stop feeling sorry for yourself. Stop complaining and stop with the lack of confidence. You are the light of the world. Whatever you are facing today, bring light to it. Let your light shine! You have come this far; darkness will never overtake you. You are the light of the world. You have a purpose bigger than you imagine. God has a plan greater than you can dream. There's a reason He placed you on a hill. Shine!

"You are the light of the world…let your light shine before others, that they may see your good deeds and glorify your Father in heaven." (Matthew 5:14-16)

My Prayer for You Today:
Father, today with your confidence and your grace we embrace our identity of being the light of the world. Thank you, Lord, that you have great plans for our lives, thank you that you have a purpose that requires us to be set on a hill, never hidden. You are so amazing and we love you so much. Be with us today as we shine in Jesus's name. Amen.

ADVOCATE

"We have an advocate who pleads our case before the Father. He is Jesus Christ, the one who is truly righteous." 1 John 2:1

Have you ever needed an advocate? Maybe you've needed an attorney to plead your case, to settle a dispute, or work the details of your divorce. Maybe you just needed a friend to stick up for you when someone was badmouthing you. We have all needed an advocate. Thankfully, we have one!

The Bible reassures that Jesus is your advocate. Jesus continually pleads your case. He is there, full of grace, interceding on your behalf. Unlike an attorney, He doesn't lose a case. He always wins in your favor. Because of Him, you never get the punishment you deserve. His grace gives you a new chance everyday. His grace makes all things work for your good. His love allows you to bask in blessings you don't deserve. Friend, you have an advocate!

Today, move through your day knowing that Jesus is your advocate. Be still. Relax. You don't have to fight your own battles. You don't have to prove your point. You don't have to be angry or scared. Jesus is your advocate! He intercedes in your favor. He steps in for you.

Be still. Jesus pleads your case!

My Prayer for You Today:
Lord, thank you that we never get what we deserve, but because of your unconditional grace and love we are always blessed with better. Thank you, Jesus, that you are our advocate. Thank you for interceding on our behalf. Thank you for standing up for us. Today we receive your love and your grace as we serve as advocates for others. We love you and praise you. Amen.

VISION

"Where there is no vision, the people perish." Proverbs 29:18

Today, wake up with a vision!

Who do you want to be? What are your dreams? Your five-year old self was fearless and never let her circumstances dictate her dreams. Who did she want to be? The eight-year-old boy you once were was strong and courageous; he fought monsters and believed in his own strength. What happened to him? Your fearless self had incredible dreams and a great vision. What were they? What is yours?

Don't walk into work today the same way you did yesterday. Have a vision. Who do you want to be? What do you stand for? Your vision may be blurry, but what God said about you is the ultimate truth. God said you are the salt of the earth. (Matthew 5:13) He said you are the head, not the tail. (Deuteronomy 28:13) God said you will lend and not borrow. (Deuteronomy 15:6) He said you are a fisher of men. (Matthew 4:19) He said you are His light in a dark world. (Matthew 5:14)

So today, have a vision! Embrace God's vision for your life. Be an agent of grace. Be who God created you to be. Build those around you. Speak words of life. Love people. Smile. Be grateful. Give others a break. Relax. Trust God. Be the light!

My Prayer for You:
Lord, today let us be new people. Transform our thinking, Father. Take captive every thought and make it obedient to you. Help us to be the light. Be with us as we love people, as we preach the gospel not with words but with our deeds. We surrender today to you, Lord. Have your way in our lives. We love you and praise you. Amen.

PRAISE HIM

"Let us continually offer to God a sacrifice of praise—the fruit of lips that confess his name." Hebrews 13:15

Today, praise Him!

Praise Him when you're happy. Praise Him through your storm. Praise Him when life is great and praise Him when you are in trouble. Whatever you do, just praise Him. Friend, praising God doesn't only involve shouting and yelling; it is not limited to singing on Sunday mornings. Praise is an attitude of gratitude. Praise is acknowledging God in every area of your life.

The Bible teaches us that "the sounds of joy and gladness" (Jeremiah 33:11) bring Him praise. Praise Him by enjoying your day. If you enjoy music, poetry, movies, or socializing, do so as a way to praise God. By simply being happy, you are praising God. Do what you enjoy to praise Him. Do what makes you smile. Your laughter praises Him. Your smile praises Him. Open your heart in different ways and praise the One who loves you.

Praise Him with your smile. Praise Him with your joy. Praise Him with your life!

My Prayer for You Today:
Father, let everything we do bring praise to you. Thank you that you love us so much that everything we enjoy in your name brings praise to you. Today we praise you with our lives. We are thankful for all the blessings bestowed upon us. Thank you for your love, thank you for your grace. We love you, Lord. Amen.

WORD MADE FLESH

"The Word became flesh and made his dwelling among us." John 1:14

Jesus is the Word made flesh!

We have all accepted it and believe it to be true for Jesus, yet today you too are called to be the "Word made flesh". Unfortunately, we have let the words of others shape us. Your mother called you selfish, so you believed it and behaved accordingly. Your critics said you were arrogant, so you believed it and behaved accordingly. You are not defined by the words of others. Just because someone calls you something doesn't mean that's who you are.

You are His Word made flesh. God said you are fearfully and wonderfully made. (Psalm 139:14) He said you are the heir of His kingdom. (Romans 8:17) He said you are the head, not the tail. (Deuteronomy 28:13) He said He will set you high above all. (Deuteronomy 28:1) He said you are a conqueror. (Romans 8:37) He said you will lend and not borrow. (Deuteronomy 15:6)

Today, let His Word reside in you so that, like the Apostle Paul, you can say, "It is no longer I who live, but Christ lives in me." (Galatians 2:20)

You are the Word made flesh.

My Prayer for You Today:
Father, today we seek to have your Word reside in us. Let ever word be from you, let your Word take root in the depth of our souls so that we may live the life you purposed for us. We open our hearts and souls to you today. We surrender all in Jesus's name. Amen.

CHILDISH WAYS

"When I was a child, I talked like a child, I thought like a child, I reasoned like a child. When I became a man, I put away childish ways."
1 Corinthians 13:11

It's time to put away your old ways!

Now that you know better, do better! God has revealed Himself to you and it's time to change the way you think and speak. It's time to grow into who God created you to be. You no longer have to live in fear. You no longer have to envy others. You no longer have to carry the burden of seeking others' acceptance. It's time to put away childish ways.

The Bible tells us, "…when completeness comes, what is in part disappears." (1 Corinthians 13:10) Likewise, when the favor of God is upon your life, put away childish ways. Your old ways no longer serve you. God has blessed your life and it's time for you to be a blessing to others. Let His love light the way to a mature, abundant, and blessed life.

Today, in the midst of your journey, put away fear and hold on to faith. Put away anger and hold on to forgiveness. Put away blaming and hold on to His grace. Put away comparing and hold on to His love. Put away worries and hold on to His promises. Put away childish ways and look to Him. He is the way, the truth, and the life. (John 14:6)

My Prayer for You Today:
Father, today in Jesus's name we put away childish ways. Lord, you know the habits and activities keeping us from prospering, today help us to identify them and put them away. We open ourselves to a more mature life in faith and in you. Be with us. Fill us now. Amen.

OVERFLOW

"My cup overflows." Psalm 23:5

Friend, God is not a god of scarcity. He is not a god of just enough. He is a God of overflow!

You are not meant to be counting pennies. He never intended for you to struggle to make ends meet. God doesn't want you to be barely making it, with mediocre health and low energy. He is not satisfied with you living unenthusiastically. God loves you too much to have chosen that life for you. He is an overflowing God. Your cup is supposed to overflow. Your life is supposed to burst excess love, joy, fun, and peace. You are supposed to experience abundance in every area of your life. That is God's vision for your life.

Today, stop talking about your lack and declare your overflow. God has promised to give you houses you didn't build and vineyards you didn't plant. (Joshua 24:13) He promises to meet all your needs according to His riches. (Philippians 4:19) He is able to bless you abundantly so that you will have all you need at all times. (2 Corinthians 9:8)

He is a God of overflow. Today, may your cup overflow!

My Prayer for You Today:
Lord, today we declare overflow in all areas of our lives. Bless us with overflow in love, joy, peace, fun, overflow in our finances, overflow in our health, overflow in our relationships, and overflow in our professional lives. Lord in Jesus's name we declare overflow in all areas of our lives because we know you are abundant and it brings you great pleasure to bless us. Father, today we are so lucky and so thankful to be your children. We love you and praise you. Amen.

BY HIS SPIRIT

"Not by might nor power, but by my spirit." Zechariah 4:6

You have an incredible spirit that resides in you and you can do all things through Him.

You don't have to shout. You don't have to demand, no need to defend yourself or fight your way to the top. You will get there. You will accomplish great things, not by your power or your might, but by His spirit. You will do great things through Him who resides in you.

Friend, understand that when you walk into a room, all of Heaven walks in with you because the Kingdom of Heaven is within you. (Luke 17:21) The Omniscient Creator is within you and wherever you go, He is with you. When you walk into a room, ALL of Heaven walks in with you!!!

Today, grasp the depth of power that is in you. Grasp the depth of His love for you. Bask in His infinite grace. You can do all things through Him. It's not your might, not your power, but His spirit! There is nothing impossible, nothing insurmountable, and nothing too big for His spirit. Tap into His spirit and soar!

My Prayer for You Today:
Father, we are so amazed by your spirit. Help us today to overcome barriers, knock down walls, take leaps of faith, and overcome our fears not by our might, but by your spirit. Thank you, Father, that you reside in us and that through you we can do anything. Today we are strong because of you, we are conquerors because of you, we are the head and we can do all things through you. Thank you, Lord. Thank you, Jesus. Amen.

BE BLESSED

"Blessed is she who has believed that the Lord would fulfill his promises to her!" Luke 1:45

You are blessed to know that God keeps His promises.

Be the type of person who believes He keeps his words no matter what. People may tell you that things will never change, and you won't make it, but be bold and blessed enough to know that God has great plans for you. Let your faith empower you to speak victory. He will do what He promises. You can do all things through Him. You will prosper. He will grant the desires of your heart. Know it, believe it, and live it!

Knowing His Word keeps you blessed and faithful. Today, forget what the critics say, forget what the news predicts; dive into His Word. His Word holds the truth of who you are and the truths of His promises. His Word reveals His plans for your life. God will fulfill His promises. Dare to believe it!

Wait, watch, and be blessed!

My Prayer for You:
Lord, we declare ourselves blessed today because we believe beyond a doubt that you will fulfill your promises. The desires of our hearts are from you and we thank you already for granting them. Your loyalty and grace continue to amaze us. We love you and praise you. Amen.

HELP

"For I am the Lord, your God, who takes hold of your right hand and says to you, Do not fear; I will help you." Isaiah 41:13

Help is here! God is your help.

No need to fear. No reason to panic. You have God as your help and your shield. Everything will work out for your good. Breathe. God promises to take hold of your right hand. He won't let go. His hold is the hold of life, the hold of deliverance, the hold of hope, the hold that breaks you free from every shackle. Do not fear—God will help you!

Today, whether you are facing difficulties at work or at home, with family or with friends, in public or in private, God promises to help you. He will never leave you. He will never abandon you. He is here. God is holding your right hand. He will guide your steps. Trust Him. Stay aware of His presence. Don't let the world cloud what He is revealing to you. You are going to be just fine. Trust Him.

Your help is here. God is here!

My Prayer for You Today:
Father, help! You promised to help us and today we are holding on to your promise. You know each and everyone of us and the specific help we need; help with our health, our finances, our relationships, our commitments, our dreams, our hopes, our aspirations. We need help with finding peace in the midst of the storm, help with finding stillness in the middle of so many battles. Come to our rescue now. Move! Do something. We declare it done in Jesus's name. Amen.

AGREE AND PRAY

"If two of you agree here on earth concerning anything you ask, my Father in heaven will do it for you." Matthew 18:19

Who is your prayer partner? It is just as important to stay away from the wrong people as it is to surround yourself with the right people. Do you have someone you call to pray with you? Do you pray with your friends?

There is power in numbers. Pray together. Get in accordance with someone and pray for something. It is written and promised that if two of us agree on something and pray for it, God will grant it. Don't keep your dreams to yourself, share them with a confidant who will support you and pray with you.

God has called us to fellowship with one another. And God rewards fellowship with answered prayer. Today send a text, call a friend, and pray. God is waiting to amaze you both. You can pray for anything, and if you believe that you've received it, it will be yours. (Mark 11:24)

Agree and pray!

My Prayer for You Today:
Father, thank you for the gift of fellowship. Thank you, Lord, that as we pray and agree on something, you promised to answer. Today we pray for open doors, for success, health, joy, and peace, for increase in every area of our lives. Fill us Father. We pray all this in Jesus's precious and holy name. Amen.

BACKSLIDING

"I will heal you from backsliding." Jeremiah 3:22

For all the times you take one step forward and two steps back, God will cure you from backsliding.

For all the times you started your workout regimen and quit, all the times you saved ten dollars and spent fifteen, all the times you left a relationship and went back, all the times you sabotaged your own success, all the times you quit drinking and smoking only to get another glass and light another cigarette, God will heal you from them!

Today understand that backsliding is a disease! You don't have to go through it alone. Take it to the One who can heal you. Seek the One who strengthens and guides you. Pray to Him who loves you. From the most mundane habits to the biggest addictions, invite God to take over and pray His healing over your backsliding. He promises to heal you, and God keeps His promises!

If you are feeling discouraged and unmotivated, God can help. If you are moving backwards, God has a plan to stop you from backsliding. Reach out to Him. Seek Him. Pray without ceasing! Turn it over to Him.

My Prayer for You Today:
Father, we are backsliding, help! Heal us from destructive habits. Free us from sabotage. Release us from ineffective practices. Thank you that you have declared us heads, not tails. Today, guide our steps forward in Jesus's name. Amen.

TROUBLE

"I have told you these things, so that in me you may have peace. In this world you will have trouble. But take heart! I have overcome the world."
John 16:33

As long as you are alive, you will face trouble. Don't let trouble fool you into believing that God is absent. Don't believe the whispers of heartache trying to convince you that He has forsaken you. Jesus foretold that trouble is part of life; take heart and find peace in Him.

Bills continue to pile, clients are overly demanding, family brings more drama, there isn't enough time in the day to get everything done, you should be exercising instead of eating that piece of cake, you can't stand your mother-in-law, your neighbor's dog just soiled your front porch, the list goes on. Trouble never ends, that's the beauty of life. Take heart. You can be in trouble and not be consumed by it. You can be in the storm and still experience His peace.

Today, if you thought God forgot about you, take heart. It's all part of the journey. Seek Him. The trouble, heartache and headache are guideposts leading you back to Him. Lean not unto your own understanding; trust Him. (Proverbs 3:5)

Nothing in your life is out of order. Consider it pure joy whenever you face trials of many kinds, knowing that the testing of your faith produces endurance. (James 1:2-3) Take heart and find your peace in Him.

My Prayer for You Today:
Lord, you know the troubles that we each face. Help us today to take heart. Thank you, Father, that we do not have to face trouble alone, as you promised to be with us every step of the journey. Today we pray for patience, for endurance, for divine peace, and for the faith to keep moving forward despite feeling tired. Be with us and keep us focused on you. Fill us with your love and grace. We need you right now. Amen.

POWER, LOVE, SOUND MIND

"For God has not given us a spirit of fear, but of power and of love and of a sound mind." 2 Timothy 1:7

Let His spirit fill you with power and love and may you be blessed with a sound mind.

Friend, God has not given you a spirit of fear. Whenever you experience fear, remind yourself that fear is not of God. Fear is the absence of faith. Choose today to embody the spirit that your Creator has given you. Circumstances may leave you trembling, people's accusations may keep you awake at night, the demands of your job may have you losing your mind, but God is not losing sleep over any of it. He is neither scared nor fazed by your situation and your needs. Tap into His power and relax.

God is love. There is no fear in love, but perfect love casts out fear. (John 4:18) Let His unconditional love cast out all fear from your life. He loves you too much to let anything happen out of order. His love is too deep and too broad for it not to cover every detail of your life. Greater is He that is in you. (1 John 4:4) With His spirit in you, you will experience perfect bliss, peace, joy, love, power, and a sound mind.

Today, if it's not from God, reject it. Open your heart and life to what He has for you. God wants to bless you with power, love, and a sound mind. Accept it today.

My Prayer for You Today:
Lord, we rebuke and break all shackles of fear. Be with us today as we move to a place of power, love, and a sound mind. Thank you for blessing us with the fruits of the spirit. We pray today that you take away everything that is not from you. We open ourselves to you fully and we thank you that you love us and have us safely in your arms. We love you. Amen.

VALUABLE

"Look at the birds. They don't plant or harvest or store food in barns, for your heavenly Father feeds them. And aren't you far more valuable to him than they are?" Matthew 6:26

You are so valuable to God. He loves you more than you can imagine and will take care of all your needs.

Nature has a beautiful way of teaching us about God's love. In the midst of winter, when the soil freezes and the birds fly south, it's easy to forget that flowers will blossom again and birds will chirp again. Similarly, in the midst of your struggle, in your life's winter season, you may forget that things will change. Your life will blossom again. You will sing again. God will always take care of you.

"Cast all your worries to God because he cares for you." (1 Peter 5:7) You are God's prized possession. He delights in you. He cares for you and loves you. You matter to God. You are valuable. The world can reject you, everyone can turn against you, but God will never leave you. The opinions of others will never change His love for you. Nothing will change His mind about you. You matter. You are valuable.

You matter to God. You are valuable to God. He loves you so very much. You matter.

My Prayer for You Today:
Father, thank you that we are valuable to you. We don't understand it, and we certainly don't deserve it, but because of who you are, you value us. Thank you. Thank you for your love, your grace, and your provision. We surrender our lives to you and rest in knowing that you always provide. We love you and praise you. Amen.

HIS TIME

"My times are in your hands." Psalm 31:15

Never late, never early, always on time. Your times are in His hands. Trusting God requires you to trust His timing.

Everything in your life is as it should be. Your blessings unfold according to His plans and His time. Trust. You are always under His watch. You are filled with His love and wrapped in His grace. Your times are in His hands. The phone will ring right on time. The breakthrough will come on time. The miracle will happen exactly when you need it. Just when you are falling apart, you will be sustained. Trust Him.

"There is an appointed time for everything. And there is a time for every event under Heaven." (Ecclesiastes 3:1) God knows the seasons of your life. He knows the right time for everything. He has appointed a time for your heart's desires. Relax.

Today, remember that your times are in His hands. You can trust God. And trust His timing.

My Prayer for you today:
Father, thank you that our times are in your hands. Father, we know that there is a time for everything under the sun and that you know the perfect time. Help us today to be patient while we wait. Help us to trust you and fill us with your strength so that we may have unwavering faith. We know that in every season, Lord, you are there. Thank you for always being with us and never forsaking us. We love you and praise you. Amen.

STEPS

"In his heart a man plans his course, but the Lord determines his steps."
Proverbs 16:9

God knows the desires of your heart. He knows your dreams and aspirations. Trust Him to guide you step by step.

Today, if you have dreams without plans, aspirations without directions, ideas without an execution strategy, take heart. The Master has a plan. Devote yourself to God and watch Him order your steps. You don't have to know how you will get there, just know that you will. You don't have to understand the process but be certain that there is one. You don't have to see the staircase but take the first step.

God has great plans for you. (Jeremiah 29:11) You are called to walk by faith, not by sight. (2 Corinthians 5:7) God has a process for your success. Trust Him. Believe. You may feel frustrated and lost, confused and stagnant, but know that God order steps, not elevator rides. The process takes time. The blessing is unfolding one step at a time. Hold on.

Let Him who knows it all and Him who loves you most order your steps. Listen to His directions.

My Prayer for You Today:
Father, you know the deepest desires of our hearts. Though we don't understand the process, we are committed to praising and serving you throughout the process. We don't see the way, but we know that you know the way. We trust you, Lord. Order our steps. Guide us into blessings, success, health, wealth, happiness, and peace. Thank you that it's already done. Amen.

HIDDEN FACE

"The Lord has hidden himself from his people, but I trust him and place my hope in him." Isaiah 8:17

If you ever feel forgotten by God, unheard and alone, continue to trust and place your hope in Him. He hasn't left you.

Life has a way of beating us up. Things come up one after another, and we wonder where God is hiding. In the midst of your pain, in the middle of your battle, He may hide His face but God will never withhold His love. He may seem distant but He will never leave you nor forsake you. He may be silent but He is there.

Today, continue to trust God. He's brought you this far! Hold on with unwavering faith. Focus on the process. He is building your character. His silence is sharpening you. His perceived distance is strengthening your mind. Be thankful for His tough love. Hope is the anchor of your soul. (Hebrews 6:19) Hope in Him. Trust in His love. Believe in His grace. Remember His omniscient power.

The One who never sleeps watches over you. Though He hides His face, He is there!

My Prayer for You Today:
Father, you know every detail; you know our coming and going, you know our pain and battle. Help us to have faith and trust in you even when we feel distant from you. Wrap us in your love and grace and remind us of your loyalty. We thank you that you mend broken hearts. We praise you. We love you. We pray all this in Jesus's precious and holy name. Amen.

HE SEES YOU

"Be careful not to do acts of righteousness before men, to be seen by them. If you do, you will have no reward from your Father in heaven."
Matthew 6:1

Your journey is inward. Stop the show. Drop the act. Your goal is to be recognized by God, not men!

We all seek recognition. Filled with good intentions, we often lose sight of the big picture and seek acknowledgement from men. We shout the loudest and recite the most scriptures only to be portrayed a certain way to people while we continue to be spiritually empty. We feed ten people and tell one hundred about it. We give to the less fortunate and brag about it. We sponsor a child and talk about it for the next ten years. God is not impressed by our bragging.

Do good and shut your mouth. Let God reward you. His blessings are far more substantial than the applause of men. Let God recognize you for your acts of righteousness. Let your actions speak of your faith without boasting. Jesus warned about praying in public and seeking others' recognition when we fast. Stop bragging and let God reward you.

God sees you. He sees your heart. No act is ignored. No smile goes unnoticed. And no helping hand is unobserved. God sees your heart. He sees your giving. He knows your acts of kindness. He sees the smallest acts of love. He will reward you. Seek solely His acknowledgement.

My Prayer for You Today:
Father, thank you that you know our hearts. Break every shackle keeping us attached to human recognition. You are the one we seek to please, Lord. Help us to stay focused on you. Inspire us to do good and we thank you that in return you will bless us. We pray for seven times the blessings today in Jesus's name. Amen.

CHOSEN AND APPOINTED

"I chose you and appointed you that you should go and bear fruit… so that whatever you ask the Father in my name, he will give to you." John 15:16

You have been chosen and appointed by the Almighty. It's not by your works, but by His grace and love.

When you are appointed and chosen for a position, you can put away your resume. Forget about an interview, no need for a cover letter, the position is yours! Therefore, stop trying to prove yourself. Relax and do your best through God's grace. No need to convince others of your worth. You have been chosen and appointed by the One who matters. Your success has already been set, so "go and bear fruit". The One who appointed you never lies. He never fails. And His promises are without repentance. Your success is guaranteed.

Ask and it will be given to you. (Matthew 7:7) Have you asked God for the very thing you have been yearning? Why do you limit yourself? Nothing is too small or too big to ask. Jesus himself guaranteed that when we ask in His name, we receive! God has chosen and appointed you. You are exactly where you should be. You have everything you need to bear fruit and to prosper.

Friend, you have been chosen and appointed. God loves you that much!

My Prayer for You Today:
Father, you know the deepest desires of our hearts; we ask that you fulfill them in Jesus's name. We know that whatever we ask in His name, we receive. We thank you for your love, thank you for your grace. Show us today how to bear good fruits. Thank you for choosing and appointing us. We know it's not by our works, but all by your grace. You are an awesome God. We love you and praise you. Amen.

SALT

"You are the salt of the earth." Matthew 5:13

Newsflash: You are kind of a big deal! You are not anybody, not a no-good chump; you are the salt of the earth! Let that soak in for a minute…you are the salt of the earth!

In everyday life, we know that salt brings flavor and taste to food. It is used for many different things including cleaning and relieving wounds, stings, bites, and poison ivy. In the physical world, salt is useful and essential. Similarly, in the spiritual realm, you are the salt of the earth! You have the power to bring flavor and life wherever you go. You have the power to heal and clean. You are the salt of the earth!

Friend, Jesus himself declared you the salt of the earth. You have the ability to radically change your environment and everyone you come in contact with. You are God's ambassador here on earth. (2 Corinthians 5:20) You are not just anybody. When you fulfill your duties as an attorney, a doctor, a teacher, a secretary, a nurse, a hairdresser, a banker, a stay-at-home mom, you are showing the world what God looks like doing everyday jobs. You are representing Him on earth. You are the salt of the earth!

Today, if you forgot how important you are, if you ever doubted your significance on earth, know that you are the salt of the earth! Your smile brings hope to others. Your attentive ear to your coworker reminds him that he is worthy. Your generosity to the beggar proved to him that God still provides. Your encouraging words spoken to that troubled teen prompted a mind change. Everything you do is significant. You are the salt of the earth!

My Prayer for you today:
Father, thank you for reminding us that we can do better, we can do more, we can serve you through serving others in ordinary ways. Thank you, Father, for choosing us as your ambassadors here on earth. We pray for renewed faith, heightened courage, divine enthusiasm as we step out today and do your work and show your love. We love you for your greatness. We thank you for your grace. We pray all this in Jesus's name. Amen.

KNOW HIM

"His divine power has given us everything we need for a godly life through our knowledge of him who called us by his own glory and goodness." 2 Peter 1:3

You have everything you need to live a godly life. Knowing God is enough alone.

Friend, you don't have to be perfect to live the life God intended for you. Your past can be crooked. You can lie, cheat, and steal and God will still love you. You could be the most hated person on earth, and yet He would still love you. God loves you. Knowing God will radically change you and the trajectory of your life. Do you know Him?

Jesus said He came not for the righteous, but for the sinners, not for the healthy, but for the sick. (Mark 2:17) God doesn't expect us to be perfect, but as you commit to His Word, as you pray and place Him first, you will be amazed at how He will completely change you.

Today, rather than beating yourself up and trying to change on your own will, get to know Him. Spend time in His presence. Read His Word. Love. As you know Him, you will change.

To know Him is to be changed by Him.

My Prayer for You Today:
Lord, more than anything we yearn to know you. Reveal yourself to us, Father. You know our deepest desires. Speak, Lord. Have your way. We surrender. Amen.

WITH YOU ALWAYS

"I am with you always, even to the end of the age." Matthew 28:20

One of God's most comforting promises is that He is with you always.

You are not alone. You do not have to go through life alone. God is with you always. He knows your circumstance. Invite him to all the details of your life. Throughout your day, be in constant communication with God. Be more and more aware of His presence. He will reveal Himself in the most beautiful and intimate ways. Speak to Him throughout the day. Utter simple phrases like "Father be with me," "Lord thank you right now," "Jesus speak for me." Speak to Him. He is always with you.

Today you don't have to do life alone. Your Creator is with you. The One who delights in you is accessible at all times. He knows your coming and going. Find peace and comfort in His presence. He is smiling at you right now. Take a deep breath. Relax. Everything is going to be ok.

God is with you always.

My prayer for You Today:
Father, we pray to feel and experience your presence today. Thank you that you love us so much that you are with us always. Lord, speak to us today, we yearn to hear from you. Reveal yourself. We love you, Lord. We praise you. Amen.

ACCORDING TO YOUR FAITH

"According to your faith, let it be done to you." Matthew 9:29

Here's a secret: the size of your miracle correlates to the size of your faith.

Friend, your limited faith puts a glass top on your blessings. Believe God for things that do not make sense. Trust His grandeur and magnitude. He is the Supreme God who created the Earth and all its' wonders. Imagine a God so amazing, capable of creating the human body, a God so powerful, so extreme, who colored the ocean with over five million species of animals. 5 million!!!! It's difficult to wrap your brain around such magnitude. So when you talk about your God, and pray for your miracle, take the lid off. God can do big things. He can do outstandingly more than we can imagine.

There's nothing impossible for God. (Luke 1:38) There isn't a miracle too big, a task too enormous, a situation too destroyed for God. Have faith in the One who is insuperable, the One who can do exceedingly above and beyond, the One like no other. Have faith enough to pray according to His ability, not yours. Have faith to ask according to His opulence.

Today your miracle is based on your level of faith. Rank up your faith. Pray big. Think big. Dream big. Imagine big. Ask big. God will amaze you!

My Prayer for You Today:
Father, the very fact that you give us according to our faith is amazing and loving. Today we ask for supernatural, unwavering faith. We take the lid off of our faith, knowing that you are too big to fathom and that nothing is impossible to you. Bless our lives in supernatural ways, Lord. We pray for exceedingly above and beyond blessings, we pray for things we can't even fathom, and we know that you will answer. We thank you in advance. We love you. Amen.

NOW I SEE

"I know this: though I was blind, now I see." John 9:25

After Jesus restored a blind man's sight, his prosecutors were questioning the healed man and asked him if Jesus was a sinner. The man simply answered "I don't know if he's a sinner, but I know this: though I was blind, now I see."

Friend, you don't have to understand how God works, you simply have to proclaim and share the blessings He's done for you. Don't focus on the way things look, just know that God can restore every aspect of your life. People will question your intention and bring up your past, but like the healed man, you will share that though you were broke, now you are abundantly blessed. Though you were sick, now you are miraculously healed. Though you were clinically depressed, now you are encouraged. Though you were unhappy, now you live in a space of deep joy. Though you were worried and scared, now you are certain and you stand in faith.

Today, in the midst of your blind relationships, blind finances, blind career, blind health, know this: God has the ability to restore every area of your life. He can touch you in supernatural ways. He can and will restore your sight. Your condition doesn't determine your destiny, your God does!

My Prayer for You Today:
Lord, today we ask that you open our eyes in all areas of our life. Open the eyes of our understanding. Take away the blindness in our finances, health, relationships, and families. We trust in your supernatural powers and know that nothing is impossible for you. Touch us, Lord. We ask all this in Jesus's name. Amen.

HOUSE

"As for me and my house, we will serve the Lord." Joshua 24:15

Decide today to serve God.

Too many of us have read this verse and been limited by our definition of the word "house." We often use it to complain about our unspiritual spouse, immature roommates, conservative parents, unruly children and weird family members. We blame our family for our inability to serve. Today, broaden your definition of "house." Your physical house may consist of other individuals but your spiritual house includes your body, mind, soul and heart. Serve Him with both houses.

God wants all of you. He wants your physical house and your spiritual house. He is concerned with everything that concerns you, from your career to the shoes you choose to wear. Let Him in your house today. Let him in all of your business. Invite Him in every part of your life. Serve Him with all your might. Do everything with a servant heart by keeping Him first and having a grateful attitude.

Today, serve God with your mind, body, soul, and heart. Serve Him with your house.

My Prayer for You Today:
Father, today we surrender all of who we are to you. We surrender our household as well as our house, our being and soul. All of it brings glory to you. Show us today how to serve you in the ordinary as well as the extraordinary, in the physical as well as the spiritual, show us how to serve you through others. Thank you for your love, thank you for your grace. We pray all this in Jesus's precious and holy name. Amen.

WITHDRAW AND PRAY

"He…often withdrew…and prayed." Luke 5:16

If Jesus had to withdraw and pray, so do you!

Prayer changes things. It is your communication to the Almighty. Thankfully, there are no specific words or rituals that you have to follow. You don't need a lengthy intellectual blurb or an exact place. God loves you so much that He makes it convenient for you to be in communication with Him. Never a busy signal, never a dropped call. He is available always. Through words, thoughts, or feelings, you have access to Him—take advantage of that!

Jesus is the perfect example for us. He often withdrew to pray. He understood the power in prayer and you would be a fool not to take advantage of that power. God is available to you 24/7. The One who watches over you doesn't slumber or sleep. (Psalm 121:4) If your life is too busy for prayer, you're in big trouble. The Bible tells us to pray and not lose heart. (Luke 18:1)

Today, withdraw and pray. Treat yourself to a conversation with your Creator. Do it on your drive to work. Do it by taking a deep grateful breath. Do it by simply being aware of His presence and love. Whatever it is, just pray!

My Prayer for You Today:
Father, thank you that you love us so much that you gave us access to you at all times. Lord you know our hearts, you know the prayers we do not have the courage to utter. Listen to us Lord. Speak to us. Reveal yourself to us today as we reach out to you in prayer. We love you for your greatness; we thank you for your grace, thank you for the perfect example of Jesus. Amen.

RENEWED MIND

"Be transformed by the renewing of your mind." Romans 12:2

Be transformed by the renewing of your mind.

Do not spend another year thinking small, thinking defeat, or thinking about your problems. Let your life be transformed by thinking God-thoughts. Thinking miracles and opportunities. Think blessings and success. You can only go as far as your mind takes you, so think BIG!

Today, take every thought captive to the obedience of Christ. (2 Corinthians 10:5) Don't let your mind play tricks on you. God has great things in store for you and it starts with your faith in Him. Have enough faith to think big, enough faith to pray big, and enough faith to believe big no matter what things look like.

We serve a supernatural God. Let your life be transformed in supernatural ways by the renewing of your mind. Think God!

My Prayer for You Today:
Father, take captive every thought. Today we take the lid off our thinking and trust you for supernatural blessings. We declare ourselves transformed and renewed in Jesus's name. Have your way right now. We praise you and love you. Amen.

HIS PLANS

"For I know the plans I have for you" declares the Lord, "plans to prosper you and not to harm you, plans to give you hope and a future." Jeremiah 29:11

God has great plans for you. Are you excited?

It's important to have hopes and aspirations aligned with God's plans for your life. His plans are higher than yours. His purpose is bigger and better than yours. So rather than cheating yourself and living a life smaller than what your Creator intended for you, align your desires with His plans.

God promises plans to prosper you, to bring you hope and a future. Thankfully, God keeps His promises. It brings Him great joy to bless you. Know that whatever God has in store for you is beyond awesome, beyond great, and beyond amazing, because that's who He is. Friend, God will bless you according to His riches. He blesses according to Jesus. We will always fall short, but He loves us so much that He blesses according to His greatness and His love. Blessings are not earned; they are gifts from a generous and loving God. Be thankful.

Today, ask God to reveal His plans for you. Trust that His plans are amazing and that you will be wowed. He has great things in store for you. Receive them now.

My Prayer for You Today:
Father, thank you that you have great plans for us. Help us to receive, accept and live according to your plans. Lord, thank you that your thoughts are higher than ours and that our lives aligned with your will are higher than we could ever dream. We open our hearts and lives to you today. Fill us. Reveal your great plans to us. We love you. We praise you now and always. Amen.

WISE TIME

"Therefore be careful how you walk, not as unwise men but as wise, making the most of your time..." Ephesians 5:15-16

Be wise and make the most of your time.

Walk and live wisely. Make the most of your time. Be selective. Let everything you do be a reflection of God's great plans for your life. Be picky! Some will say you have changed, others will think you are indifferent, but your focused effort will make you more effective, and bring you more peace while experiencing more blessings in all areas of your life.

Let your life reflect who you are. Let every activity and endeavor be aligned with His great purpose for your life. Let the Master's plan be your master plan. Make the most of your time by giving Him all of your time. Take God out of your box. Everything in your life is part of His plan. His plan is not only reflective on Sunday mornings; His plan includes your career, your hobbies, your relationships, your down time, and your social life. He is in everything. Let every aspect of your life be aligned with His master plan.

Friend, God has a purpose and a plan for your life. The more aligned you are with His plan, the more peace and enjoyment you will experience. The Bible tells us that God gives perfect peace to those who keep their purpose firm according to His will. (Isaiah 26:3) Commit to making the most of your time.

Let the Master's plan be your master plan.

My Prayer for You Today:
Father, today we commit our time to you. Have your will in our lives. Bless us with wisdom and discernment to always be living according to your will. Thank you, Lord, that your plans are greater than our plans, your thoughts higher than our thoughts, and for that we turn every plan, every thought and all of our time to you. Thank you that you are good. We are so grateful and humble. Thank you for your love. We praise you and love you. Amen.

FORGET AND STRAIN

"Forgetting what is behind and straining toward what is ahead."
Philippians 3:13

Leave the past in the past. Whatever happened last year, last month or last week is not a crutch to your blessings right now. Your past does not dictate your destiny. Leave it behind.

Decide today to hold on to the blessings and forget the rest. Dump the disappointments and failed plans. Burry the worries and struggles. Look forward to what is ahead: greater blessings, greater growth, greater adventure, and greater peace. Take inventory and leave people, things, and circumstances behind. Everyone is not meant to move forward with you. Leave the useless, energy-sucking baggage behind and open yourself to better. Open your heart to a better you and a bigger life filled with favor, love, and blessings.

Jesus warned: "no one who puts a hand to the plow and looks back is fit for service…" (Luke 9:62) You can't reach for your dreams while holding on to your past. You can't stand with one foot in hope and one foot in regrets. Jump in fully and faithfully. Forget your past and press on to a brighter, bigger, more blessed future.

Today, forget the drama, burry the disappointment, suffocate the failures, and plant seeds of prosperity, love, and abundance for a blessed tomorrow.

Be blessed!

My Prayer for You Today:
Lord, thank you that your Word tells us to forget the past and press on. Today we take your advice. Fill us with new ambition, new courage and new enthusiasm as we seek you with great expectations. We thank you for your love; we praise you for your greatness. Amen.

LISTEN

"Whoever listens to me will dwell secure and will be at ease, without dread of disaster." Proverbs 1:33

God is always speaking to you. Are you listening?

When you listen to God you will reside, be settled, live in, be housed, and stay secure. You will be at ease. Life will be simple and smooth. Nothing will move you. Too often we choose to listen to our fearful minds or our messed up friends instead of listening to God. We worry about the rug being pulled from under us. We seek the counsel of our dysfunctional family. When you have an Almighty God, Alpha, and Omega always available to you and always speaking to you, why listen to anyone else?

Those who choose to listen to God will live with no fear. Even if the rug is pulled from under you, you will be supported. That's how God works! Friend, God will never steer you wrong. Listen to Him. Know and do His Word and flourish. You will recognize His voice. The sheep knows the shepherd. (John 10:14).You will know when God is speaking to you. It will bring you peace. He will speak to you in ways only you understand. Everything you do will prosper.

Today, be still and listen to Him. You will never be the same.

My Prayer for You Today:
Father, we yearn to hear from you. Today we pray for the courage not only to hear you, but to listen. We pray for the ability to not only recognize your voice, but to follow it. Thank you that you speak in ways we understand. We're listening, Lord. Have your way in our lives, in Jesus's name we pray. Amen.

GREATER

"You will see greater things than these." John 1:50

Jesus's miracles were amazing, yet He warned, "You will see greater things than these." Wow!

Rejoice, you will see greater things than those you have seen before. God has great plans in store for you. "Truly, truly I say to you…you will see the heavens opened." (John 1:51) This is a reason to celebrate. This should bring you great joy and excitement. Think of all the wonderful things God has done for you. Now just imagine, He will do greater things than those. Wow!

God is going to open the floodgates of heaven unto you and pour out blessings you will not have enough room to store. (Malachi 3:10) I'm excited for you. Lay your hopes and dreams at His altar today. Stand in faith. Stand in great expectations. He will do greater. He will do bigger. He will do more amazing things!

Today, pray for greater: greater joy, greater peace, greater health, greater wealth, greater purpose, greater adventure, greater pleasure, greater revelation, greater meaning, greater relationships, and greater blessings.

In Jesus's name, declare and profess "greater" in every aspect of your life starting now.

My Prayer for You Today:
Lord, we are so excited for the things you have in store for us. You continue to amaze us with greater things. Thank you that it only gets better. We are so excited and so thankful. Thank you, Lord. We open our hearts and lives to greater in Jesus's precious and holy name. Amen.

A GOD LIKE YOU

"For since the world began, no ear has heard and no eye has seen a God like you, who works for those who wait for him!" Isaiah 64:4

There you have it: no ear has heard and no eye has seen a God like our God.

In a world where everything fades and change is a constant, it's hard to fathom a God that never changes. It is even harder to comprehend a God who loves us no matter what. Nothing you have done and nothing you will do will ever change God's mind about you. He loves you now and always. That's hard to understand, especially when we often stop loving ourselves for our mistakes. There is none like Him.

Today, know that God is working for you. He works for those who wait for Him. Don't take matters into your own hands. Watch His blessings unfold beautifully in your life. He loves you, so what else would you expect? He loved you before you were conceived. (Jeremiah 1: 5) He has a plan for your life to prosper and give you hope. (Jeremiah 29:11) That's love. That's Him. That's God.

God works for those who wait for Him. He is working for you. Relax into His love. Have confidence in His promises. He loves you!

My Prayer for You Today:
Father, it's hard to fathom your love, but we accept it today. Thank you that you love us no matter what. Thank you, Father. Let your love change us today in Jesus's name. Amen.

FOUNTAIN OF LIFE

"For with you is the fountain of life; in your light we see light." Psalm 36:9

Look no further, with God is the fountain of life!

Whatever you are looking for today, you will find it in Him. You won't find it at the mall, nor in another piece of cake, but you will find it all in Him. Your worth, peace, love, purpose, meaning, confidence, and strength are with God. Seek Him and find it all. Whatever you desire today, go to the fountain! He is everything and can give you anything. God is the fountain of life!

Today, don't let the blessings blind you of the Blessor. Look no further. Your fountain of life is with your Creator. Let His light shine through you and for you. Let Him guide you and direct your path. He loves you and will bless you with the desires of your heart.

Your fountain of life is in Him!

My Prayer for You Today:
Lord, you continue to amaze us. In you we have all we need and want. Thank you for your generosity and your love. Today we open ourselves to you; let your light shine and change us. May we never be the same in Jesus's name. Amen.

EVERLASTING ARMS

"The eternal God is your refuge, and underneath are the everlasting arms." Deuteronomy 33:27

His everlasting arms are always open wide to welcome you back home. His arms are ready to rescue you and uphold you. Find refuge in Him.

God is your eternal refuge. To seek refuge in temporary places is not refuge at all. Imagine running from one house to another in the midst of a tsunami. True refuge and real shelter is in stable and unshaken ground. Only God can provide you a shelter that never fails. Only He is your eternal, unshaken, all-powerful refuge. In Him there is no variance; He is the same yesterday, today, and forever. (Hebrews 13:8)

Today, run to the arms of the One who loves you. Anchor your soul to His everlasting love. In Him you will find security like no other. God is your provision. He is your protection. Seek Him for guidance and love. In Him resides your peace and joy. His unfailing love will heal you. Through prayer and submission, find refuge in Him.

May His everlasting arms wrap you in love, grace, and peace today and everyday.

My Prayer for You Today:
Father, thank you that in you we find refuge. Remind us today that our only security is in you. Help us to keep focus on you. Fill us today with your love. Wrap us in your grace and give us peace. We love you and pray this in Jesus's precious and holy name. Amen.

GOD IS IN YOUR MIDST

The Lord your God is in your midst." Zephaniah 3:17

God is in all the details of your life. God is at your core. Relax!

Today, in the midst of your chaos, your worries, your fears, your disappointments, your dysfunction, breathe and find God at your core. He is at the center of your being and your life. Despite your struggle, there He is. Despite your heartache, there He is. Despite your loneliness, there He is.

The Lord your God is in your midst. At the core of your being resides the magnificent, omniscient, powerful God of the universe. Nothing can shake you. Nothing can overpower you. With God you are invincible.

Live from your core knowing that God is at your core. May you be empowered to stand taller, reach higher, love stronger, and live fuller.

My Prayer For You Today:
Father, thank you that you are in our midst. Thank you that at the core of our being, there you are. Lord, I pray that we remember this as we strive for more. Let this bring us encouragement and confidence to face the world and conquer our dreams. Thank you, Father, for your unconditional love. We love you. We praise you. Amen.

SACRIFICE

"He who did not spare his own Son, but gave him up for us all, how will he not also, along with him, graciously give us all things?" Romans 8:32

As I studied this verse, I could not fathom giving up my son for anyone. For those of us who are parents, we understand the level of sacrifice it takes to give up a child.

If God loves you so much that He did not spare His son, what will He not do for you? Your deepest desire doesn't measure up to the depth of His sacrifice. God already showed you that He would give you all things. There isn't anything He wouldn't do for you. Name it, and He'll give it to you. He already gave His son, anything else is small and insignificant in comparison.

Today, I pray you understand in the depth of your soul how precious you are to God. He loves you so much that He did not spare His son. He put everything on the line for you! He values you that much. If you ever feel unworthy, unimportant, or not enough, remember His sacrifice. When the world rejects, blames, and disappoints you, remember you have the One who loves you so much that He did not spare His own son for you.

God loves you this much!

My Prayer for You Today:
Father, we cannot fathom the level of sacrifice you took for us. Wow. Your love amazes us and humbles us. Thank you, Father, that you love us enough to give your own son. For that we are forever grateful. Thank you that your sacrifice gives us confidence that you will graciously give us all things. We praise you. We love you. Amen.

FRUIT OF THE SPIRIT

"Whoever sows to please the Spirit, from the Spirit will reap eternal life."
Galatians 6:8

Today, sow seeds of the Spirit rather than seed of the flesh. Please God and not the world. In Him you have eternal life.

The fruits of the Spirit are love, joy, peace, patience, kindness, goodness, and faithfulness. (Galatians 5:22) If your activities bring forth other feelings such as competition, jealousy, anger, strife, and deception, you will know that they are not of the spirit but of the flesh. Surround yourself with those who bring out the best in you and participate in activities of the spirit.

Take time today to bear and share the fruits of the spirit. Share your love, joy, peace, patience, and kindness with all those you encounter. Sow God-seeds! With God, you will never be disappointed and never be forsaken. You will reap eternal life.

My Prayer for You Today:
Father, fill us today as we yearn to sow seeds of the spirit. Help us, Father, to see the best in everyone and every situation. Fill us today with your peace and your love and use us to bless others. We surrender ourselves to you. Have your way. We love you and praise you. Amen.

BLESSINGS AND RESPONSIBILITY

"To whom much is given, much is required." Luke 12:48

There's a great sense of responsibility attached to your blessings. You can't have one without the other.

Too often we pray for breakthroughs, promotions, health, and success without realizing that blessings bring about greater responsibility. The more you are given, the more is required of you and the more challenges you will encounter. The Bible gives us many agricultural examples, such as "whatsoever a man sows, He will reap." (Galatians 6:7) Jesus gave the parable of wheat and weeds growing together. (Matthew 13:24-29)

Friend, remember that your wheat will grow along side weeds. Your success will grow with more trials. Your gifts will be accompanied with stress. You can't have one without the other. As you grow in your faith, do not get discouraged when your faith is tested in big ways. The stronger the faith, the stronger the test. Take heart.

Today, God is requiring much of you because He has done so much for you. He has even more in store for your life. Hang in there. Fight the good fight. Give yourself and your time. If you needed a sign today, this is it!

God loves you. He requires more of you because He has so much more in store for you.

My Prayer for You Today:
Father, thank you that you trust us so much that you are blessing us with more. Help us to give more of our time and our love. Be with us today as we answer your call. We love you, Lord. We pray all this in Jesus's precious and holy name. Amen.

SIGN

"Therefore the Lord himself will give you a sign…" Isaiah 7:14

Friend, God is always speaking to you. Are you listening?

Too often we minimize and dismiss signs from God. Beware that signs come in different ways, from an idea, to a phone call, to an open door. Pay attention to the signs. If today you pray for guidance, He may give you a sudden idea. Pay attention. Do not dismiss anything, from a simple text to a related article that catches your attention. Do not spend more time thinking and worrying about the answer without realizing that it is in front of you. Pay attention.

God speaks your language. He gives you signs that make sense to only you. Listen. He speaks to you in a still quiet voice. He knows what you need and already has your answer. Tune in to Him. He cares for you and hears you.

Throughout your day today, pay attention. Pray for signs and observe. They will come in all sorts. Be brave: ask for a sign!

My Prayer for You Today:
Father, you know the deepest desires of our hearts. Today we ask for a sign; show us, Lord. Let us know that you have heard our prayers. Answer us with clear signs. Guide us, Father. We yearn to hear from you. We pray all this in Jesus's precious name. Amen.

RELAX INTO HIM

"God will make perfect that which concerns me." Psalm 138:8

Keep a good attitude. God will work everything out for your good.

It is easy to get discouraged when things look faint. You want things a certain way and feel stuck in the way that they are. Everything seems out of sync. There's something missing and you know it. Today, let it go! God will make perfect that which concerns you.

Cheer up! Look at the bright side of things. You've come this far. Find a reason to smile. Breathe. Listen to music. Experience God in everything. Delight in the smallest details. Bishop TD Jakes often says: "God establishes patience, character, and concentration in the school of 'nothing seems to be happening.' Take the class and get the course credit; it's working for your good."

Today know that God is working things out for you. He is concerned with everything that distresses you, from a hangnail to your career. He makes everything work together for your good. (Romans 8:28) Cast your anxiety on Him, because He cares for you. (1 Peter 5:7)

Relax into Him.

My Prayer for You Today:
Father, we surrender all to you. Help us to be at peace and trust you in everything that concerns us. Be with us today as we relax into your grace and loving hands. Reveal yourself to us, Lord. Touch us in ways only you can. We thank you for your love. We praise you for your grace. Amen.

COMING RIGHT UP

"And we are confident that he hears us whenever we ask for anything that pleases him. And since we know he hears us when we make our requests, we also know that he will give us what we ask for." 1 John 5:14-15

God hears you and knows the desires of your heart.

Have you ever gone to a restaurant, placed your order, and had the waiter answer, "Coming right up?" Do you then ignore the answer and continue to order your pan-seared salmon over and over and over again? That seems absurd, unnecessary, and plain annoying, correct? Yet we do that when it comes to our prayer life. Over and over, we pray and beg God for the same things. We are not satisfied with praying once for something, and we continue to place the same order. Like the waiter, God heard you the first time and answered, "Coming right up!"

God is in the blessing-serving business! Your desires are his orders. It pleases Him to grant you the desires of your heart. Matthew 7:11 specifies, "If you… know how to give good gifts to your children, how much more will your Father in heaven give good gifts to those who ask him!" God hears your prayers. He knows the deepest desires of your heart and has answered, "Coming right up!"

Today, praise Him while you wait. Thank Him already for the blessings. He will give you the desires of your heart. Your blessing is coming right up! Trust Him and have faith while you wait.

My Prayer for You Today:
Father, thank you that you have heard our deepest prayers and have already answered. Thank you, Lord, for granting the desires of our hearts. Thank you that, like a waiter, you've taken account of our order and will deliver all good things to us in due time. You amaze us. We love you. We give you praise now and always. Amen

GOD'S POWER

"... so that your faith might not rest on human wisdom, but on God's power." 1 Corinthians 2:5

What is your faith based on? Statistics? The news? Or is your faith based on miracles? Blessings?

Too often we look at life from a human perspective. Things have to make sense and add up. We want things to correlate. We want to predict certain outcomes. Though there's nothing wrong with patterns, it's important to remember that we live by faith, not by sight. Sometimes things are not going to make sense, but they will workout. God doesn't need your bank account to add up in order for Him to provide. He doesn't need to listen to what the doctors learned in med school. He is the true healer.

Rest your faith on God's power that is inexplicable. Trust in His infinite capabilities. Know that He has no limit. When things don't add up, lean on Him and trust Him. Miracles are easy for Him. His ways are higher than our ways and His thoughts higher than our thoughts. We don't have to rely on what people say. We can trust God to be at work in our lives.

Today, remember to rest your faith on God's power, not human wisdom. Humans may be wise, but God is all-knowing. Humans may suggest, but God directs our path. Humans may know facts, but God knows the beginning and end. Lean not on your understanding, lean on Him. Have faith in His power!

My Prayer for You Today:
Lord, help us to rely and have faith in your power. Thank you for filling our lives with people to love and support us. Reveal the truth to us, Father. Let your power be revealed in our lives. We need you now. Fill us, Lord. We surrender all to you and praise you for guiding our steps. We love you. Amen.

GROW

"I planted the seed…but God has been making it grow." 1 Corinthians 3:6

You are in a growing season; take heart!

In the process of growth, things often look dark. It may seem like nothing is happening but God is surely at work. He is growing you, shaping and preparing you for blessings. In the midst of darkness, understand that God is preparing your heart to accept and handle His promises.

Today, continue to plant seeds of love, joy, peace, abundance, bliss, and success. Continue to hope and dream knowing God is making all things grow in your favor. Do your part and let God develop the rest. You are on the right track. Your destiny is unfolding one step at a time. Keep the faith. Believe. Things are working out in the invisible. Trust Him.

My Prayer for You Today:
Father, thank you that as we sow good seeds you make them grow. Thank you, Father, that you are a God who multiplies. Thank you for enlarging our territory, thank you for unfolding our dreams. Thank you for everything that you are doing even when we can't see or feel it. We trust you fully and completely. We trust your time. Thank you, Lord. Amen.

CELEBRATE YOU

"… by the grace of God, I am what I am." 1 Corinthians 15:10

In the world of copycats and wanting to be different than what you are, today, show your gratitude to God by embracing who you are! You have made it this far, been shaped and molded by every experience and by the grace of God. You are who you are and He loves you perfectly.

God loves variety. In a world with thousands of types of fish and flowers, infinite numbers of galaxies, and every human being having a unique fingerprint pattern, it's evident that God loves diversity. He created every single person with unique gifts and talents. Stop the comparison and embrace your uniqueness. Nothing about you is exactly the same as your neighbor. You are amazing. You are special. And you are so fabulous.

Every experience, every detail of your life is singular to you. God made you who you are; embrace it! By His grace, you are wonderfully and fearfully made. (Psalm 139:4) Today celebrate God by embracing who you are. His grace brought you this far and His love made you who you are.

Love and celebrate God by loving and celebrating yourself!

My Prayer for You Today:
Father, thank you for your attention to details. Thank you, Father, that you created each and every one of us as individuals. You never cease to amaze us, Lord. Thank you that your grace brought us this far and you will continue to bless, protect, provide and guide us as we continue to praise and thank you. Today help us to celebrate you by accepting, celebrating and embracing who we are. We pray this in Jesus's name. Amen.

JOY

"A joyful heart is good medicine." Proverbs 17:22

Heal yourself with a joyful heart!

The holidays can be a stressful and depressing time for those of us living in the midst of a storm. We stress over family, gifts, traveling, and crowded malls. Like much of our lives, we lose the bigger picture and fall victim of the small details. What is meant to bring us joy suddenly becomes stressful and we quickly forget to be grateful for simply being alive.

Your joy is with God. You can make a decision right now to be joyful. It doesn't depend on your circumstances, it has nothing to do with the stress you are experiencing, but it has everything to do with the One who loves and cares for you. Because your joy depends on Him, you can always experience it. He will forever be with you. Be joyful in Him.

Today, find peace and stillness in the midst of a stressful season of life. Let your joy heal you and remind you of what really matters: gratitude, love, peace, and bliss. Spend time with loved ones. Things may not be exactly how you want them, but let joy forever be in your heart.

My Prayer for You Today:
Father, today we ask for stillness and peace. Bless us with a joyful heart that continues to seek you, Lord. Thank you, Father for another year, another season, we are so grateful for your blessings. We love you, Lord. Be with us today as we enjoy our day peacefully and joyfully in Jesus's name. Amen.

TOUGH AND SOFT

"I am sending you out like sheep among wolves. Therefore be as shrewd as snakes and as innocent as doves." Matthew 10:16

Here's your wake up call: God knows that you are living among difficult people. He knows you have to deal with people's attitudes and issues. Yet today He wants you to be as shrewd as snakes and as innocent as doves. He is sending you out in the world like a sheep among wolves. Take heart. You can handle it.

People will piss you off. They will lie to you and about you. They will try to manipulate you. But you are smart enough to handle their games. You can see beyond their disguise. And like an innocent dove, you will handle every situation with compassion and kindness. God wants you to have tough skin and a soft heart. He wants you to see people's intentions and love them anyway. God wants you to recognize when others are trying to take advantage of you, and serve them anyway. He wants you to be smart enough to see how people are trying to hurt you and soft enough to still open your heart to love and support them.

God knows you are dealing with wolves. He has equipped you and is with you. He never gives you more than you can handle. He will reward your kindness. He will give you beauty for ashes. (Isaiah 61:3) He will give you double blessings for your trouble. (Isaiah 61:7) Take heart and treat others based on who God is and what He has done for you.

Today with God, grow tough skin and a soft heart!

My Prayer for You Today:
Father, thank you today that you know our situations. You also know the difficult people in our lives, you know our daily struggles of being Christ followers in the midst of wolves. Help us and be with us today as we continue to let your light shine through us in the way we love, support, and live with others. Fill us with your strength. Speak through us and for us. We pray all this in Jesus's name. Amen.

THERE HE IS

"I am with you and will watch over you wherever you go." Genesis 28:15

Wherever you are, there He is!

God is with you wherever you are: at church or at the strip club, at home with your spouse or at your mistress's house, with you and your friends or with you and those you dislike. This I know for sure: wherever you are, God is there!

Today, be aware of His presence and let it bring you peace, not fear, comfort, not anxiety. You are never alone. God watches over you every second of every day. Whether you are aware of His presence or not, God is there. You have a constant companion. Find strength in knowing that you can handle anything with Him.

In the midst of your joy or your pain, your health or sickness, God will never leave you nor forsake you. He is with you to the very end of time. (Matthew 28:20) He knows your situation, understands the depth of your pain and the profundity of your desires. He knows you inside and out and He delights in you.

You are never alone, wherever you are, there He is!

My Prayer for You Today:
Father, thank you that you will never leave us nor forsake us. Thank you, Lord, that with you we can handle anything that comes our way. Today, we rebuke all feelings of loneliness and open our hearts and minds to the awareness of your presence. Fill us today with your love and your grace. We praise you now and always. Amen.

UNSHAKEN LOVE

"Though the mountains be shaken and the hills be removed, yet my unfailing love for you will not be shaken nor my covenant of peace be removed." Isaiah 54:10

Unshaken, unbroken, unmoved—that's God's love for you!

In the world of disappointments, disagreements, pre-nuptials, and breach of contracts, it's difficult to find unconditional agreements, unshaken commitments, and unmoved loyalties. Friends often betray and family members sometime deceive—that's human nature—but God is always loyal, always true, and His love is unshaken. Wow!

It's difficult to fathom His unfailing love. Friend, this means, at your worst, committing the most atrocious act, saying the cruelest words, God still loves you, and surprisingly, He still will bless you with peace. Some of us cut others out of our lives over a misunderstanding or an insignificant offense, but not God. "Nothing in all creation will ever be able to separate us from the love of God." (Romans 8:39)

Today, find peace in His unfailing love. Nothing you have done or will do can shake His love for you. He loves you with no conditions, no pre-nuptials, and no reservations. He simply loves you!

Unshaken, unbroken, unmoved—that's God's love for you!

My Prayer for You Today:
Father, you are so awesome. Your love for us brings us a deep sense of gratitude and humility. Thank you that despite our missteps, our human nature, you love us perfectly and wholly. Thank you, Father, that you are so good that you have promised us perfect peace. Thank you. Thank you. Thank you. Amen.

SEE HIM

"So we fix our eyes not on what is seen, but on what is unseen. For what is seen is temporary but what is unseen is eternal." 2 Corinthians 4:18

Fix your eyes on Him, who is eternal.

Life has a wonderful way of making us lose focus on what is important and eternal. We focus on our current situation and immediate needs at the expense of what matters most: the unseen. You focus on your coworker's rude attitude, without seeing the pain. Your spouse's lack of communication frustrates you, yet their insecurities go unnoticed. What is unseen tells a brighter story than what is seen.

Friend, fix your eyes on what is not seen. Decide today to walk by faith, not by sight. Anchor your soul in Him and in hope. (Hebrews 6:19) Commit to seeing the unseen in yourself and in others, only then will you experience the splendor of His creations, the wonders of His love, and the grace of His presence.

Today, do you see Him in the midst of your everyday life? Are His love and grace apparent in the individuals you encounter? Do you see His promises in the heart of your situation? Do you see your heart in the palms of His hands?

See Him!

My Prayer for You Today:
Father, today we pray to see you and your wonders in the midst of our everyday lives. Let your greatness be evident in every area of our lives. Help us to focus on you who is eternal and true. Reveal yourself to us today in the deepest and most intimate ways. We yearn to see you. We love you. We praise you always. Amen.

VISION

"Where there's no vision, the people perish." Proverbs 29:18

What is your vision?

Refuse to perish, get clear on your vision!

Friend, a vision is more than a to-do list—it is a to-be list. What's your vision for your life this week, this month, this year? Who do you want to be today? A vision gives you something to hope for, to live for, to dream about. A vision wakes you up in the morning energized and with ambition. A vision gives you purpose.

Today is the day for you to be who you've always wanted to be. Today is the day to take a step, no matter how miniscule, towards what you want to achieve. Lao Tzu said it best: "The journey of a thousand miles begins with a single step." Take a step toward your vision. You've talked long enough about freeing yourself of anger and pain, you've said a million times you'll start a healthy lifestyle. Today is the day! Wait no more. Take one step toward your vision.

God has great things in store for you. Decide today to walk by faith, not by sight. For those of us unable to get a vision because we are deeply blinded by disappointment, hurt, heartaches, and heartbreaks, God has given us a great vision: to be more like Christ!

Envision it and watch it concretize with God!

My Prayer for You Today:
Father, today for those of us without a vision, I pray that you show us our gifts and our talents and our purposes in order to develop a vision that is aligned with your will. For those who already have a vision, I pray that you enlarge their territory, bring to life their dreams, and give them the desires of their hearts. We surrender all to you, Father. Thank you that your vision for us is bigger than we can imagine, fill us with courage and ambition to do your work. We love you and praise you always. Amen.

HE REMAINS FAITHFUL

"If we are faithless, He remains faithful, for He cannot disown himself."
2 Timothy 2:13

You have the right to remain faithful. Anything you say can and will be used against you to create fear, doubt, and anxiety. Similar to our Miranda Rights, too often we incriminate and crucify our faith with the words we speak, leaving us faithless, scared, lost, and depleted.

Luckily, even when we lose faith, God remains faithful, because that's who He is. This verse is encouraging because even when we are doubtful and scared, God is certain. When we are unkind and cruel, He remains loving. When we are deceitful, God remains loyal and true. No matter the circumstance, God remains flawless. You may feel like you are in the dark, but in Him there is no darkness. (1 John 1:5) He is the same yesterday, today, and forever. (Hebrews 13:8)

Today, find strength in knowing that God never loses His rank. He remains the Alpha and Omega. He continues to orchestrate life in your favor. He loves you and will never leave you nor forsake you. Nothing you do will change His character. His favor is upon you and He delights in you—always!

Remain in Him.

My Prayer for You Today:
Father, thank you that when we fall short, you are there to lift us. Thank you that when we are faithless, you remain faithful. We cannot fathom how flawless you are but we are so grateful that you are a loving and faithful God. Today, help us to remain in you no matter what our circumstances look like. Fill us with your grace, bathe us in your favor and wrap us in your love. We need you. Thank you for hearing us. We praise you and love you. Amen.

BE FILLED

"...a man full of God's grace and power performed great wonders and signs among the people." Acts 6:8

With God, you can do anything.

Friend, whatever fills you determines your performance. We can safely assume that if you decide to fill your car with water or apple juice, you will need a new car very soon. And if you are thirsty and decide to drink a cold glass of gasoline, your body will not function very well. Similarly, what you fill your mind and spirit with determines your performance. This verse specifies: only "full of God's grace and power" is a man able to perform great wonders. It is Him in us that creates wonders.

If your life is not where you want it to be, if you want more than what you have, ask yourself: "Am I full of God's grace and power or am I simply full of myself?" Your honest answer to this question will bring about incredible changes. You can do anything through Him. (Philippians 4:13) And with God all things are possible. (Matthew 19:26)

Today, remember: it is all about God in you! Fill yourself with Him, His love, His grace, His power, His peace. And the way to do that is through prayer and spending time in the stillness of His presence. Be in the spirit, not the flesh. Live in love, not in fear. Read His word, not tabloids. When you do so, your life will transform and you will perform great wonders.

Full of Him there's nothing you cannot do!

My Prayer for you Today:
Father, today we pray for your grace and power. Fill us, Lord. Use us as vessels to perform great wonders, Lord, to love the unlovable, to serve the immoral and disenfranchised. Have your way with us. We surrender our lives in your hands. Fill us with your love now. Amen.

PRAY

"Pray without ceasing." 1 Thessalonians 5:17

Friend, never stop praying!

When things fall apart, pray. When things come together, pray. When you're lost, pray. Found, pray. Happy, pray. Sad, pray. Rich, pray. Broke, pray. Healthy, pray. Sick, pray. Whatever you do, never stop praying! Too often we pray when life is cloudy and forget to pray when the sun is out. We run to Him when we are heartbroken and forget Him when we fall in love. Good, bad, and ugly, pray without ceasing!

Because God is love, He will never forsake you. Whether you pray every hour of every day or you never pray, He will continue to love you and bless you because of who He is. But friend, your life will be so much more enjoyable, abundantly blissful, and inexplicably peaceful if you run to Him in prayer in all circumstances. Be assured that He hears you and answers every time. Keep on praying.

Today commit to praying without ceasing. Don't place God in a box or on a schedule. Pray at all times. Talk to Him in the shower, on your way to work, at lunch, in between text messages; talk to him with a deep breath, a sigh, a tear, a smile. Whatever it is, pray! He understands your unspoken prayers. Today, pray!

My Prayer for You Today:
Father, we could never stop thanking you for your goodness. We don't have enough words to sing your praise, but today we turn to you in gratitude and in love. We seek you unceasingly, Father. Speak to us Lord. Be with us every minute of every day. We surrender all in Jesus's name. Amen.

OPEN/SHUT

"What He opens no one can shut and what He shuts no one can open."
Isaiah 22:22

Your blessing is in God's hands, no one else's.

You don't need to kiss anyone's behind, or beg and plead. What God has for you is for you. Don't let people belittle you and make you believe they hold your opportunity. He alone holds the key! Your blessing comes from Him. Breakthrough, dream job, dream home, spouse, the children you yearn for, your increase, your success—all of it comes from Him.

Friend, what God has for you is for you. No one can take it away. Relax! Trust Him! If it's yours your enemy cannot take it away from you. It cannot be stolen. It cannot be cursed out of your life. God has the final say. What He opens no one can shut and what He shuts no one can open.

Today, trust God. The door will open up for you at the right time. Stop chasing people and opportunity. Chase God. Everything will come to you through Him. Sit back, relax, and trust Him.

My Prayer for You Today:
Father, today we pray for discernment and wisdom to know when you have shut a door. And we pray for faith to trust you to open the floodgates of Heaven upon our lives. Thank you that what you have for us will always be ours. Thank you, Father that your promises are without repentance, nothing we do can make you change your mind and for that we are so grateful. Today we pray for open doors, for opportunities, for breakthroughs and growth in Jesus's name. Amen.

AS HE IS

"As He is, so also are we in this world." 1 John 4:17

The Message version of this scripture says this: "Our standing in the world is identical with Christ's." If you were asked to describe Christ, and you said, "He is loving, a healer, patient, kind, forgiving, graceful, powerful, everlasting," you would be correct. And I'm here to remind you that those words also describe you!

Friend, you are God's ambassador in this world. (2 Corinthians 5:20) Be empowered knowing that you can do great work. Besides, Jesus himself said we could do greater work than Him. (John 14:12) Do for others what God has done for you. At your job, in your family, love one another like God loves you. Give and forgive. Listen and accept. Love and support. You might be the only Jesus someone comes across.

Today, in the midst of your everyday life, find confidence in knowing that as He is, so also are you. Nothing is too big for you. You are worthy of amazing things. You are loveable and deserving of love. You are full of grace. You are powerful. Someone is waiting to be touched by you—go out there and do His work today!

My Prayer for You Today:
Father, thank you that you love us so much that the power you gave to Jesus is also given to us. Wow! You amaze us, Lord. Help us today to remember our worth and our power, which are found in you. Let your love encourage us to do your work. Be with us today as we step out in faith. Use us as your vessel. We surrender all to you in love. Amen.

HUSH

"Why are you afraid? Do you still have no faith?" Mark 4:40

Jesus asked those questions when His disciples panicked in the midst of a storm. Awaken by his frightened disciples because the boat was quickly filling up with water, Jesus spoke to the storm: "Hush, be still."

Friend, when Jesus is in your "boat," you have nothing to be afraid of! This story is filled with powerful lessons on how to react in the midst of life's storms. If you focus on the storm your natural reaction is to panic, but when you have God in your life you, like Jesus, you can sleep through storms. You find rest in Him despite the wind, despite the water, and despite turbulence. You can rest because you know that God is able to calm any storm.

Why are you afraid? Do you still have no faith? God has shown you his faithfulness over and over. Why do you still doubt Him? Why are you afraid? Storms are natural occurrences of life. They do not last forever, nor are they ever too much for God. In an instant He can calm any storm. The object of your faith is Him! Focus on Him, not the storm!

Today make a decision—when storms come you will not jump ship. Believe that with God in your boat, in your life, you will make it to the other side. God's plans will prevail no matter what. Believe it. Don't lose your faith in the midst of the storm. Rest in Him. Know that He will never leave you nor forsake you. Rest.

My Prayer for You Today:
Father, today in the midst of our storms help us to find rest in you. Hush the storms in our lives. Still the wind like only you can. Father, I pray today for those of us in the middle, in the valleys of life, that we may seek and find you, that we may anchor our lives to you. Thank you that you are preparing us for better. We love you for your faithfulness; we thank you for your love. Amen.

ROOTS AND ROCK

"Let your roots grow down into him and let your lives be built on him. Then your faith will grow strong in the truth you were taught, and you will overflow with thankfulness." Colossians 2:7

Deep roots stabilize. A house built on the "Rock" withstands any storm. Are you rooted in Him? Is your life built on Him?

It's easy to build a life on vanity. It's even easier to be rooted in ego and the world. The problem with such a lifestyle is that it will leave you unfilled, thirsty for more and when the storm hits and the rug is pulled from under you, you will panic, unable to stand, and you will believe that God has forsaken you.

When you are rooted in God, storms will still come but they will never uproot you. You may be shaken, but never overtaken; bruised, but not broken. With Him, you will weather any storm. Matthew 7:25 reminds that a house built on the Rock will not collapse. Build your house, and you will never again fear a storm.

Today commit to being rooted in Him through prayer. Be aware of your intentions and make certain every action stems from a place of love, not fear. Build your life to serve, not to impress. Choose to love, not to compete. And remember to seek Him first every time and in every thing.

Let your roots grow down into Him and build your life on Him.

My Prayer for You Today:
Father, show us how to grow deep roots into you. We yearn to serve and love you, Lord. Show us. Use us today as a vessel for your work. Fill us with creative ideas, ambition, and courage to do your work. Have your way in our lives. We praise you and trust you with every detail. Thank you. Amen.

SPEAK

"The Lord spoke to Moses saying: speak to the rock and it will pour out its water." Numbers 20:8

Friend, take note that God told Moses to speak a miracle into existence. Wow!

Your life is one word away from change. You have the power to speak that word. God is so amazing that He has given you the power of miracle. The power of life and death, the power of creation is in your words. Amazing!!! God told Moses to speak to the rock and the rock would pour out water. An impossible task became possible through words. You can do the same.

Speak to the rocks in your life. Don't talk about it, or speak around it, speak specifically and directly to the rocks in your life and watch them burst open, flooding you with blessings. Speak to your pain. Speak to your debt. Speak to your brokenness and your fears; speak! The same power that God gave Moses has been given to you. Life and death are in the power of the tongue. (Proverbs 18:21)

Today, speak life to yourself! Speak success. Speak abundance. Speak joy. Speak divine peace. Speak bliss and love into every area of your life. Speak overflows of blessings. Speak laughter and light to yourself today. Be blessed!

My prayer for You Today:
Lord, thank you that you have given us creative power through our words. Today, let us all be aware of what we are creating with our words. Father, today I speak abundance and blessings into each person reading this, I speak breakthroughs and opportunities, I speak health, wealth, and happiness and I thank you that it is already done. We love you, Lord. Amen.

LOVE AND FEAR

"There is no fear in love; but perfect love casts out fear, because fear involves punishment, and the one who fears is not perfected in love." 1 John 4:16

God is love. Reread this scripture by replacing the word "love" with "God." "There is no fear in God, but God casts out fear, because fear involves punishment and the one who fears is not perfected in God."

Friend, God is love (1 John 4:8) and where He is, fear is not. Fear and love cannot coexist. Darkness and light cannot coexist. God is love and God is light. In Him there is no darkness, in Him there is no fear. (1 John 1:5)

Today, let this scripture illustrate God's love for you. God is not afraid of your situation. He is not worried about your enemies. He is not scratching his head wondering how to heal you. He is certainly not out of ideas on how to grant you your deepest desires. He is ready. God is willing and able to casts out all things that stand against your happiness and destiny. He will make all things work together for your good. (Romans 8:28)

Remember: Love and fear cannot coexist. You will know that it is love when you have no fear. Move, breathe, and sprout from love…move, breathe, and sprout from God.

My Prayer for You Today:
Father, thank you that you are love, and that in you there is no darkness. Thank you, Lord, that fear is not of you. Thank you, Father, that nothing fazes you and that nothing is impossible to you. Today we pray for discernment and wisdom to know how to move from a loving place. Take over. We lift our lives to you, trusting every detail in your hands. We love you. Amen.

SEARCH YOUR HEART

"Tremble and do not sin… search your heart and be silent." Psalm 4:4

Scripture is full of powerful messages for everyday life. Be frightened, shake and shiver in the face of adversity but keep good character. Be still.

In the midst of anger and everyday situations, we tend to lose our common sense. When tested, we abandon our spiritual attributes and react foolishly. This is our call to chill out, to be silent, and to focus inward despite often trembling in fear and anger. Rather than reacting, search your heart.

Today, spend time searching your heart. Search your heart for solid ground. Search your heart for the safest place. Search your heart for light. Only in your heart will you find compassion, forgiveness, self-control, peace, joy, love, acceptance, abundance, and beauty. In the depth of your heart, you will find God.

My Prayer for You Today:
Father, show yourself to each and every one of us today. In the midst of chaos, help us to be still and search our hearts for you. Thank you, Lord, that our blessings of peace and love are always available to us in the present moment. You continue to amaze us, Father. Thank you for your grace, thank you for your love. We surrender all to you. Amen.

THANKSGIVING

"Enter his gates with thanksgiving, go into his courts with praise. Give thanks to him and praise his name." Psalm 100:4

Today, take time to reflect on the many blessings you have received. As you reflect, thank Him.

Friends, more than anything let thanksgiving be a way of life for you. Rather than celebrating the holiday once a year, let your life be a testimony, a sacrifice of continual thanks to the Blessor who has given you so much. Enter His presence with thanks. Thank Him for bringing you this far. Thank Him for keeping His promises. Thank Him!

Today, may your heart be filled with gratitude. May you be reminded of His love which never fails. Give Him thanks for the simplest things. Give Him thanks for everything. His love saved you. His grace embraces you. Do you need any other reasons to thank Him?

Today, thank God!

My Prayer for You Today:
Father, today we thank you for so many blessings. Thank you, Father, for your grace and your love. Thank you for always being there. Lord, today like everyday we are humbled by your unconditional love that never fails. Thank you, Lord. Thank you. Thank you. We love you. Amen.

SPIRITUAL MILK

"Crave pure spiritual milk so that you will grow into a full experience of salvation." 1 peter 2:1-5

Friend, the old cliché "you are what you eat" is also applicable to your spiritual life. Crave spiritual milk and grow in spirit, love, peace, and joy.

What you feed your mind will reflect in your life. If the only things you dwell on are depressing news, friend drama, and Facebook non-sense, the quality of your life will be poor. Dwell in positive messages, indulge in great books, tune in to the Word and watch your life and spirit grow.

Today, crave spiritual milk. You will certainly find it in the Bible, but do not limit yourself there. Whatever is true, noble, right, pure, lovely, admirable, excellent, praise worthy, (Philippians 4:8) indulge in that. Some of us find it in music and art, others find it in flowers or at the beach, in books or with great friends, in stillness or in laughter. Whatever uplifts you, brings you hope, peace, bliss, and love, commit to doing those things.

Crave spiritual milk; crave God!

My Prayer for You Today:
Father, thank you that you know how to show yourself to each and everyone of us through our different interests. Today we crave you, Lord. Speak to us in ways only we can understand. We thank you that we can find you in everything, in the broken glass or in a diamond, in the valley as well as the mountaintop. Have your way with us. Touch us today so that we may never be the same. We crave you. We love you. Take over now. Amen.

BE FREE

"And you will know the truth. The truth shall set you free." John 8:22

The truth is God loves you perfectly right now as you are. Nothing you do can increase or diminish His love for you.

Do yourself a favor today and let go of people pleasing. Let go of fear. Let go of proving yourself. The One who loves you perfectly doesn't need the approval of others to bless you. Let His truth give you freedom to live the life you choose, to do the things you enjoy, and to be who you are, wonderfully and fearfully made.

God's truth sets you free. You don't have to worry about Him loving you one day and crucifying you the next. God does not promise you the world one day and betray you the next. His unconditional love is the basis of our freedom. What God has for you is for you! What He says about you is the truth forever! His love is with you until the end of time.

Today find freedom in His truth. He is everlasting. He is love. His word is forever. His promises are without repentance. You are free to dream, live, love, and be whatever you desire. You are free to be you. You are accepted and loved despite your flaws. Your freedom is in the truth of who He is. Be loved, be free, be you!

My Prayers for You Today:
Father, thank you so much that your truth sets us free. We believe what you say about us. We rebuke all fear of judgment and old habits of people pleasing and we open our hearts and lives to accepting your unconditional love. Thank you that what you say about us is the truth. We are fearfully and wonderfully made with a spirit of power, love, and self control. Today, help us to live in your truth. We love you and praise you. Amen.

EXCEEDING ABUNDANTLY ABOVE ALL

"Now all glory to God, who is able to do exceeding abundantly above all that we ask or think, according to the power at work within us."
Ephesians 3:20

Guess what? Whatever you ask or think, God is able to do you far more!

Friend, if you pray for crumbs, God is able to give you loaves. If you pray for money that jingles, He's able to give you stacks. If you pray for half, He can give you a whole. If you pray for just enough provision, He's able to give you barns! Pray for the job and He will entrust you with the company. Pray for the paid bill and He will clear out all your debt. Pray for the spouse and He will bless you with the family.

Today, get ready to be amazed! God has amazing blessings in store for you. Take Him out of the box. Think your highest thought and pray your most daring prayer. He will outdo them both. I dare you, do it! He is able to do exceeding abundantly above all that we ask or think. What have you asked for today? What are you thinking?

God wants you to know that He's heard your prayers and He has answered. He will amaze you. Thank Him already. His thoughts and His ways are higher than yours. (Isaiah 55:9) I'm excited about your blessings today.

Exceeding abundantly above all that you ask for...after all, what else would you expect from the Omniscient, Alpha, and Omega? Receive His blessings now!

My Prayer for You Today:
Father, you never cease to amaze us. Thank you, Lord, that you can do far more than we can fathom. Today we open our hearts and mind to be amazed by your blessings. We thank you, Lord, that your thoughts are higher than our thoughts. You know our highest dreams, our biggest desires, Lord. Surprise us with more in Jesus's name. We thank you that it's already done. We praise you. We love you. Amen.

FIRST

"But seek ye first the kingdom of God, and his righteousness; and all these things shall be added unto you." Matthew 6:33

God first, then the rest!

Don't wait until you get the job, marry the spouse, get the big break, buy the house or get healthy before placing Him first. The Bible specifies to seek Him first, and then all other things will be given to you. Don't place the cart before the horse. Seek Him first.

The story in the Bible of Peter walking on water has always touched me. The idea of doing the impossible when focused on God is amazing and inspiring. As soon as Peter focused on the wind and his circumstances, he started to sink. Likewise today, focus on God in order to accomplish the impossible in your life. With your eyes on Him, all things will be added to your life and you will lack no good thing. That's the truth!

Today before calling your friend for advice, before stepping your feet on the floor, before doing anything—seek Him. Spend time with the One who is all-capable, all-knowing, all-giving. Find stillness in Him. He knows your desires. He understands your needs. And God will grant them all once you fix your eyes on Him.

My Prayer for You Today:
Lord, today help us to put you first. We seek you, Lord. Thank you for answered prayers, thank you for blessings. Renew us today and inspire us to do the impossible as we focus on you. We love you, Father, we praise you. Fill us with your divine peace. Amen.

SMILE

"Look at the birds of the air; they do not sow or reap or store away in barns, and yet your heavenly Father feeds them. Are you not much more valuable to Him than they are?" Matthew 6:26

Nature has a way of telling us the truth. In the midst of your busy day, take time to observe the natural evolution of the world around you.

Birds sing and fly effortlessly. Seasons change seamlessly. Autumn leaves fall with ease. Yet we get worried and anxious about the unfolding of our lives. Like the birds, God will take care of you. Your life will unravel in a beautiful, divinely fashion. Eggs hatch when ready, flowers bloom at the perfect time, and likewise your life evolves perfectly, as it should. Trust the Supreme Intelligence, the Creator of this divine process; trust God.

Let nature remind you of your divinity. Let the natural world around you bring you back into His awareness. He is in complete control. There is a bigger process at play. He will leave nothing undone. Trust Him. You are valuable to Him. He will take care of every detail. Let go. Breathe. Rest. Relax. Laugh.

Today, smile as you observe the perfect unfolding of your miracles.

My Prayer for You Today:
Father, you amaze us. When we think of nature, birds, fish, the ocean, WOW! Wow, Father, you amaze us. We surrender the unfolding of our lives to you. Fill us with your peace today as we let go and smile. Remind us of your love. Thank you that everything is as it should be. Thank you that you leave nothing to chance. Thank you, Father, that your love takes everything in consideration and that you make everything work together for our highest good. We praise you, Lord. We love you. Amen.

CERTAIN OF THE UNSEEN

"Faith is the assurance of things hope for, the evidence of things not seen." Hebrews 11:1

Today, know beyond a shadow of a doubt that what you are seeking is seeking you. What you desire is already on its' way to you. Have faith.

Faith is not only knowing God can answer prayers, but it is believing that He will answer your prayers. Get rid of doubt. Do not let time discourage you. Faith is the evidence of things not seen. You haven't seen the case, or the job, you haven't met your spouse nor encountered the miracle, but have unwavering faith that all prayers will be answered. Know in the depth of your soul that God will answer your prayers. Have faith.

Today, be assured that the desires of your heart will come to pass. Accept it in the spiritual realm and watch it materialize in your life. Pray for it and say it. Declare your blessings before seeing them. Romans 4:17 reminds us to call those things that are not as though they are. Declare your prayers answered today. Call out your blessings!

Be certain of the unseen; be certain of God!

My Prayer for You Today:
Father, today we have faith that you will answer our prayers. Father, we lift up our hopes of love, abundance, wealth, health, joy, happiness, and peace to you today. We know that you hear us and that you will answer. We trust you, Lord, even when we don't understand. Thank you for being faithful and amazing. We declare blessings over our lives today in Jesus's name. Amen.

DELIGHT IN THE BLESSOR

"Take delight in the Lord and He will give you the desires of your heart."
Psalm 37:4

Today, rather than ranting and raving about your desires and most wanted wishes, rant and rave about God and watch your desires manifest in your life.

We can all talk with great details about our dream homes, ideal spouse, and fantasy vacations. We easily delight on the blessings but forget to delight in the Blessor. We rant and rave about what God has done and forget to appreciate who He is. If you think His blessings are wonderful, you ought to get to know Him. He's even better, sweeter, and greater than your biggest blessing!

Today, delight in the Blessor, rather than the blessings! Delight in Him, His grandeur, His flawless character, and His unfailing truth. In the midst of delighting in Him, your deepest desires will come to pass. When you focus on Him rather than what you want, He will surprise you with bigger, better, and greater.

Delight in Him and watch your dreams come true!

My Prayer for You Today:
Father, remind us to focus on you. When our minds wonder, bring them back to you. Father, you know the deepest desires of each and every one of us, we surrender them to you knowing that nothing is impossible to you and we ask today that you surprise us with bigger, better, and greater. Amaze us, Lord. We praise you. We thank you for your love and your grace. You are amazing. We pray all this in Jesus's precious and holy name. Amen.

PEACE

"Thou will keep in perfect peace, whose mind is stayed on thee: because he trusted in thee." Isaiah 26:3

Peace comes from our ability to focus inward, our ability to focus on God.

There isn't a magic pill, a list of accomplishments, or a specific amount of cash in your bank account that will bring you perfect peace. I have yet to find it in a shopping spree or a piece of cake. Your level of peace is directly related to your ability to keep your mind on God. The scripture specifies: "whose mind is stayed on thee." Notice that it doesn't say: "who doesn't have issues or problems." No matter the circumstances, keep your mind on God. In Him is your peace.

Friend, you have to first win the battle in your mind before winning it in your life. Counting your problems only brings anxiety. Counting on the One who is bigger than our troubles bring peace. Peace comes from fixating our mind on God. Today make it a task to keep your mind on Him. When your mind wonders and your harmony eludes, use your breath to return to Him. You are one deep breath away from His presence and His divine peace.

Today, take time to breathe Him and experience His peace.

My Prayer for You Today:
Father, today we fix our minds on you. Thank you that you love us so much that you give us the ability to connect and feel your peace instantly. Your love continues to amaze us. We love you, Father. Have your way in our lives. We trust you with every breath of our being. Wrap us in your grace now and always. Amen.

SECURITY

"You need not be afraid of sudden disaster or destruction... for the Lord is your security. He will keep your foot from being caught in a trap."
Proverbs 3:25-26

Relax. God is your security.

No more fears, no more worries, no more contemplating how a colleague is trying to trap you. It's impossible to trap God's children. God is your shepherd and security. You cannot be trapped. Don't lose sleep over the lies and deceit; they may trip you temporarily but they cannot trap you. God will keep your foot from being caught in a trap.

God is your security. You are well equipped and capable of handling anything that shows up in your life. He has your back. The Almighty is fighting for you. He knows your coming and going. He is in complete control. Relax. The One who keeps you safe does not sleep. He will never leave you nor forsake you. He loves you this much.

Today, in the midst of your everyday life remember that you are loved and you are protected. Nothing can touch you. God is with you. He has empowered you. Go out there and get your blessing!

My Prayer for You Today:
Father, thank you that you are our security and will never let our feet get caught. Thank you, Father, for loving us so much. We surrender today to you. Empower us; fill us with courage and motivation to do your work, to fulfill your purpose. We lift up our needs to you. We love you, Father. We praise you. Amen.

CAPTIVE

"Take captive every thought to make it obedient to Christ."
2 Corinthians 10:5

If it's in your head, it controls your life. Today, take captive every thought and think God!

So many of us rehearse tragedies, quarrels, and fears in our minds all day long. We hear one negative word and let it spiral out of control in our minds for the entire day. Our unfocused minds literally drive us crazy and cause us stress and great despair. We replay stories, conversations, and nonsense over and over in our minds and wonder why we are worried, anxious, and plain nuts.

Take captive every thought. Become aware of your thoughts and align them to what God says about you. It doesn't matter if you think you're fat and ugly, God says you are fearfully and wonderfully made. (Psalm 139:14) Your mind may tell you that your plans never come through, but God has plans for you to prosper, to give you hope and a future. (Jeremiah 29:11) Your mind may tell you that God doesn't know the details of your life, but the Bible says He even knows the number of hairs on your head. (Luke 12:7)

Today, don't let your mind fool you. Take captive every thought. Think God. When a thought comes up that doesn't align with the Word, speak God-thoughts. Remember what He's already done for you. Say a prayer. Bless your life. Thank Him. And like the Apostle Paul said, "Whatever is true, whatever is honorable, whatever is just, whatever is pure, whatever is lovely, whatever is commendable, if there is any excellence, if there is anything worthy of praise, think about these things." (Philippians 4:8)

My Prayer for You Today:
Father, take captive every thought today. Take over our minds, Lord. We declare transformation today by the renewal of our minds. Lord, we surrender our week to you and thank you for blessings already. Be with us, order our steps, and protect our thinking. We praise you, Lord, and we love you. Amen.

SPOKEN

"...for the mouth of the Lord has spoken." Isaiah 1:20

Great news: God has spoken today regarding your situation!

The wait is over; God has spoken. He spoke against your illness, against your struggle, against your worries and your fears. God has spoken: strength, healing, joy, peace, and abundance. His blessings are yours today. Receive them!

When God speaks, miracles happen. Listen to Him. He has spoken. He declared you the head and not the tail, victor and not victim, blessed and not cursed. What happened to you was part of His big plan. Let it go. Stop replaying the past. He has spoken into your destiny. Stop reliving the hurt. He mends the brokenhearted.

Today, remember that He has spoken. You have His favor. Do not defend your position. He has already spoken for you! His words are spirit and life (John 6:63) and will not return void. (Isaiah 55:11)

God has spoken; now relax!

My Prayer for You:
Lord, thank you that your word never returns void. Thank you that with one word you can change everything. Thank you for speaking into our lives today, Father. We believe you and thank you for changes, for miracles, for blessings without measure. You amaze us, Lord. Thank you for everything. We praise you. We love you. Speak! Amen.

WILLING AND OBEDIENT

"If you are willing and obedient, you will eat the good things of the land." Isaiah 1:19

This is God's promise to you, if you are willing and obedient, good things will come your way. Are you willing and obedient?

Friend, too many of us want the promise without the process. We want the fruit without having to plant the seed. We desire the success without the headache. Today, be willing to work. Be willing to pass the test. Be willing to serve and love. Be willing to listen to God and to be obedient to His word. Have the hard conversations. Make the sacrifice. Follow Him. And you will have the desires of your heart.

God promises that He will withhold no good things from those who do what is right. (Psalm 84:11) He will open the floodgates and pour out so many blessings that you will not have enough room to store them. (Malachi 3:10) Be obedient to Him today. What is He asking you to do? Be willing to obey Him in the smallest way—maybe through your patience with your spouse, your attention to your neighbor, or through giving help to your annoying colleague. Be willing to do His work today. He will reward you.

Today, go out there willing and ready to do God's work. Don't wait for the big event, do His work in every small possible way. Obey. Love. Serve. Give. Forgive. And get ready to be blessed!

My Prayer for You Today:
Father, today we are willing and ready to obey you. Speak to us. Give us the courage and tenacity to obey you even when it's hard. Fill us with your strength. Help us to serve you through serving others. Inspire us with your love. Use us to bless others, and in return, we pray for blessings upon every aspect of our lives. We love you and praise you. Amen.

BE STILL

"Be still and know..." Psalm 46:10

Friend, stillness speaks. Be still and know that He is God!

God speaks in silence. The answer is there. Listen. Be still. Shut your mind and your mouth. Spend time in the quietness of His presence. Listen. He is speaking to you. Your answer is awaiting you. Be still.

Your gut is correct! Something inside tells you what you already know. Your gut is telling you He is God. He will never forsake you and never leave you. He loves you and is orchestrating life in your favor. His grace has cleaned your slate. You are empowered. You are worthy of all good things. He will grant every desire of your heart. He is God. Believe it.

Today, breathe! Be still. Listen. The One in you is great, powerful, and omniscient. Be still enough to feel His presence. Take a deep breath. He is ordering your steps. He loves you right now as you are. He has already answered your prayers. Be still.

My Prayer for You Today:
Father, we yearn to hear you. Speak to us Father; we are listening. Today, help us to shut out the noise and to be still long enough to feel your presence and recognize your voice. Be with us as we seek to know you better and to serve you more. We thank you for your unconditional love and amazing grace. Have your way with us, Lord. Amen.

CONTENT

"I have learned the secret of being content in any and every situation. I can do all things through Him who is my strength." Philippians 4:12

The secret of being content is knowing who you are in God. Connecting to the divine in you will always bring you contentment, joy, love, and inexplicable peace.

Do not spend another day seeking it outside of yourself. You won't find it in your spouse nor your children. It is not at work, not even at church. You can't buy it at the store nor borrow it from a friend. The secret is in you. The divine is in you!

In the midst of debt, disappointments, failures, successes, ups and downs, connect to God in you. All of a sudden time will be still. You will realize that everything you ever needed has always been in you. The Omniscient, Alpha and Omega, Beginning and End, all of Him is in you, ignited as this everlasting flame. No one can take it from you. It is yours till the end of time. (Matthew 28:20)

Today, remember that the secret of being content is your relationship and connection with God. Lean a little closer to Him through prayer and meditation. Enjoy a cup of coffee, a delicious meal, or a meaningful conversation all while connecting with Him. See and feel Him in everything you do. You will forever be content.

My Prayer for You Today:
Father, thank you that everything we ever need is found in you. Thank you, Lord, that you are so giving, so loving that you have placed it all in us. You amaze us. Help us today to see and feel you in everything we do. We yearn to connect with you, Lord. We call on you today to fill us and color our lives. We need you. We love you. Amen.

IN HIM

"In God I move and breathe and have my being" Acts 17:28

In the midst of your everyday chaos, remind yourself that in Him you move, breathe, and have your being.

Too often we move and breathe in chaos, stress, and foolishness. We find ourselves blinded by heartache, disappointment, and headaches. Life's pettiness has a way of consuming us. The decision is ours: be consumed by life or be infused by it; drown in chaos or bathe in grace; be paralyzed by darkness or emboldened by the process.

God is a god of order, love, and grace. Move in Him. Breathe His love. Have your being in His grace. All of a sudden, you will experience synchronizing events, things will fall together perfectly for you in perfect timing. You will understand His unfailing love and know divine peace. Once you receive the promise, you will be grateful for the process.

Today, remember to move, breathe, and have your being in Him.

My Prayer for You Today:
Father, today we rebuke all heartache, pain, and disappointment. We are committed to the process and know that it will bring about the promises. Thank you that you are a God of order and that everything is exactly as it should be. Thank you, Father, for your love and your grace. We love you, Lord. Soothe us and fill us today in every way. We pray all this in Jesus's precious and holy name. Amen.

GROWTH

"It's not important who does the planting, or who does the watering. What's important is that God makes the seed grow." 1 Corinthians 3:7

Wherever you are right now, know that God planted you there. He is growing you. Hang in there!

Friend, being planted can often feel like being buried. Take heart; you have not been buried, rather you have been planted. God planted you in your specific circumstance, within your relationships, your family, that dead end job. He planted you right where you are today to grow your seed, to enlarge your territory, to develop your dream. Hang in there!

Today, in the midst of darkness know that God is making your seed grow. He is growing the dream He planted in your heart. He is growing your relationship and your faith. He is growing the seed of your destiny. Now is the time to walk by faith, not by sight. When darkness hits, know that He is the light. Growth is traumatic, but hang in there. It will all be worth it.

Hang in there and let Him grow your seed!

My Prayer for You Today:
Lord, this sucks! We know that growth is worth it, but the process hurts. Help us today, Father, to hang in there with faith and expectation. Soothe us, Lord. We don't understand what's going on but we trust you, Lord. We surrender all to you. Have your way with us. We love you and praise you. Amen.

LET GO AND TRUST

"Do not worry about your life… who of you by worrying can add a single hour to his life?" Luke 12: 22-25

Friend, plans fall apart, people disappoint us, and life may seem blurry, but the Bible calls for us not to worry about our lives. God has it already figured out.

Trust the process of life. There is a bigger order in place that you may not understand. Trust that God is orchestrating things in your favor. When you do not get what you were hoping for, thank Him because He was planning something better. Everything is in order. He is a God of order. The tears, the heartache, the pain, they are all part of the process to shape you and prepare you for your blessings.

Today, things may seem uncertain and painful; you may be disappointed, hurt, and heartbroken but God restores. He is a God of restoration. He will restore you. He will grant the desires of your heart. He has seen your tears; He knows your needs and is working on them right now. Trust Him.

Let go and trust.

My Prayer for You Today:
Father, we do not understand. We didn't see the heartache and pain coming, but we trust you. We surrender all to you right here right now. Fill us with faith. Fill us with assurance that you are in control. Keep our eyes focused on you now more than ever. We love you, Lord. Have your way with us. In Jesus's precious and holy name we pray. Amen.

PEACE

"You will keep in perfect peace all who trust in you, all whose thoughts are fixed on you." Isaiah 26:3

When you trust God, you will experience an unexplainable, serene calm and peace. Fix your thoughts on Him and be at peace.

Friend, when you trust God, you know that everything is in order. Things happen the way they should, and despite challenges, your life is unfolding perfectly according to His will. When you trust Him, you are able to be at peace with whatever and whoever shows up in your life. Circumstances may change, yet your mind is on God and your heart is at peace.

Serene peace means that "A thousand may fall at your side, ten thousand at your right but it will not affect you." (Psalm 91:7) Your circumstances do not determine your peace, God does. "For God is not a God of disorder but of peace." (1 Corinthians 14:33) Seek Him and you will be at peace. Think His thoughts and you will experience His divine peace no matter what you are going through.

Today, in the midst of busyness, in the midst of chaos, spend time with Him and receive His peace.

My Prayer for You Today:
Father, today we open ourselves to your peace. Fill us with your deep calm and peace. Keep us still enough to hear your voice. Be with us today. Reassure us that every thing is in perfect divine order. We trust you with every fiber of our being, Lord. Thank you for right here right now. We surrender all to you in Jesus's precious and holy name. Amen.

PRISON OF FEAR

"I sought the Lord and he heard me and delivered me from all my fears."
Psalm 34:4

God is able to deliver you from your fears. If you are like me, often paralyzed by fear and anxiety, turn it over to God.

The hard conversation you are avoiding, the next step you are evading, the doctor's visit you keep escaping—all of the circumstances that cause you fear and anxiety—turn them over to God. Feeling fear is normal, but let your faith in God break the cage and set you free from fear. There is nothing to be afraid of; God has it under control.

God hasn't given us a spirit of fear but of power and self-discipline. (2 Timothy 1:7) Today, as you face your fears, let God speak and move through you. You can do all things through Him. (Philippians 4:13) You have the fruit of the spirits and are empowered by Him. (Galatians 5:22) Go out there and speak! Reach for your goals. Be assertive and persistent. Fight for what you want. Break out of the prison of fear and step into His grace.

Remember His words: "fear not for I am with you; do not be dismayed for I am your God. I will strengthen you and help you. I will hold you with my victorious right hand." (Isaiah 41:10)

My Prayer for You Today:
Lord, take away our fears right now. We know that you haven't given us a spirit of fear but of power and self discipline. Today we step into your grace, let it empower us to dream bigger and live fuller. We have faith in you, Lord and trust your plans. We need you now. Move into our lives and bless every fiber of our beings in Jesus's name. Amen.

APPROVED

"Obviously, I'm not trying to win the approval of people, but of God. If pleasing people were my goal, I would not be Christ's servant." Galatians 1:10

You have God's approval! God thinks you are amazing and awesome. Stop trying to prove it to people.

We have all played the role of a fool trying to gain the approval of the world. Too often we are affected by other's opinions, their ideas, and we seek their approval. People are just as lost as we are, yet we seek to please them! Once you decide to only seek God's approval, people will reject you. Take heart, Jesus was also rejected!

Today in the midst of your everyday life, remember that your work is God's work. Stop trying to win the approval of people. You already have God's approval and favor upon your life. Work with all your heart. Do good. Speak His word. Love. Serve. Be of good cheer and leave the rest to God.

In the end, it doesn't matter who rejects you, it only matters that God loves you and sees your heart. He has already approved you. Now go out there and be great!

My Prayer for You Today:
Lord, keep our eyes focused on you. Today we thank you for your approval. Let your love inspire and guide us today to do our best and to love like you love us. Father, today we surrender to you our loved ones, the sick, the tired, the depleted. You are a God of restoration and we ask for restored health today. Pour out your blessings, Lord. We love you and need you now. Amen.

WAIT

"Those that wait upon the Lord shall renew their strength." Isaiah 40:31

It is in the waiting that strength is produced. There's power in waiting and in the process. As you wait upon the Lord today, let your strength be renewed!

Friend, faith begins where your ability ends. When you have a problem too big to solve, it's a God problem. When neither your status nor your money can solve the problem, it's time to turn it over to God. Wait on Him. Renew your strength through patience and faith.

Today, God wants you to know that your strength is in the waiting. In the in-between stages of life, your character is being built. It's all part of His plans for you. Trust the process. Wait faithfully. Wait with a great attitude. Wait with expectancy. Wait knowing that He is scheming something big and wonderful for you. Wait knowing that He is amazing. Wait knowing that He is God.

My Prayer for You Today:
Father, today we wait upon you with great expectancy. You know our needs, you know our dreams and aspirations; speak, Lord. Be with us today and renew us, as we tend to become weary, impatient, and depressed. Fill us with your strength and your courage. We need you now. We pray all this in Jesus's precious and holy name. Amen.

SPIRITUAL GIFTS

"You have every spiritual gift you need." 1 Corinthians 1:7

You have every spiritual gift you need. It's not outside of yourself, it's not at church, it's not in your pastor, not in your guru, it's in you! You have it!

Too often we feel more secure in others' abilities than our own. We lie to ourselves and believe that our friends are more spiritual than us. We think our pastor definitely has more gifts than we do. And surely God answers our gurus' prayers faster than ours. Those are lies. If anyone is special, we all are. If anyone has spiritual gifts and abilities, we all have them too. Some of us tap into our gifts through faith, while the rest of us look outward.

God doesn't favor one person over another. The Bible tells us that God causes the sun to rise on the evil and the good, and sends rains on the righteous and the unrighteous. (Matthew 5:45) You have spiritual gifts, just like your pastor. You have spiritual power, just like your mentor. You have the ability to bless and heal, to curse and destroy. Jesus himself said that, if we believe, we can do even greater works than He did. (John 14:12) Amazing!

Today, beware of your spiritual gifts. They reside within you. You have everything you need. You are able to do great things. You can do all things through Him! (Philippians 4:13)

My Prayer for You Today:
Father, thank you for our spiritual gifts. Thank you, Father, that you have equipped us for greatness. We thank you. Help us to recognize and utilize our spiritual gifts. Thank you for your love. Empower us now, Lord. Lead us and guide us in Jesus's precious and holy name we pray. Amen.

STICK TO IT

"Perseverance must finish its work so that you may be mature and complete, not lacking anything." James 1:4

Stick to it! Don't give up! What you are going through is maturing you and preparing you for your blessings!

We live in a quick-fix society: drive-throughs, microwaves, instant weight-loss schemes. We are programed for impatience. If it can't happen now, we move on to something else. God doesn't work that way. In the journey of life, with challenges and disappointments, He teaches us to rely on Him. He builds our faith and matures us for our blessings. When you receive your blessings too early, it's a curse. Push through. Stick to it. Be dedicated.

God is shaping and molding you. Stick to the course. Pray and keep on praying. The testing of your faith produces patience. (James 1:3) Those who persevere inherit the promises. (Hebrews 6:12) God knows your journey and every detail is necessary. Trust Him and trust the process.

Today, stick to it! The One who started the good work in you will bring it to completion. (Philippians 1:6)

My Prayer for You Today:
Father, though it's not always enjoyable, today we thank you for maturing us and for perseverance. Help us to be patient and to trust the process, to trust you. Thank you that you are preparing us for our blessings. Be with us today as we stick to the course when we want to give up. Fill us with a sense of purpose, motivate us and bless us. We love you. Amen.

HIGHER

"My ways are higher than your ways and my thoughts higher than your thoughts." Isaiah 55:9

Too often things happen that are beyond our control. We make plans and prepare only to be forced to do things differently. When you've done all you can, trust that God's ways are higher than yours.

Stuck in traffic, missing an important meeting, delayed flights, lost luggage—everyday events can leave you frustrated and irritated. Use the small inconveniences of life to practice your faith. Go with the flow. Trust that there is a bigger process at hand that you do not understand. Breathe, relax; it really is not that important!

Friend, God is always speaking to you. He reminds you that His ways are higher than yours even in everyday events. Let Him control the small details. Leave it to Him to guide your steps; after all, you know that all things work together for the good of those who love God. (Romans 8:28)

So today, listen. Pay attention to what God is telling you in the small events of life. Go with the flow. Don't push. Breathe. Relax. He is in control. Everything is exactly as it should be.

My Prayer for You Today:
Father, help us today to surrender to you. Everything is in your hands. Have your way with us, Lord. Let your plans persevere. Thank you that your plans are higher than ours. Take us to the next level in Jesus's name. Amen.

LOVE, LOVE, LOVE

"Nothing can ever separate us from God's love. Neither death nor life, neither angels nor demons, neither fears for today nor our worries about tomorrow—not even the powers of hell can separate us from God's love. No power in the sky above or in the earth below—indeed, nothing in all creation will ever be able to separate us from the love of God."
Romans 8: 38-39

Friend, I cannot write it enough: God loves you, period! I pray you understand the depth of His love. You may have been brainwashed to believe that God is upset at you, or that He loves you less when you behave unethically. That is the world's biggest lie. Nothing, not one thing, can cease God's love for you. He loves you.

It doesn't matter what you have done or what you will do; nothing, will ever separate you from God's love. Murder can't separate you. Lies can't either. Manipulation or fornication won't stop Him from loving you. Cheating or stealing won't do it either. None of these things can separate you from God. God loves the sinner and hates the sin. He loves you no matter what.

Today, let His love inspire you to make better choices. Let God motivate you to be kinder and more caring to yourself and others. Let love be your greatest aim. (1 Corinthians 14:1)

God loves you so much.

My Prayer for You Today:
Father, thank you that nothing can ever separate us from your love. You amaze us Lord. Thank you. We cannot begin to understand the depth of your love, but today we open our hearts to accept it. Thank you, Lord. Father, today we choose to be inspired by your love and to love others like you love us. We praise you for your love. We surrender our lives to you. Have your will with us. Amen.

NOTHING HIDDEN

"Nothing in all creation is hidden from God. Everything is naked and exposed before his eyes, and he is the one to whom we are accountable."
Hebrews 4:13

God knows everything. Nothing is hidden from Him.

Your pain is not hidden from God, and neither is your joy. He knows everything. You are accountable to Him. People will judge you for your pain and envy you for your success. Relax. God knows your heart. Your secrets and your intentions are clear to Him. Seek to please Him; you only ever have to answer to Him.

The good news is that the One who you are accountable to does not judge you. He doesn't look down on your pain. He knows your success and sees past your boasting. He loves you with your flaws. Your accountability is to Him. Continue to seek Him and love Him.

Today, remember that nothing is hidden from God. You can hide your pain, addiction, guilty pleasures, and successes from the world, but you can never hide anything from God. You are exposed before Him and He loves you. Stop the front, take off the mask, and be vulnerable.

God sees you and loves you! Nothing is hidden from Him.

My Prayer for You Today:
Father, thank you that you see us as we are, exposed and naked and you love us anyway. You know our hearts, our secrets and intentions and you love us anyway. Help us to accept your love and to open our hearts to you. Today, Lord, we need your courage to be vulnerable, to take off the mask and to live the life you intended for us, full of truth, blessings, and light. We pray all this in Jesus's precious and holy name. Amen.

SEASONS

"Even the stork in the sky knows her seasons." Jeremiah 8:7

Just as different seasons bring different weather, different seasons of life bring different circumstances. We can suffer through the winter months knowing that spring is around the corner. Today, rather than being overwhelmed by your season, find hope knowing that your spring season is just around the corner.

Tough times do not last, but spiritually tough people do! If you find yourself in a tough season, with endless difficulties, know that this too shall pass. God has a spring of blessings in store for you. God is close to the brokenhearted. (Psalm 34:18) The heartache will pass. The tears will dry. And trouble will leave you. Hang in there with God.

Today, know your season! People change, things change, but God remains the same. Anchor your life to the One who has no season. Hope in the One who never changes. Hang on to the One who knows no darkness. In Him all your seasons will be blessed and every footstep will be firm.

Let every season be God-filled!

My Prayer for You Today:
Father, today we anchor our lives to you. We need you for stability; we need you for abundance. Lord, open the floodgates of heaven upon us, so that we may know seasons of success, blessings, and prosperity. Bless everything we touch. Be with us today as we proclaim your greatness and hope in you. We love you. Amen.

RELY ON HIM

"… but this happened so we might not rely on ourselves but on God…"
2 Corinthians 1:9

You have thought of everything, you are running out of ideas, now it is time to turn it over to God. Let the roadblocks remind you to rely on God and not your own strength.

Friend, when you've done all you can do, when you've made the right choices, met the right people, and nothing seems to work, it is a reminder that you cannot rely solely on your efforts. Rely on God. The distress and success happen so that you may rely on Him. When you are spiritually mature, you realize that you can't even take credit for your success because if it weren't for the grace of God, it would not have happened. Likewise, when challenges surface, this too happens so that you may rely on God.

When you are out of options, pray and wait faithfully on God. He is always on time. He knows your situation and is guiding you. He hasn't let you down yet. And He will not forsake you now. He has brought you too far to ignore you. Pray and wait faithfully. Rely on Him fully.

Today, do not take the challenges personally. Challenges are guideposts. Challenges force you to seek your Creator. Focus on Him. Rely on God and watch all obstacles disappear. He is all you've got and all you'll ever need. Rely on Him.

My Prayer for You Today:
Father, today we turn inward to you. We know that our own strength cannot carry us; we need you. Help us to realize our limits and to know when to hand it all over to you. Be with us, Lord; fill us with your wisdom and guidance. We pray faithfully today knowing that you hear us and that you know the details of our needs. Thank you for already answering. We love you. Amen.

STAND AND WIN

"Stand firm and you will win life" Luke 21:19

Your perseverance will be rewarded. Hold on to your dreams, have faith, stand firm, and you will win.

Keep on keeping on! Do not let inconveniences change your mind. You may have to change your plans, but hold on to your dreams. Keep on seeking, keep on growing, and keep on believing. Your perseverance will be rewarded.

Stand on the Rock today. Stand firm in God's promises. Believe what He says about you. He says whatever you ask for in His name, you will get. (John 14:13) Stand firm. Stand in faith. Don't let the storms knock you down. Don't let the critics discourage you. Don't let your thoughts fool you. God will do what He says He will do!

Today, if you dream of being a success, if you want to win life, if you want to be happy and at peace, stand firm on God. You don't have to understand it all when you know the One who created it all. You don't have to know the way when you know the One who is the way. Stand on Him.

Stand and win!

My Prayer for You Today:
Father, today we stand firm in you. We need you, Lord. We are choosing to believe your promises despite what the circumstances look like. Be with us today as we keep on keeping on. Give us the courage to stand strong and confident in your name. We love you, Father. We praise you in Jesus's name. Amen.

CONNECT TO HIM

"...apart from me you can do nothing." John 15:5

Some of your plans may succeed temporarily, but to ensure eternal success you need to commit your ways to God because apart from Him you can do nothing.

You have spent a considerable amount of time trying to make things happen on your own. You made the phone calls, specified every detail, and overanalyzed everything, only for things to change and for your plans to drown. God is the master planner. Apart from Him you can do nothing. Connect to Him. He will guide you through your intuition.

With God all things are possible. (Matthew 19:26) Connect to Him. When you connect to Him through meditation and prayer you are able to do great things. All of a sudden things fall together perfectly for you. Your success comes naturally and with ease. All of a sudden you meet the right people, you live out your dreams and desires. Focus on God, who is all-knowing, and with Him you can do all things.

Commit to Him so that, like Paul, you can say, "I can do all things through Him." (Philippians 4:13)

My Prayer for You Today:
Father, we know that apart from you we can do nothing. Be with us today; inspire us and fill us with your courage and strength. We need you, Lord. We surrender our lives today and ask you to take over. Your plans are bigger than ours and your power more than ours. We need you. We praise you, Father. Amen.

HE DOESN'T CHANGE

"For I am the Lord, I change not." Malachi 3:6

Children grow up, life changes, but God remains the same forever.

Relax today knowing that God will not and has not changed His mind about you. He thinks you are amazing. He knows you are worthy and nothing can change His thoughts. Whenever you are feeling down, depleted, and discouraged, remember what God thinks of you. He doesn't change His mind because you ate the last cookie. He doesn't think you're a loser because you didn't keep your word. He certainly doesn't stop loving you because you did something unethical. He will never change His mind about you.

God loves you, period. Today, give yourself a break. Stop beating yourself up over your mistakes. Stop identifying your perceived inadequacy. You are beautiful, smart, and a creation of the Almighty. You deserve to be loved. You are worthy of peace, joy, abundance, and prosperity.

God loves you and hasn't changed His mind about you. Smile.

My Prayer for You Today:
Father, thank you that you love us and haven't changed your mind about us. Thank you, Father, that despite our inadequacies you will continue to bless us and lead us. Thank you that you do not change. Today, help us to accept your grace. We love you. Amen.

NOT ASHAMED

"For I am not ashamed of the gospel…" Romans 1:16

Don't be ashamed of God and what He's done for you. After all, you wouldn't want God to be ashamed to bless you, would you?

Too often we share our lives, our careers, likes, and dislikes with those around us but are ashamed to talk about our faith. We talk about our outward journey but keep our spiritual journey to ourselves. We refrain from talking about how God has revealed Himself in our lives. We tell stories about our neighbors and celebrities, but we don't share stories about Jesus. Even more, sometimes we are ashamed of our blessings. We keep our experiences a secret, our faith under wrap, and our blessings to ourselves.

Don't be ashamed; speak up! God has been too good to you for you to keep it a secret. Remember the time God showed up at the midnight hour and answered your prayer? If it weren't for His grace, you wouldn't be here. Don't be ashamed of the gospel. Proclaim the good news. You don't have to be that annoying God-person, but you do have to proclaim Him through your interactions, your positive outlook on life, your love for people, and your service to the world.

Today, don't be ashamed of the gospel. Speak of His love and His grace. Tell your story. Share your faith. Someone is waiting to hear the good news from you. Share what God has done for you. Don't be ashamed. God is not ashamed to love you and bless you despite your past.

My Prayer for You Today:
Father, fill us with the courage to share your good news with the world without feeling ashamed. Thank you, Lord, that we are not ashamed of your love and your blessings. We surrender our lives to you, Father. Guide our steps. Be with us today, we need you. We love you, Lord. Amen.

CONFIDENCE

"Blessed is the one who trusts in the Lord, whose confidence is in him."
Jeremiah 17:7

What God has for you is for you. Stop worrying about losing your blessings. Too often our insecurities blind us and make us act like fools. We are so afraid of losing the ones we love that we drive them away with our insecurities. We feel so inadequate about our abilities on the job that we sabotage our success. Our lack of confidence spoils our lives.

Friend, insecurities are an indication that we lack trust in God. If we remember who we are in Him, we would feel confident. If we remember that He orchestrates life in our favor, we would feel surer. If we recall His love for us, we would never feel insecure again. Our confidence is in Him. You can trust in the One who created heaven and earth. He's shown you before His magnitude and power; trust Him and remember what He has done for you.

Today, be confident in Him. You may not have all the answers, but you know the One who does. You may not understand the situation, but you know the One who orchestrated the circumstances. You may not know how the future will unfold, but you know the One who holds the future. Be confident. You are blessed. God is on your side. He will never leave you nor forsake you. His blessings are without repentance.

Release insecurities. Stand firm and confident in God.

My Prayers for You Today:
Father, too often we feel scared and insecure. Today we rebuke all feelings of fear and open our hearts to confidence in you. Help us, Lord, to meditate on your promises so that they reside in us and erase all feelings of insecurity. Be with us as we stand boldly against challenges and confidently against difficulties. We need you. Fill us today. We love you and pray all this in Jesus's name. Amen.

HEART NOT MOUTH

"Out of the abundance of the heart, the mouth speaks." Matthew 12:34

Today, God wants you to pray with your heart. For all of us who have uttered loud prayers with no results, let us express silent prayers from our hearts.

Prayer is less about what your lips say and more about what your heart whispers. We have all been fooled by the praising words of a hypocrite and disappointed by the empty promises of a statement, but rest assured that the heart never fails, never deceives, and cannot lie. Connect with your heart and speak from your heart. Let the sincerity of your heart pour out in prayer.

No one understands your heart better than God. Like Hannah, pour out your soul to God. (1 Samuel 1:15) Do not let your circumstances make you stop praying. Pray with your heart—it is the key component of your prayer. Today, understand that an open heart is louder than an open mouth. Speak to Him heart-to-heart.

Today, God is listening to your heart, not your words. Speak!

My Prayer for You Today:
Father, you know our hearts better than we do. We open our hearts to you, pouring out our souls, screaming for your love and grace. Hear us, Father. Listen to our hearts. We need you now. Move in our lives, leave nothing untouched, bless every fiber of our heart, body, mind, and soul. Our hearts scream your name. We love you. Amen.

BLESSINGS FOR TROUBLE

"I promise this very day that I will repay two blessings for each of your troubles." Zechariah 9:12

God will reward you for all your troubles. For all the times you have been betrayed, hurt, lied to, and misled, God will repay two blessings for each of your troubles.

Let go of the grudge. Forget the pain. Release the anger. Open yourself to double the blessings. God will repay you for your patience and endurance. God knows the nights you spent in fear and in tears. No need for revenge on those who betrayed you and spoke ill of you. God kept count and will repay you in blessings.

God promises, "Instead of shame and dishonor, you will enjoy a double share of honor. You will possess a double portion of prosperity in your land, and everlasting joy will be yours." (Isaiah 61:7) So today, rather than focusing on all the trouble you are facing, look ahead to the blessings to come. Nothing goes unnoticed and no trouble will go unpaid.

Today, as you list your troubles, remember to multiply them by two and count your blessings. Smile knowing that for every trouble you will receive double blessings!

My Prayer for You Today:
Father, today we look ahead to the blessings to come. Thank you that you are a God who repays our troubles with blessings. We thank you that you are great; we praise you for your grace. Thank you that we are so loved by you. We surrender all to you and open ourselves to love, grace, peace, and joy. Be with us today as we count our blessings and not our troubles. Thank you. Amen.

FAITH AND PATIENCE

"**...do not become spiritually dull and indifferent. Instead follow the example of those who will inherit God's promises because of their faith and endurance.**" Hebrews 6:12

Faith and patience will reward you with God's promises. Today, keep the faith and be patient.

The testing of your faith produces patience. (James 1:3) You have been praying for a breakthrough, praying for answers, waiting on a miracle. Today, keep on praying and do not lose faith. It's easy to lose faith. You have been praying for years for the same thing, yet God hasn't answered. Have you lost faith?

God wants you to know that the answer is coming. Do not become spiritually dull, defeated, and tired. Keep on praying faithfully. Believe that He will answer you. God is growing your seed of patience. It will happen. His promises are *yes* and *amen*. They will come to pass. Keep the faith.

Today, follow the example of those who will inherit God's promises. Be faithful and patient. His blessings are without repentance. (Romans 11:29) Keep praying. Keep knocking. Keep seeking. God has great things in store for you.

My Prayer for you today:
Father, today fill us with faith and patience. We know that you answer prayers, Lord, but sometimes we feel impatient. Forgive us. Today we ask that you answer now. Give us a sign today, Lord. Speak to us. Thank you for your favor and grace. We love you. Amen.

TODAY

"So don't worry about tomorrow, for tomorrow will bring its own worries. Today's trouble is enough for today." Matthew 6:34

Today, focus on today. God has tomorrow already figured out; enjoy today.

Our focus on tomorrow robs us of our peace and joy today. We spend hours worrying about how things will be in the future only to miss God's blessing today. Forget about when you lose weight. Enjoy your health today. Be happy today. When the kids grow up it will be easier, but enjoy them now. Be grateful now. Today take a deep breath and enjoy the now.

Friend, life will only unfold in a string of todays. God promises to provide daily bread, not a lifetime supply of bread all at once. Similarly, His mercy is new everyday. He will bless you and fill you daily. Focus on today. Let go of tomorrow, you can deal with it tomorrow. Today, be filled with gratitude knowing that He is with you, blessing you, answering your prayers, and loving you right now.

Love Him today!

My Prayer for You Today:
Father, thank you for today. Thank you that we don't have to worry about tomorrow, since you hold tomorrow in your hands. Fill us today. Give us our daily bread today. We need you now, Lord. Speak to us and bless us. Thank you that it's already done in Jesus's name. Amen.

QUALIFIED

"Give joyful thanks to the Father, who has qualified you…" Colossians 1:7

God has qualified you! Wow! The God of gods has qualified YOU! If that doesn't make you feel special, nothing will.

See, it doesn't matter that you didn't finish school, or that you grew up in a dysfunctional family, or that you've lied, cheated, and slept your way to the top. God has qualified you! You are qualified to get all the blessings, all the joy, all the peace, and all the desires of your heart. He qualified you to share His love, to tell your story and to serve your neighbors. You do not need a college degree or fancy letters behind your name. His grace is enough. His love is sufficient. His favor qualifies you.

Today, hold your head up high. Nothing is above you. You are qualified. Sit at the head of the table. Speak. The work has been done for you. You have been stamped with His favor. You are qualified. Give thanks to Him. Be confident. God has qualified you.

Go-on-with-your-bad-self. You are qualified!

My Prayer for You Today:
Father, thank you that you have qualified us. You continue to amaze us, Lord. We are so thankful for your stamp of approval. Remind us today of your favor so that we are not blinded by our needs to be recognized by the world. Father, today we pray that you throw open the flood gates of heaven and pour out so much blessings that we will not have enough room to store. Thank you, Lord, that it's already done. We love you. Amen.

THIRSTY

"Those who drink the water I give will never be thirsty again. It becomes a fresh, bubbling spring within them, giving them eternal life." John 4:14

Contrary to popular belief, the things we seek will not satisfy us. They may bring happiness for a season, but only God can quench your thirst permanently. With God you will never thirst again.

Friend, you are thirsty for God, yet settle for anything. You thirst for love and settle for a mediocre relationship. You think status and career will fulfill you, only to be thirsty once again. Surely once you graduate from school or retire you will no longer be thirsty; yet once again, you thirst. Getting married and having a family will certainly satisfy your thirst, but after that season you find yourself thirsty again. Have you ever been thirsty for cold spring water and settled for spoiled milk? We settle for spoiled milk everyday in our lives. Stop it!

If you are tired of being thirsty, turn to the only One who can quench your thirst forever. Today, turn to God. He will give you more than you need. You will thirst no more. Seek Him first. He loves you and promises you eternal life in Him. The world may satisfy you for a season, but only God gives eternal life. Hang on to Him.

Today, why settle for spoiled milk when you can have a fresh, bubbling spring within you, giving you eternal life? Let God bless you!

My Prayer for You Today:
Father, today we turn to you in our need for fulfillment. Thank you, Father, that with you we will thirst no more. Forgive us for searching for you in the world, when all along we carry you in our hearts. We need you today, Father. You know our needs, and thirst, and only you can fulfill them. Speak, Lord. We praise you, Father. We love you. Amen.

YOURS FOREVER

"My health may fail, and my spirit may grow weak, but God remains the strength of my heart; he is mine forever." Psalms 73:26

The only constant in life is God. When everything changes, God remains the same. God is the strength of your heart, forever.

Our emotions change from day to day. Our circumstances change from season to season. What was important to you then is now irrelevant. What brought you joy then is now insignificant. Find strength in the One who never changes and who is yours forever. No one can take God away from you. They can't will you out of Him. They can't curse you from Him and cannot lie nor scheme you out of His love. Your strength comes from Him.

God is yours forever and remains your strength. When friendships fade, relationships end, health fails, and spirit weakens, God will continue to shine and empower you. Today, hold on to Him. Let go of the pettiness, the mundane, and the ridiculous and hold on to the Omniscient, the Powerful, the Alpha, and the Omega. Fix your eyes on Him who knows no darkness. Focus on the One who loves you and will never fail you.

God is yours forever; rejoice!

My Prayer for You Today:
Father, help us to remember what is important: you. Thank you that nothing can separate us from you. Thank you, Lord, that neither schemes nor lies can change your love for us. Be with us today as we focus our eyes on you and let go of pettiness. We surrender all to you. We praise you in Jesus's name. Amen.

HE IS HERE

"Don't be afraid…take courage, I am here!" Matthew 14:27

Those were Jesus's words to Peter the night Jesus walked on water. No matter your circumstance, take courage, because God is here.

Friend, storms are inevitable. We will all face storms of disappointments, health scares, frustrations, loss, tragedies, but be assured; take courage, because your God walks on water. There is no storm too big for God. Because we rely on His strength, we do not have to be afraid.

God is here. Wherever you are, there He is. He is in the midst of your joy as well as in the depth of your pain. God is with you on your hospital bed as well as your dream vacation. Wherever you are, there He is. You have nothing to worry about. Don't be afraid; take courage!

Today, when the winds of fear and the storms of trouble are brewing, know that God is with you. Your lifeguard walks on water. You will never drown. God is able to calm any storm. He loves you. He will never leave you nor forsake you. He is with you today and always.

Take courage. He is here.

My Prayer for You Today:
Father, thank you that you are with us right now. Thank you that you will never leave nor forsake us. Father, calm our storms. We need you today. Do not let us drown in the struggles of everyday life. We surrender our lives to you. We praise you. Amen.

ALL THINGS

"And God is able to bless you abundantly, so that in all things at all times, having all that you need, you will abound in every good work." 2 Corinthians 9:8

Let's get something clear today, the lies we have been told about not having it all, are just that—lies. With God you can and will have it all… in all things, at all times, having all you need.

Here's another reality: God is not broke. God has it all, abundantly and will meet all your needs. We tend to think of God in a limited way, which causes us to envy our neighbors and hoard our blessings. You can rejoice and be happy for others because their blessings will never reduce yours. God has an abundant supply. His bank account will never run dry. His blessings are without limits. Relax! Be happy for your neighbor's new job. God will bless you with yours as well. Congratulate the new fiancés. Your spouse has already been picked out for you. Celebrate others' blessings knowing that God will bless you similarly.

Remember: God is able to bless you abundantly, so that in all things at all times, having all that you need, you will abound in every good work. The Bible doesn't say "in some things… sometimes… having some of the things you need…" God promises blessings in all things, at all time, having all you need. All means all. Yes, all includes your health, finances, relationships, family, career, fun, peace, school, vacations, business, car, house, shoes, etc. All leaves nothing out. God will bless you in all things.

Today, remember that God leaves nothing out. You are blessed in all things.

My Prayer for You Today:
Father, you amaze us. Thank you that you leave nothing out, that you will bless us in all things, from the smallest needs to our deepest desires. Thank you, Father, that in all things, at all times you have your blessings and favor upon us. We love you for that and praise you for being good all the time. Our lives are in your hands, Lord. May your will be done at all times. We surrender all in Jesus's name. Amen.

PERFECT BOND

"Beyond all these things put on love, which is the perfect bond of unity."
Colossians 3:14

Today, God is calling you to love the difficult and the unlovable. Let love be your greatest aim because it is the perfect bond of unity.

As we seek to be closer to God, let love be our practice. It's easy to speak the word of God. It is not so easy to love. We all have the family member who is difficult to love; the coworker who doesn't deserve our love; the hater who will only get our disgust. God also loves those individuals. Thus, if they are children of God, we are called to be in unity with them.

Today, ignore the comments and love. Be patient and love. Shut your mouth and love. See beyond the actions and love. Forget about the past and love. Don't worry about what it may look like and love. Commit to love no matter what, because God first loved you.

God is love. He is the perfect bond of unity. Love!

My Prayer for You Today:
Father, thank you that you first loved us. Today, we commit to loving the unlovable. Thank you for filling us with your love in order to love those around us. We love you, Father. We praise you. Amen.

FOREIGNERS

"Live out your time as foreigners here." 1 Peter 1:17

We are here on earth as foreigners. We are God's ambassadors. Today, let us remember our status and not get caught up in the pettiness of life.

What would happen if you walked in to work today with the idea of being a foreigner? Foreigners like tourists are able to enjoy sceneries and experiences knowing that they will leave this place and return home. Foreigners speak a different language. They know enough to communicate and get by, but hold on to their culture and language. Likewise, live as a foreigner in your everyday life. Enjoy every experience without clinging on to any. Speak the language of love.

Friend, home is your relationship with God. Home is your connection to divinity. You are not a foreigner to your Creator. Today, live in connection with Him. The One who strengthens you and cares for you yearns for a connection with you. The One who knows your needs and formed you in your mother's womb seeks to be your intimate friend. God is home; everything else is foreign.

My Prayer for You Today:
Father, help us to focus on you and live our time here as foreigners. Remind us to keep our eyes on you and not get distracted by the pettiness of life. Be with us as we grow spiritually and in all areas of our lives. We lift our needs to you knowing you hear us. Thank you for already blessing us. We love you, Father. Amen.

TASTE AND SEE

"Taste and see that the Lord is good. Oh, the joys of those who take refuge in him!" Psalm 34:8

God is good. You have already tasted his goodness. You know the miracles He has already done in your life. Take refuge in Him.

Today, remember what God has already done for you. If it weren't for His grace, where would you be? You know He is good. So why do you doubt now? Take time to enjoy His presence. Delight yourself in His grace. Wrap yourself in His love. Surrender all to Him. Take refuge. Trust and let go.

Friend, God is in charge of your life. He is good and all things are orchestrated according to His goodness. Let go. Find joy and peace in knowing that God doesn't leave anything to chance. He is working things out in your favor. He knows every detail of your life. Take refuge in Him. He loves you and cares for you.

Taste and see that He is good!

My Prayer for You Today:
Father, today we thank you for all the miracles, all the times you showed up and made things happen in our lives. Father, today we surrender our lives to you and take refuge in you. We thank you for your goodness. We praise you for your grace and we adore you for your unconditional love. Thank you. Thank you. Thank you. We pray all this in Jesus's precious and holy name. Amen.

YES AND AMEN

"For all the promises of God in him are yes, and in him Amen." 2 Corinthians 1:20

God keeps His promises! Through Christ He filled us with His grace and today we are able to declare yes and *amen* for all promises.

Yes, God has great things in store for you. Amen that those things are on their way. Yes, God will deliver you from all circumstances. Amen that with Him all things are possible. (Mathew 19:26) Yes, in this life you will face trials. Amen that He has conquered the world. (John 16:33) Yes, you may be weary and faint. Amen that those who trust in the Lord will soar on wings like eagles. (Isaiah 40:31)

Today, know that all of His promises for your life are yes. Yes, you will succeed. Yes, He will grant you the desires of your heart. Yes, what you are going through is temporary. Yes, He will deliver you. Yes, you are blessed financially. Yes, you will get married. Yes, you will finish school. Yes, you will be healed. Yes, you'll get the house. Yes, your business will prosper. Yes, yes, yes!

Shout *amen* and thank God for keeping His promises!

My Prayer for You Today:
Father, thank you that you love us so much that you keep your promises. Today we shout yes and amen boldly, knowing that Christ already did all the work and paid the price. Thank you, Lord. We are so excited and eager to see how you move in our lives. We love you, Lord. We praise you. Amen.

TAKE HEART

"Therefore we do not lose heart. Though outwardly we are wasting away, yet inwardly we are being renewed day by day." 2 Corinthians 4:16

Here's the deal: things may look the same in your life, but in the spiritual realm they are very different. God is blessing you and renewing you everyday. Accept it first in your heart and it will manifest in your life. Take heart!

Think back on a time you needed financial help and worried about paying a bill. You couldn't sleep, worried, stressed, and then decided to call your parents for help. Your parents promised to put a check in the mail. All of a sudden you were able to sleep, you smiled, and moved on. Nothing in your outwardly situation changed. You had not received the check yet, but knowing that the check was in the mail allowed you to smile and be stress free. God works the same way. When you pray, He answers and the blessing is on its way. Though outwardly things look the same or even worst at times, He is blessing you spiritually, inwardly, and the check is in the mail!

Friend, you are not the same person you were last year, last week, or even yesterday. You are more blessed, filled with more faith, empowered more with His grace and you are being strengthened day by day. Take heart. God is working on your heart. You are well equipped to go through everything you are facing today. He is with you. He would never forsake you. Take heart!

Today, be aware of God. Be renewed by Him. Be aware that He is pouring out His blessings on you spiritually as we speak and it is only a matter of time before the blessings materialize in your life. Take heart!

My Prayer for You Today:
Father, fill us with your strength. We need you, Lord. Forgive us for often feeling faint and weary when we have an all-powerful God who never loses strength. Fill us, Lord. Be with us. Renew us. Pour out your blessings in every area of our lives, and in every fiber of our being. We thank you, Lord. We adore you, Father. Amen.

GOOD NEWS

"Everything that has happened to me has helped to spread the Good News." Philippians 1:12

Friend, let your testimony spread the good news of God's love and grace. Nothing just happens. There's a purpose for everything and today tell your story so as to bring the light of God's amazing grace in your life.

You have an audience. People are watching you. People observe the way you behave. People witness the unfolding of your life. Your story and your pain serve as someone else's medicine. Let your faith and response to life's circumstances spread the good news of God. The greatest sermon you will ever preach is the way you choose to live your life.

God wants to use everything that has happened to you to spread His love. The heartbreak taught you that God is close to the brokenhearted. (Psalm 34:18) The financial hardship taught you that God will supply all your needs according to His riches. (Philippians 4:19) When you were down and broke and needed the impossible, you realized that with God all things are possible. (Matthew 19:26)

Today, don't keep secret His miracles. Share the good news with others. Someone is waiting to hear your story. Spread the good news! Share your testimony! Let others know what God has done for you.

My Prayer for You Today:
Father, like Paul, everything that happened to us serves to advance your Word. Thank you for the opportunity to share your love and your grace. Give us the right words and the correct actions as we spread the good news. Fill us with your grace. We love you. We praise you. You continue to amaze us. Speak to us today and pour out your blessings on us. We need you. We pray all this in Jesus's precious name. Amen.

REBUILD

"The glory of this present house will be greater than the glory of the former house... and in this place I will grant peace." Haggai 2:9

If you begin to rebuild God's house, which is your heart, your former days will be nothing compared to your latter days. God promises to bless you and grant you peace.

Too often people want to label us based on our past; when you start putting God first in your life, critics will remind you of your old ways. You decide to go back to school and the haters talk about all the times you changed your major and took a break from school. You are led to a new job, and rather than supporting you, others criticize you for being unstable. The world will remind you of your past, but God will give you a glimpse of your future.

God promises that if we begin to rebuild our lives, restore our hearts, commit to different ways, our lives will grow greater and better. It doesn't matter what you've done, begin today to rebuild your life and put God first. At the core of your being lives the Omniscient Creator who is waiting to pour out all of His blessings on you.

Today, rebuild yourself. Trust God. Pray. Push a little harder. Dream more. Fight. Pray some more. Seek Him. Dedicate your ways to Him. Serve. Be a blessing. Love. God will grant you peace beyond understanding and everything you touch will prosper. Trust Him.

My Prayer for You Today:
Father, today we are committing to rebuilding your house and our lives in Jesus's name. Thank you that your grace grants us a clean slate. We submit our ways to you, Father. Be with us as we follow the example of Jesus today in everything we do. We trust you, Lord. We surrender all to you. Speak! Amen.

WALK IN HIM

"Whether you turn to the right or to the left, your ears will hear a voice behind you, saying, "This is the way; walk in it." Isaiah 30:21

Pray to hear God's voice as He directs your path. Pay little attention to directions but rather focus on His voice.

God has a way of directing our path and speaking to us in subtle ways. The gut feeling that helps you make a decision is God's voice. The doubtful thought that tells you to rethink your ways is God's voice. The rejection from the world is God's direction. In the grand scheme of things, whether you turn right or left, God will always speak to you. Tune in to His voice. Walk under His direction.

Today, may you operate in faith knowing that you have a God who will not let you go astray. As you decide to listen to His voice and follow Him, you will be walking in His greatness. His voice leads you to walk in His love. Your path will unfold beautifully in front of you one step at a time. Trust Him today to lead you. Commit your ways to Him. (Psalm 37:5) He is the light of the world, whoever follows Him will never walk in darkness. (John 8:12)

Walk in Him!

My Prayer for You Today:
Father, we need you today as we walk the circle of life. Help us to always walk in you, under your protection, with your direction. Be with us today as we tune out the voice of the world and listen to you. Lead us to our best lives, to our dreams and aspirations. Lord, we pray today that you break all chains and that you grant us freedom to love, be at peace and soar in Jesus's name. Amen.

GOD SAVES

"What must I do to be saved?" ... "Believe in the Lord Jesus and you will be saved, you and your household." Acts 16:31

It is that simple: when you believe in God, you will be saved. Today, if you are looking to be saved from your circumstances, from heartache or headache, believe in God and you will be saved from your situation.

God is so great that He doesn't require us to work off our wrong doings in order to save us from our circumstances. He loves us so much that he spared us from punishment. His grace does all the work. Jesus's crucifixion took care of our punishment. The work has been done for us. All we have to do is believe in Him.

Today, if you're looking to be saved from your circumstances, depression, heartache, headache, disappointment, failure, whatever it is, turn to God. If you believe in Him, He will save you from your circumstances. God loves you that much. He has great things in store for you. It's time for you to align yourself with Him. Praise and worship are your weapons. Turn to Him. Pour out your soul to Him. Praise Him in the midst of your pain. He loves you and will save you. Trust Him.

God saves!

My Prayer for you Today:
Father, today we believe. We believe that you and you alone can save us from our circumstances, from any and everything we are facing. We believe in you Lord. We believe in your love and in your grace. Today, we pour out our soul to you expecting miracles, expecting saving. Speak to us, Lord. We need you. Thank you for the gift of salvation. We surrender our lives to you in Jesus's holy name. Amen.

HIS WORDS ARE FOREVER

"Heaven and earth will disappear, but my words will never disappear."
Matthew 24:35

God's words will endure forever.

Friend, today you may be in a valley, but you will not stay there. You may be on the mountaintop, but things will surely change. Who you trust today may betray you tomorrow. A stranger today may become your most trusted confidant tomorrow. The point is everything in life changes except God!

God's words will last forever and will never change. What God says about you will surely come to pass and His love for you will remain perfect today and forever. In your search for stability and safety hold on to the One who doesn't change. Anchor your hope and dreams onto Him alone.

Today, hold on to God's words. His words say that He loves you perfectly and that He will never leave nor forsake you. His words say that you are blessed and that no weapons formed against you will succeed. His words say that He has plans for you to prosper. His words assure you that He cares for you and that His love is made perfect in weakness. Hold on to His words, which will never disappear. Hold on to Him.

My Prayer for You Today:
Father, today we are holding on to your words. We believe what you say about us and what you promise about our lives. Thank you that you are the same yesterday, today, and forever. We trust you, Lord. We stand on your words and on your love. Bless us today as we continue to seek only you. We love you. We need you. Amen.

GOD FIRST

"Seek ye first the kingdom and His righteousness and all things will be added unto you." Matthew 6:33

Life has an order. God has an order. He comes first in everything. Seek first the kingdom of God and all good things will come your way.

Friend, if you don't put God in the proper place—first—your life will always be out of order. You will be chasing success, recognition, love, acceptance, finances, only to be left tired, disappointed, and unfulfilled. The moment you take your eyes off of God is the moment you try to be the god of your life. All of a sudden you place more value on the created things than on the Creator. It is not going to work.

God has an order. He comes first in everything. And when you place God in His correct place you are able to weather any storm. Your circumstances may be tough but you will stand strong like "a tree planted by streams of water… whatever you do prospers." (Psalm 1:3) You can lose your dream job or the love of your life and know that you will always have the courage to rebuild, to start over, and to prosper through Him.

Today, place God in the correct order. Place Him first in everything. Give Him the first minutes of your day. Give the first of your finances. Give Him the first of your love and your thoughts. Put Him first. After all, you wouldn't want Him to put you anywhere else on His list.

God first!

My Prayer for You Today:
Father, today we place you first in every area of our lives. Thank you that by doing that we stand firm on you and on your love. Help us, Lord, it's not that we don't want to put you first but often life blinds us; teach us how to place you first. Be with us as we seek you, Lord. Take over. We pray all this in Jesus's precious and holy name. Amen.

LISTEN

"He who has an ear, let him hear what the spirit says…" Revelations 3:22

Do you have a spiritual ear to hear what God is saying to you? Have you positioned yourself to hear His voice?

Friend, who you listen to has influence on your life. If you listen to friends who worry about the economy, your life will reflect their voice. If you listen to friends who are full of drama and shenanigans, your life will be full of drama. If you listen to good counsel, your life will be full of wisdom. And when you listen to the voice of God your path will be straight.

God is constantly speaking to you. He speaks through people and circumstances. He speaks through the Bible and prayer. God is always speaking. Are you listening? Do you have an ear for Him or for the world? Friend, God spoke to Abraham. He spoke to Noah and Jonah and Sarah and Esther, so why wouldn't He speak to you?

Today, draw close to God in order for you to hear His voice. Spend time in prayer. Be still. Ask and keep on asking. Seek Him and keep on seeking. Knock in prayer and keep on knocking. You will hear His voice. You will experience His love. You will be blessed. You will see the miraculous. You will know His love.

Today, listen!

My Prayer for You Today:
Father, today we seek to hear your voice. Speak to us, Lord. Speak! We are listening. We have ears for your voice. Lord, we declare today that we are the head and not the tail, that no weapons formed against us shall prosper. We surrender all that we are and all that we will be to you. Shape us and mold us through your word. We love you, Lord. Amen.

TODAY IS THE DAY

"Now is the time of God's favor, now is the day of salvation." 2 Corinthians 6:2

Today is your day of deliverance, of receiving God's blessings. It is your day of salvation. No more waiting; today is the day!

Friend, you don't have to wait until you are good enough. You don't have to wait until you've prayed enough, or when you're out of school. You don't have to wait until you lose weight, get more money, get married, get divorced, retire, sell the house, or buy the house. You do not have to wait for any specific event; today is the day! Now is the time for God's favor to pour all over your life. Receive it. Receive Him.

It doesn't matter where you come from. It doesn't matter what you've done. It doesn't matter how many people you've slept with, or how many times you lied and cheated; you are covered by His grace. You have the opportunity to be made new today. Friend, it doesn't matter how you started. It matters how you finish. The Apostle Paul started as a murdered and finished as a great teacher of the gospel. Jesus Christ started in a manger and finished as a savior. You too have great potential and will finish victorious. Today is your day of salvation!

God has a great purpose for your life. Put Him first. Let Him lead you. Put your fears behind you and walk in faith today.

My Prayer for You Today:
Father, thank you that today is the day! Thank you that today you will fill us with your grace and love, you will lead us to make the right decisions with the right words and the right people. Thank you that today you will reveal your purpose for our lives. We are so thankful, Lord. We love you. We praise you. Amen.

REMARKABLE SECRETS

"Ask me and I will tell you remarkable secrets you do not know about things to come." Jeremiah 33:3

God has remarkable things in store for you. The things to come will surprise you and take your breath away. Ask Him what they are.

Friend, it is perfectly normal to wonder about things to come. It is, however, not necessary for you to worry about things to come. Your past has conditioned you to think of secrets in a bad way. Your family kept a secret from you that hurt you, your spouse kept a secret from you that destroyed your relationship. Today know that the remarkable secrets of God will bless you and push you forward.

God has remarkable secrets about things to come and today, if you want to get a glimpse, ask Him! He will give you clues and revelations that will only make sense to you. Maybe someone will text you something out of nowhere, or a street sign will suddenly trigger an idea. Whatever it may be, God will speak to you in your language. Ask and open your heart to His answers.

The things to come will bring you increased joy, deep peace, abundance, deliverance, divine health, and prosperity. His remarkable secrets include opened doors, financial blessings, rewarding relationships, success, bliss, and love. Receive them today.

It is no secret that God has remarkable secrets in store for you!

My Prayer for You Today:
Lord, today we agree and ask in Jesus's name about the remarkable secrets of things to come. Show us, Lord, what you have for us. Speak to us today. Give us clues and ideas. We are so excited about the remarkable things you have in store for us. We know that they are awesome and purposeful. Tell us, Lord. We thank you in advance. You continue to amaze us. We love you, Lord. Amen.

NO SEPARATION

"Not height nor depth, nor anything else in all creation will be able to separate us from the love of God." Romans 8:39

God loves you perfectly right now just the way you are. Nothing can change that. Nothing can separate you from His love.

Walk in His love today. If only you would understand the magnitude of His love, you would walk a little taller, speak with more confidence, dream bigger and love stronger. Nothing can affect you. Nothing can change His love for you. Be inspired by that today and dream!

Friend, when you live in the awareness of His love, you will understand that life is working for you. Every situation, every circumstance is working to grow you and lead you to your destiny. Every step is used to grant you the deepest desires of your heart. Wow! Amazing, right? His love is that powerful: that even while you are sitting in traffic, complaining about being late, He is orchestrating things in perfect, divine timing. His love is that powerful. He doesn't leave anything to chance. He blesses in all circumstances.

Today, walk in His love and know that nothing can separate you from His love. Even the lies you tell yourself—you're not good enough, you're bad, you've sinned too much—even those lies cannot separate you from His love. Amazing, right? He is amazing!

Today, walk with more confidence, stand up tall and dream big knowing that the Omniscient, Alpha, and Omega loves you so much.

My Prayer for You Today:
Father, today we find confidence and inspiration in your love. We are inspired by the depth of your love and we thank you that you are always leading us to our best lives and granting the desires of our hearts. Thank you, Father for everything. We surrender all to you. Use us for your glory. Bless everything we do. Be in our thoughts and in our actions. We love you, Lord. Amen.

SHEPHERD

"Be shepherds of the church of God" Acts 20:28

We are called to look after, grow and invest in the church of God. Friend, do not confine the idea of church to a building. The first church you belong to is your family. How are you being a shepherd within your family?

You are a shepherd of the Church of God whether you go to church daily or you haven't stepped a foot in church your entire life. A shepherd actively tends to the needs of the church, guiding and serving family and friends. Understand that your words make a difference. Your care is needed. And your love will shepherd others to God.

"Where two or three are gathered in my name, there I am in the midst of them." (Matthew 18:20) God is in the midst of your family. He is amongst your celebrations with friends as well as in the gathering of people at a church. Let us be shepherds in all situations and circumstances, spreading His love and speaking His word.

Today, be a shepherd within your inner circle. Love. Serve. Praise. Forgive. Mend. Tend to needs. By doing so, you will be building the church of God.

My Prayer for You Today:
Father, thank you that we always have the opportunity to be shepherds. We accept that title with pride and confidence today, knowing that you will give us the right words to mend relationships and love others like you love us. Guide us. Help us. Bless us. We pray all this in Jesus's precious and holy name. Amen.

GOD SAVES NOT CONDEMNS

"For God did not send his Son into the world to condemn the world, but to save the world through him." John 3:17

Friend, we are too quick to condemn others, while we ask God for His grace and deliverance. God does not condemn. He saves.

We have all done it: pointing out the fault of others, judging them based on their actions while we judge ourselves based on our intentions. Likewise, people have judged us, spoken ill of us, instilled guilt in us while hiding behind the veil of helping us. This behavior is not of God.

Jesus was the perfect example of a servant who never condemned. Jesus, He without sins, could have judged those who were cheaters and adulterers, but rather He was the example for us: forgiving, blessing, and saving sinners. Likewise, in your life, instead of condemning those around you, take time today to love them. Forgive them and accept them. "For in the same way you judge others, you will be judged and with the measure you use, it will be measured to you." (Matthew 7:2)

Today let us set the bar on loving and forgiving others and ourselves. God doesn't hold any of our wrong doings against us; may we do the same.

God saves and does not condemn. Thank God for that!

My Prayer for You Today:
Lord, thank you that you save and you do not judge us. Help us today to give the same treatment to others. Forgive us for being so quick to judge. We need you, Lord to be more forgiving, more accepting and more loving. Be with us today. Fill us with your presence, your love, and your grace. In Jesus's precious name we pray. Amen.

ROAR

"Even strong young lions sometimes go hungry, but those who trust in the Lord will lack no good thing." Psalms 34:10

Take inventory of your life; be grateful because you may be hungry, but you will lack no good thing.

Lions symbolize strength and passion, yet even strong young lions sometimes go hungry. Likewise, the roaring inside of you may be faint due to disappointment, tiredness, and lack of hope, but today is the day to feed the lion in you by trusting Him. The lion in you is still alive; hungry, but alive; dormant, but present; faint, but well-able.

Trust God today and get roaring again. Let your faith in His word feed the lion in you. The lion in you lacks no good thing. Today is the day for you to roar again: roar toward your dreams, roar to abundant life, roar to a better future in Him, roar to improved relationships, dream jobs, divine peace, and perfect joy. The lion in you is hungry for Him. Trust Him to fulfill all your needs according to His riches.

Today, be reminded that those who trust in God will lack no good thing. Pick yourself up. Rebuild if needed. Feed your dream with His word. Get your roaring back. Trust Him to provide. Breathe. Pray. Love. Hope and be blessed.

Roar!

My Prayer for You Today:
Father, we need you right here right now. Feed us, Lord, with your everlasting love. You know better than us what we need; we are relying solely on you. We trust you with our lives, we trust you with our dreams. Speak to us, Lord. We love you. We praise you. Amen.

GOD BUILDS

"Commit to God and to the word of his grace, which can build you up and give you an inheritance among all those who are sanctified."
Acts 20:32

Commit to God and be blessed. He builds and provides. As His child, you will inherit His riches. It's a win-win situation!

The Word of God will build you. We all have that person who we talk to, and after hanging up the phone, we feel depleted, confused, worried, and depressed. We all know the coworker who complains vainly about the economy, financial strains, and the darkness of life. While the word of men worries us, His word brings us peace and assurance. Listen to Him not them.

You will never be in the Word and feel depleted. God's Word builds. It will build your faith, confidence, relationships, and family. It will bring you peace, deep joy and assurance that your life is in His hands. His Word will remind you that you are the heir of the kingdom, the beneficiary of His everlasting love and unfailing grace.

Today, make the choice to listen to Him. Do not be reluctant to end a conversation that doesn't build you up. Commit to Him. Listen and speak His word. It's easy to decipher God's voice: if it divides, stresses, or brings fear, it's not from Him. If it builds, brings hope, soothes, and conveys divine peace, then it is His Word. Choose to listen to Him.

God builds!

My Prayer for You Today:
Father, today may we be built by your word. Help us to decipher your voice from the noise of the world. Thank you that a shepherd knows his sheep, and likewise, you know us, Lord. Thank you for hearing our voice, thank you for building us and preparing us for the blessings you have in store for us. Help us to commit to you and inherit your kingdom and your grace. We need you now. We love you. Amen.

FAITHFUL

"Let us hold unswervingly to the hope we profess, for he who promised is faithful." Hebrews 10:23

God is loyal.

Because throughout your life you have been disappointed, let down, and betrayed, you tend to let those experiences affect your faith. You have a hard time believing that God will come through for you. You often doubt that He hears you and loves you. Thankfully, God is not like your family and friends. He is loyal. He does not waiver. He does not change His mind and no matter what you do, He still loves you.

Hold on unswervingly to His promises. Do not let circumstances diminish your hope and faith in Him. The Apostle Paul said it best when he said, "None of these things moved me." (Acts 20:24) Do not doubt His faithfulness because of the betrayal of men. God is faithful. Hope in Him. Pray to Him. Lean on Him. Trust in His promises and hold on to His love despite your hurtful past.

Today, know that God is faithful. If He placed a desire in your heart, it will surely come to pass. Understand that He is the same yesterday, today, and forever. (Hebrews 13:8) His love for you will never change, never diminish, and never fade, no matter what you do. His promises are without repentance. (Romans 11:29) Victory and abundance will be yours because He promised them. He never lies and is faithful. Trust Him.

Remember, God is faithful!

My Prayer for You Today:
Father, we are so lucky that you are faithful. Help us to remember your character and not be blinded by the hurt and betrayal of men. We hold on to your promises of victory, prosperity, bliss, joy, and divine peace. Guide our steps, Lord. Be with us as we face today boldly, holding on to your love, grace, and promises. Thank you that you are faithful. We love you. Amen.

SUDDENLY

"All the people rejoiced over what God had prepared: for the thing was done suddenly." 2 Chronicles 29:36

Suddenly things change. Suddenly life is totally different. In a blink of an eye everything is altered; that is God's power over our lives.

You have prayed years for a miracle, months for answers, days for guidance, and nothing has yet to happen. Do not lose heart. God is able to change things suddenly. In a blink of an eye, what you thought was a desperate situation becomes the perfect circumstance. The cancer suddenly disappears. The financial issues suddenly vanish. The heartbreak suddenly mends. The relationship is suddenly restored. And surprisingly all of your hopes, dreams and desires suddenly happen.

Friend, we often put God in a box thinking that miracles are difficult and that it takes time for things to happen. Some things may take time, yet other things may happen suddenly. "With the Lord a day is like a thousand years and a thousand years are like a day." (2 Peter 3:8) Therefore time is your illusion. Believe that things can and will change for you suddenly.

Today I pray for your "suddenly": may God suddenly put the right people in your life, may He suddenly deliver you from the family drama, suddenly free you from financial worries, suddenly bless you with the answer you are looking for, suddenly bring you the new job, suddenly award you your deepest desire, and suddenly open the door at which you have been knocking.

Today, may God suddenly answer your call!

My Prayer for you today:
Father, we believe that you are capable of all things suddenly. May you answer our sudden calls. All those things that seem impossible and that we have been praying for, may you suddenly answer, Father. We believe in your ability and declare it done in Jesus's name. Amen.

STRENGTH

"Be strong in the Lord and in the strength of his might." Ephesians 6:10

Be strong in God. You don't have to get through on your own strength, rely on His might.

Your responsibilities may be heavy—meetings, paperwork, home duties, phone calls, deadlines, errands, bills, and more—straining your peace and causing you to feel tired and burdened. The demands deplete your energy. Before long, you feel drained and tired. Thankfully, God is your strength.

Rely on His strength to sustain you. Ask to be filled with His courage in order to go through your days infinitely enthusiastic and energized. Take time to meditate and renew your strength in Him. Be strong in God. When life's responsibilities are pulling you in different directions, find strength in prayer and stand strong on His promises. Breathe.

Today, be strong in God. Fulfill your responsibilities for Him and through Him. Remember that you can do all things through Him. (Philippians 4:13) Work as though you are working for God, not for men. (Colossians 3:23).Be filled with His love and His strength.

My Prayer for You Today:
Father, we turn to you for strength. Help us, Lord, as we get tired and burdened. We need you to help us, to fill us with energy and strength to do your work. Be with us today as we enthusiastically face our days full of hope, standing strong on your Word. Thank you, Father, that it's already done. We love you. We praise you. Amen.

SALT

"You are the salt of the earth." Matthew 5:13

You are the salt of the earth. You bring flavor and spice to the world around you. You are needed to do God's work here on earth. You are the salt!

You matter. What you do, the words you speak, the attention you give, all of it matters more than you realize. Your smile, your personality, your mannerisms, all of it influences the lives around you. You bring joy and hope to those you love. You remind them of God's love and grace. You matter that much.

Today, God wants you to know that you are the salt of the earth. God wants you to know that He chose you to do His work, to spread His light, to share His love. God thinks that much of you. God left nothing to chance. He placed you with the right people, within the right circumstances, under the right roof for you to shine and spice the earth. You are that important!

You are the salt of the earth!

My Prayer for You Today:
Father, thank you for choosing us to do your work. Thank you, Lord, that you love us so much and value us so much to declare us the salt of the earth. Lead us in everything we do to be the light and to do your work. Fill us today with purpose, perseverance, and enthusiasm as we proclaim your love and grace. We love you. Amen.

DOERS NOT HEARERS

"Be doers of the word, and not hearers only, deceiving yourselves." James 1:22

You know someone who is all talk. Maybe you are that person. It is not enough to know the Word of God, you must act according to the Word.

Let your actions speak. Don't just talk about loving and serving others, do it! Your actions will demonstrate the love of God. When people see you smile despite a breakup, when you still serve and treat your coworker with respect despite their betrayal, when you continue to tithe and give to charity despite your financial struggle; these actions will speak of your faith and trust in God.

Be a doer of the Word not only a hearer of the Word. When you are obedient to the Word, you will be blessed. (John 13:17) Others will look to you for assurance that God keeps His promises. You will live your testimony, reminding others and yourself that, despite life's uncertainty, you stand on the certainty of His love, His grace, and His faithfulness.

Today, do the Word. Love. Forgive. Serve. Tell the truth. Give. Trust. Bless others. Be patient. Hope and dream.

My Prayer for You Today:
Father, today we decide to be doers, not just hearers. Help us as we need your guidance and support to be obedient to your Word. Lead us, Lord. Be with us as we love others and serve you today. We surrender all to you. We trust you and love you. Amen.

NOT A HAIR

"Not a hair on your head will perish." Luke 21:18

Wow! This is powerful! Nothing you do will perish. Nothing regarding you will fail, not even a hair on your head.

When you put God first in your life, plans may change, inconveniences may happen, you may lose your job, maybe get knocked out for a season, but your victory is guaranteed. God loves you too much to let you perish; that will not happen, not on his watch.

Speak victory over your life. Do not let depression or your circumstances overwhelm you. Your battles are not your own. Your baggage is not too heavy. God knew you were strong enough with Him to handle them. Put on His armor and get back in the fight. You will not perish, not even a hair on your head! God is with you. You cannot lose.

Today, declare boldly that you will not perish, that your healing has already been declared, that you have already been delivered by the One who knows your name, who knows the number of hairs on your head, and who created you in your mother's womb. His plans for you will bring you victory, peace, love, joy, and abundance. He loves you. Stand on His love and soar!

Not even a hair on your head will perish. He loves you that much!

My Prayer for You Today:
Father, you amaze us. Thank you, Lord that you love us so much that you will not let us fail. Today we surrender our lives to you knowing that you have great plans for us. Lead us, Lord, guide us and make a way. Fill us with your courage and your strength as we stand boldly on your promises. We will not be shaken, Father. We trust you. We praise you. We love you. Amen.

MASTER'S PLAN

"The heart of man plans his way, but the Lord establishes his steps."
Proverbs 16:9

When things do not go according to your plan and when what you hoped for is not what happened, trust the Master's plan.

You may spend days planning an event, months planning an affair, and years planning your career only for circumstances to deviate from your plans. All of a sudden, the people you expected did not show up. Your finances are not where you thought they would be and things seem to be falling apart. This is the time to trust God. He leaves nothing to chance and though things are not according to your plans, they are according to His master plan.

God has a way of reminding us that He is in charge. He knows exactly how to alter plans in order for us to trust Him. The amazing thing is, when things go according to His plans, they turn out better than we could have imagined. All of a sudden, the altered plan led to a better outcome, everything turned out even better than what you planned. Trust Him.

Friend, if God knows even the number of hairs on your head (Luke 12:7), how much more does He know? In the midst of making plans, remember that He establishes your steps. When things are not going as planned, remember the Master's plan is the master plan. Relax. Enjoy the process. Breathe. Let go. He is in total control. Learn the lesson while He changes your plans for the better.

Today, let Him who knows it all establish your steps.

My Prayer for You Today:
Lord, thank you that in the midst of our plans, you order our steps. Thank you, Father, that you know better than we do and your plans far surpass our plans. Help us today to let go of our plans and to trust you. Lead us, guide us and be with us. We thank you for the lessons, we thank you for the blessings. We praise you, Father. Amen.

CAST YOUR WORRIES ON HIM

"Cast all your worries on him because he cares for you." 1 Peter 5:7

There you have it: give God all your worries and anxiety. He cares about you and will take care of them. Cast it all on Him!

Let this scripture free you from taking care of others' problems. Too often people cast their issues and problems on you, expecting you to solve them. Feel free to let others know that you are not the one. Remind them to cast their worries onto God. Accordingly, rather than expecting others to solve your issues, cast them on to God. He is the One. Do not put the burden on your spouse, parent, or friend; God is well able to take care of whatever you are going through.

"Cast your cares on the Lord and he will sustain you; he will never let the righteous be shaken." (Psalm 55:22) God will sustain you and make your path straight. Trust Him with your worries. Talk to Him about your fears. Surrender all the details of your life to Him. He loves you so much and will move mountains to bless you.

Today, when life worries you, do not call Joe, John, or Suzanne; call God. Pray. Cast your fears on Him. He knows you. He understands you and He loves you more than you can understand. Free those around you from the burden of carrying your worries. It is no one's job but God's. Let go of the expectations that your children should take care of you, that your spouse should solve your problems. God is more than happy to take care of all your needs according to His riches. Cast them on Him.

My Prayer for You Today:
Father, today we cast all our worries and anxiety on you. Thank you that you love us so much that you carry all our burdens. Today we surrender all to you. We trust your timing, we trust your hand in orchestrating all the details of our lives. Thank you for your unconditional love. Thank you for your grace and your peace. We love you. Amen.

REMEMBER THE LESSONS

"The things you have learned and received and heard and seen… practice these things, and the God of peace will be with you." Philippians 4:9

Every situation has taught you something. Remember the lesson. Remember what God has done for you and live according to the miracles and blessings He's bestowed upon you.

We tend to only seek God when our lives are out of control. We yell out to Him when we need deliverance and a miracle. However, when life is flowing for us we quickly forget His word and what He's done for us. If you do not want to experience the same challenging circumstances, hang on to the lessons! Put into practice what God has done for you. When He humbled you during your time of need, it was to become more compassionate of your neighbor. When He delivered you from the abusive relationship, it was for you to depend on Him and experience His love.

Whatever lesson God has taught you, this year or in prior years, keep them close and in practice. Remember how He augmented your faith. Recall how He guided your steps to meet the right people at the right time. Remember how He made everything work for your good. Take time today to make a list of the lessons God has taught you and decide to practice them.

In the end, God has taught us all the same lessons under different circumstances. He's taught us about depending on Him, about love, patience, forgiveness, peace, joy, and faith. He's taught us over and over to trust Him. God has taught us that He is in control. Today, remember His lessons and experience His peace.

My Prayer for You Today:
Father, thank you for the lessons. Thank you, Lord, that you have taught us to love beyond measure, and to trust you with every fiber of our being. In our struggles, we thank you; in our success, we acknowledge you. Thank you that every situation has been orchestrated for our greater good. You continue to amaze us. We praise you from the bottom of our hearts and soul. Thank you, Father. We love you. Amen.

GRACE

"You are not under law but under grace." Romans 6:14

Friend, God's grace gives you the freedom to be at peace with your past. It doesn't matter where you've been, who you've hurt, what you've said, God's grace provides you with a clean slate.

People will hold your past over you to oppress you. You will find ways to think yourself out of blessings because of what you've done. You often feel unworthy, not good enough, and small because of what others have said about you and what you choose to believe about yourself. Stop it! You are not defined by your past, not even by your destiny. You are defined by God's love and grace for you. Accept it!

Live freely under His grace and allow others to do the same. Grace means forgiveness, it means a clean slate, and it means starting over without judgment. Grace means letting yourself and others off the hook, it means the freedom to make mistakes and know that nothing can diminish God's love for you. His love is perfect and whole right now. Your mistakes will never take an ounce away from His love and your good deeds cannot add an ounce either; His love is perfect right now.

Today, may you know and experience His grace in every aspect of your life. May you laugh a little louder, smile a little brighter, and love a little deeper knowing that your Creator and Father loves you so much that He gave you the freedom to live under Grace. Wow!

My Prayer for You Today:
Father, thank you for your grace and your love. You amaze us. Thank you that you love us so much that you give us your grace and love. Help us to give grace to others and to ourselves. Be with us as we love deeper today in your name. Fill us, be with us, and guide our steps. We love you and praise you. Amen.

STUMBLE NOT FALL

"The steps of a man are established by the Lord… though he may stumble, he will not fall, for the Lord upholds with his hand." Psalm 37:24

Every step you take is ordained and established by God. If you need a sign today, this is it: you are where you are supposed to be.

Every failure, every tear, every struggle is part of the grand scheme of things. Do not be discouraged. What seems like a complete failure is preparing you for something better. Trust Him. Trust yourself. Trust where you are in life. Your current situation is not a curse. It is preparation. You will stumble, you will take a wrong turn, but you will not fail.

Credit your past experiences for your wisdom today. Your failed relationship taught you to put God first. Your financial struggle assured you that He is your true provider. The betrayal of your close family members taught you that only God is loyal. You can always count on Him. The loss of your job taught you that God has a bigger purpose for your life. Everything you have been through and are going through and will go through is ordained and orchestrated for your greater good. Trust Him.

Today, step out in faith, knowing that failure is impossible for a child of God. Follow your dreams. Have a vision. Go for it. Be ensured that God will establish your steps and He will never leave you nor forsake you. Stop the excuses, quiet the fears, shut out the doubts, and trust Him.

With God, failure is never an option. Go for it!

My Prayer for You Today:
Father, today we are stepping out on faith, trusting that you establish our steps. Thank you for conspiring on our behalf. Thank you, Father, that failure is not an option for us. Today we rebuke all thoughts of doubt, insecurity and fear. We open our lives to you knowing that you have a bigger plan for us. Thank you for your guidance, thank you for your wisdom. Amen.

HE UNDERSTANDS

"The Lord searches every heart and understands every desire and every thought. If you seek Him, he will be found by you." 1 Chronicles 28:9

God understands you. Do not spend another day trying to explain yourself. The One who matters already knows.

Too often we feel misunderstood and judged by our peers, and sometimes even mocked for our dreams. Take heart, God knows your heart. He understands every thought and every desire and knows your deepest intentions. Seek Him to find your dreams. Stop sharing your thoughts with people who do not matter. Share them with Him.

Whether you are dreaming of a business, thinking of the next big idea, desiring a new home or a new relationship, God knows your heart and has already answered your prayers. He grants your desires and doesn't judge your negative and crazy thoughts. He understands. He knows. And despite it all, He loves you.

Today, shut your mouth to people and speak to God. He will never share your secrets and will never judge you. Spend time in prayer sharing your biggest dreams and your deepest desires. Open your heart to Him who listens.

Speak to God!

My Prayer for You:
Lord, forgive us for seeking other's opinions by sharing our dreams with them instead of you. Today we open our hearts to you, spilling all our dreams, hopes, and aspirations. Thank you for your understanding and thank you for granting our desires. We seek you, Father. We need you. Fill us with your presence and your love. We praise you and we love you. Amen.

VISION

"Where there is no vision, the people perish." Proverbs 29:18

What is your vision for your life? For the next five years? For next year? For this week? It's easy to be discouraged when you don't know where you're going. Dream, anticipate, have a vision!

Friend, your vision is your prayer to God for your life. Too often we want God to change our situation but we have no vision for our lives. When you have a vision for your life—the type of work you want, the family you desire, the person you want to become—all of your dreams and thoughts are silent prayers to the Almighty. Your vision gives you hope and a reason to go on. It's easier to wake up in the morning when you have a vision for your day. It's easier to sit through a meeting, suffer through a call, and deal with a difficult individual when you realize the purpose behind every situation and every action.

Have a vision for your life that scares you. Dream big! Let your vision be so big that only God can grant it. Know what you are doing and why you are doing it. Let every action be purposeful, every word meaningful, and make every moment count. Pray that God enlarges your vision while He blesses you with dreams come true.

Today, if you do not have a vision for your life, get one! Have a vision for your week and your day. Turn your vision to God in prayer. Your assignment is to dream and leave the rest to God. He will direct your steps (Proverbs 16:9) and will give you the desires of your heart. (Psalm 37:4)

My Prayer for You Today:
Father, today we turn over our vision to you. Enlarge it, bless it, and grant us the desires of our hearts. Guide our steps, Father, and be with us as we live on purpose and journey to our destiny. Fill us with enthusiasm, courage, and strength as we vivaciously live our vision moment by moment, day after day. Thank you for hearing our prayers and answering. You amaze us. We love you and praise you. Amen.

LOVE IS THE WAY

"If I have all faith, so as to remove mountains, but do not have love, I am nothing." 1 Corinthians 13:2

We have all heard ourselves and others say, "Love will find a way;" today reprogram your mind to say, "Love is the way." We can have everything, but without love we are nothing.

Love is the way! It is the way to forgiveness, happiness, peace, and true abundance. You can have all the faith in the world, but if you don't love others and yourself how will this faith be expressed? Love will help you commit to a cause. Love will challenge you to stand for something bigger than yourself. Love will make you persistent and persevere. Love will mend old wounds and risk new ones. Love is the way!

Today, as you move through your day with love, remember that love is the glue. God is love. Write a love letter. Mend a relationship. Forgive. Smile. Enjoy the sunshine. Love life. Love yourself and love God.

Be blessed in love!

My Prayer for You Today:
Father, we seek so much to love but are often blinded by our human tendencies. Open our minds and heart today to love and accept without judgments. Help us to give and forgive without conditions. Be with us as we step out in love and acceptance. Soften our hearts and nurture us. We need you. We love you. Amen.

HUSH YOUR STORM

"He got up and rebuked the wind and said to the sea, "Hush, be still." And the wind died down and it became perfectly calm." Mark 4:39

Whatever storm is going in your life right now, God has the power to hush it!

In the Bible, Jesus rebuked the wind and everything was perfectly calm. Jesus also said that we are capable of doing the same work and even greater work than Him if we believe. (John 14:12) Thus you have the power to hush the storms in your life. Speak it!

Circumstances do not define you and storms should not bring you fear. You have the power to bless your life in His name. Speak His word over your situation and hush the family drama. Hush the financial distress. Hush the health scare. Hush the business trouble. Hush the school stress. Hush the relationship commotion. Whatever your storm may be, hush it with God.

Today, remember that with a mustard seed of faith you can move mountains. Have faith in God and His power in your life. Believe that He can and will hush the storms in your life. Seek Him to make everything calm. He will give you divine peace.

Believe in Him and hush your storms!

My Prayer for You Today:
Father, today we hush every storm in our lives in Jesus's name and speak peace and joy. We believe in you and thank you for the miracles and blessings. Thank you, Father, for everything. Be with us today as we walk in your victory. Amen.

BE LOVE

"Rooted and established in love" Ephesians 3:17

Let everything you do be rooted and established in love, because God is love.

Life is too divine for you to be anytime but loving. Let everything you do and say come from a loving place. Speak your peace in love. Stand your ground in love. Share your opinion in love. Set your intention on love. When you do that, the family drama suddenly becomes an opportunity to express your love. The business quarrel is yet another chance to disagree in a civil and loving way. Your response to every challenge will always be ethical and effective without being tarnished by selfishness, anger, and jealousy.

Establish your ways in love. Let every action and word be rooted in God. Let Him in every detail of your day-to-day business. See yourself and others with reverence and love. Be kind. Be patient. Your life will be so much more divine.

Today, don't settle for being loving, be love!

My Prayer for You Today:
Father, today we are rooted and established in you, thus in love. Let every action and word come from you. Help us to see others and ourselves like you see us. Be with us as we face our day-to-day lives with love. Be in every interaction and every conversation. We love you. We praise you. Amen.

DO IT FOR GOD

"When you did it for the least of these brothers and sisters, you were doing it for me." Matthew 25:40

Be encouraged today, whatever you do for others you are doing for God. Take Heart.

People can easily disappoint you. Their lack of gratitude and appreciation can be frustrating and often hurtful. However, Jesus said that whatever you do and have done for others, you did for God. The family member you helped during a hard time who now doesn't talk to you, the coworker you trained and befriended who backstabbed you, the business partner you invested with who cheated you. Do not hold a grudge, God saw it all. You were doing it for Him and your reward will come from Him.

Today, continue to do good deeds. Help someone. Befriend a neighbor. Assist a coworker. Give your time. Share your expertize. Spread your love. Listen to someone in need. In doing so, you are doing it for God. It's about you and Him. You would do anything for God, correct? Today, do it!

In the end, your reward will come from Him. He will pour so many blessings on you that you will not have enough room to store them! That's a promise from God, and He keeps His promises. Try it!

My Prayer for You Today:
Father, today fill us with courage and love to continue to do your work as we help our brothers and sisters. We choose to serve you by serving them. Help us to take heart and not lose enthusiasm. Be with us today. Thank you that you have promised us blessings beyond measures. We thank you for your love and your grace. Fill us, today; in Jesus's name we pray. Amen.

HAVE FAITH

"And without faith it is impossible to please God, because anyone who comes to him must believe that he exists and that he rewards those who earnestly seek him." Hebrews 11:6

Do not waste your time praying if you don't believe God answers prayers. What's the point?

God rewards those who earnestly seek Him. Don't be fooled, you can't have superficial, fake faith, and think that will work. It doesn't work. Don't pretend like you are seeking God when you are really seeking His blessings. Seek Him. Yearn His presence and have faith in His power and love. You can't go around believing God only when life is good. Have faith—believe He exists and loves you no matter what your circumstances look like.

Pray faithfully and boldly today. Believe that God knows your situation and sees your struggle. Trust Him in all you do. Believe that He will reward you. He will answer your prayers and He will never leave you nor forsake you. Believe that beyond a shadow of a doubt. Whether you are in a season of plenty or of want, have faith.

Today, when things look clear as mud, and there's no light at the end of the tunnel, believe that He will make a way and will be the light. Trust that He will reward your struggle. He leaves nothing to chance and every thing is perfectly orchestrated for your victory. Have faith not in His blessings, but in Him, His love, His power, His grandeur, His magnitude. Have faith!

My Prayer for You Today:
Father, today we believe in you. We know that you reward those who earnestly seek you and today we seek you. We seek your presence and your love. We have faith in you, Lord, and trust you with every fiber of our being. We know that you love us and you are orchestrating life in our favor. We thank you for that. We praise you. We love you. Amen.

REST IN HIM

"Come to me, all of you who are weary and carry heavy burdens, and I will give you rest." Matthew 11:28

Friend, you have been carrying your burdens long enough. Today it is time to hand them over to God and find rest in Him.

The family drama, health issues, financial distress, business pressure, kids, parents, in-laws, personal frustrations are all weighing on you and affecting your well being. The emotional stress is tiring and draining. It is time for you to hand it to God. Let go and let God!

Find rest in Him knowing that He is taking care of your burdens. Your weight is one prayer away from being lifted. And your rest is one prayer from being granted. Pray! Hand all your worries to God. He is able to do all things. You cannot keep stressing over every little thing. You cannot control what others say or do. Bless them and hand it all over to God. Rest in your faith in Him. Rest in His love for you. Rest in knowing that nothing in His control can ever be out of control. Rest in Him.

Today know that God is able to give you divine rest and peace no matter your circumstances. When you put your faith in and trust in Him, you will experience deep peace and inexplicable rest. He is in control and works things out in your favor.

Rest in His love!

My Prayer for You Today:
Father, today we ask that you lift up the burdens. You know what is weighing us down and today we rebuke all spirit of fatigue and weariness. We surrender all to you and find rest in you, Father. Take over. We need you. Fill us with your divine peace and wisdom. We trust you. We love you and we pray this in Jesus's precious and holy name. Amen.

ENRICHED

"For in Him you have been enriched in every way—with all kinds of speech and with all knowledge." 1 Corinthians 1:5

There you have it: in God you are enriched, enlightened, augmented, and well prepared. If this does not increase your confidence, nothing will!

In God, you will find the right words and all the knowledge in order for you to prosper, thrive, and live the blessed life you are destined to live. Do not search for the words and knowledge anywhere but in Him. In Him you have been enriched in every way. The hard conversation you have been avoiding—today is the day, God will give you the right words. The decision you have to make, He has enriched you with all the knowledge, make it today!

Today is the day! God has enriched you with the right words and all the necessary knowledge. Don't wait another moment. If you were praying for a sign, this is it! Make the call. Start the conversation. Ask for what you want. Speak your mind in love. Do not settle. You have been enriched in every way.

In Him you are enriched!

My Prayer for You Today:
Father, today we pray for the right words and all the knowledge in order to take the next step in reaching our goals and mending relationships. Speak for us and through us, Father. We surrender all to you. We need you right now. Thank you that you continually enrich and enlighten us. We praise you for your goodness; we are humbled by your love. Thank you. Amen.

WORTHLESS THINGS

"Turn my eyes from worthless things, and give me life through your word." Psalm 119:37

What you pay attention to shapes your life. Keep from paying attention to what is worthless and open your mind and heart to Him who gives life.

Other people's business, the office gossip, the friends' quarrel, other's finances and secrets are some of the most worthless things you can choose to focus on. If it doesn't build you and doesn't inspire you to be more, stop paying attention to it. What someone thinks and says about you is none of your business and shouldn't get your attention. The One who matters the most already has His stamp of approval on you. Focus on Him.

Too much of our energy and time is spent on worthless things, stupid ideas, and nonproductive issues. Choose today to turn your eyes on things that matter, like how you can serve and build a neighbor, how you can love and forgive a family member, how you can grow spiritually and live without judgments. Turn your eyes on matters of the heart and spirit because that's where you will find God, who is all loving and all worth it.

Today, decide to focus on what matters. What you focus on grows and as you focus on love, faith, peace, and joy, those will grow abundantly and you will enjoy a life worth living.

Ignore the worthless and focus on the Worthy. Focus on God!

My Prayer for you Today:
Father, keep us from paying attention to what is worthless. Fill our lives, minds and hearts with worthy causes, people, and adventures. Show us how to seek you and focus on you in all circumstances. We need you. Today we choose to focus on what matters, Lord. We choose love, light, forgiveness, peace, and joy. Thank you that it is done in Jesus's precious and holy name. Amen.

MAKE PERFECT

"The Lord will make perfect that which concerns me." Psalm 138:8

God is taking care of everything that concerns you. Sit back, relax, and let Him who is the most powerful take care of all your needs.

God is in all the details of your life, from the most mundane to the most extraordinary. He promises to make everything work together for your good. (Romans 8:28) He is concerned with everything that concerns you. He will make perfect your health, finances, family, friends, career, dreams, and aspirations. Just trust Him!

Today, whenever you feel worry and fear creeping in, declare boldly, "God will make perfect that which concerns me!" Don't let your thoughts run astray; quiet them down with His Word. God is working everything out right now. If it bothers you, stresses you out, and is in regards to you, your Creator is already aware and taking charge. Breathe!

Everything is perfectly as it should; God is too perfect for it not to be! Let Him who is magnificent work everything out perfectly for your good. He loves you that much.

My Prayer for You Today:
Father, thank you that you are making perfect everything that concerns us. Thank you that you care that much for us. Help us today to hold on to your word and not our worries and fears. Be with us today as we face the world, standing boldly on your truth. Thank you for your love and your grace. We praise you. Amen.

SHINE

"You are the light of the world.... let your light shine before others, so that they may see your good works and give glory to your Father who is in heaven." Matthew 5:14-16

You are the light of the world. Yes, you! Though you think you are insignificant and small, you are the light of the world!

Your actions and your words are important. They have the power to build others and light their world. Your light is a testimony of God's love. Let it shine and light the world. Friend, today someone who is in need of God's love will come in contact with you. You will be their only source of hope. Let your light shine! Let God's words and love be evident in your actions and words.

We are God's children and He uses us to represent Him. How are you representing Him in this world? Are you full of hope and love? Are you ready to serve and help others? Do you bring light to every situation and every person? You have the power. You are the light of the world.

God placed you specifically at your job, within your family, among your friends, in your neighborhood as the light. You are not there by coincidence. Bring light to those around you. Light up their lives with your actions and words. Remind them of God's love for them. Be kind to them and forgive them despite of their selfishness. Do not hold a grudge, you are the light! Do not curse them, you are the light! Do not be impatient and rude, after all, you are the light!

Today, shine!

My Prayer for You Today:
Father, thank you that you thought so much of us that you declared us the light of the world. Wow, you amaze us, Lord. Help us today. Be with us as we let your light shine through us. Use us today within our families, at work, in our communities as the light. Thank you for the privilege of serving you. We surrender all to you, Father. We love you. Amen.

HE MAKES THINGS GROW

"So neither the one who plants nor the one who waters is anything, but only God, who makes things grow." 1 Corinthians 3:7

God makes things grow. Our work is valuable, yet our labor would be in vain without His blessings.

Today I pray that God makes all things grow in your life. May your relationships prosper, your labor be rewarded, your children thrive, your business blossom, your efforts be compensated. May God grow your faith, your success, your love, your peace, and your joy so that everything you touch is blessed and anything you take on grows.

Whether you are in a season of planting, watering, or harvesting, let God grow things in your life. Put Him first in all your endeavors. Rely on Him and His timing. Pray, pray, and pray some more. God will direct your path and bless you in every area of your life; all you have to do is turn your plans to Him.

He makes things grow and will grow every area of your life! God bless you!

My Prayers for You Today:
Father, today we acknowledge you in everything we do. We know that you are the Alpha and the Omega. We need you right now. Bless every area of our lives, Father. We surrender every part of our being and declare ourselves bigger and better in Jesus's name. Thank you for your blessings, thank you for your grace. We love you for your goodness. Speak, Lord! Amen.

TODAY

"This is the day that the Lord has made; let us rejoice and be glad in it."
Psalm 118:24

Today is the day for you to be happy and grateful. Do not put it off another day—rejoice and be happy today!

Friend, you are not promised tomorrow. Too often we put our hopes in the uncertainty of tomorrow. We wait to be happy when goals are achieved. We wait to rejoice when we finish school, when the kids are out of diapers, when it's time for retirement. Those days are not certain; what is certain is today! You're alive and breathing, so take time to be glad and rejoice.

God loves you so much that He gave you today. Don't wait until next month or next year to enjoy and celebrate. Be glad today. Give thanks today. Rejoice today. Live today. Laugh today. Love today. Be blessed today!

My Prayer for You Today:
Father, thank you for today. We are glad for your love and for another opportunity to speak of your love. Thank you for the time with family and friends. Thank you for this wonderful journey. We praise you for your love, we thank you for everything and we surrender all to you, Father. We love you. Amen.

RENEW

"So if the old way, which has been replaced, was glorious, how much more glorious is the new, which remains forever!" 2 Corinthians 3:11

This message is for you. You are stuck in the "good old days" mentality. Wake up! Your past is not better than your future. What God has in store for you is so much more glorious and magnificent. The "good old days" are gone and the blessings to come will surpass those of the past.

Do not get stuck in the past. Do not mourn over someone or something God has taken away from you. Whatever it is, God will replace it with so much more. The new relationship will not compare to the old. The new friend is so much more loyal. The new job is more fulfilling. Your new way of thinking frees you to reach higher heights.

Where you are right now, God circled on the earth for you. Trust Him. Trust your position. Trust your failures. Whatever you have lost made space for the new. Rejoice! In trusting God, you will forever hold faith, divine peace, joy, and love in your heart.

Your life is so much more than it used to be. Thank God for that!

My Prayer for You Today:
Lord, today we trust you to replace everything we've lost with so much more. Thank you, Father, that you are a God of renewal and you are constantly renewing us with more and better. Thank you for renewed faith. Thank you, Father, for renewing our minds. We trust you. We love you. May your will continue to be done. In Jesus's name we pray. Amen.

POWER OF THE TONGUE

"Death and life are in the power of the tongue, and those who love it will eat its fruits." Proverbs 18:21

Watch your mouth! What you say affects your life more than you realize. Words have power. Death and life are in the power of the tongue.

Rather than speaking words of defeat like "I'm never going to make it," "Nothing good ever happens to me," "Go figure, I'm not lucky," "I'm fat," "I'm not good enough," speak words that build! Words have the power to kill. They kill dreams, joy, peace, self-esteem, relationships, and they kill your hope and your faith.

Today, let your words give life! Speak words that build and give hope, words that inspire and encourage, words that are based on God's truth and His love. Don't wait for someone else to speak to you, tell yourself today "I am blessed," "God is on my side," "I got this," "Nothing can shake me, I stand on God's Word," "I'm fearfully and wonderfully made."

Death and life are in the power of the tongue. Choose life today! Be blessed!

My Prayers for You Today:
Father, today we choose life by speaking words based on your Word. We choose life by speaking of your love and grace. Thank you, Lord, that you have declared us blessed. Thank you that we are fearfully and wonderfully made. We declare life today in Jesus's name. We love you, Lord. We surrender all to you. Amen.

TRUST IN HIS NAME

"Some trust in chariots and some in horses, but we trust in the name of the Lord our God." Psalm 20:7

Some trust in the world and in shenanigans; today, trust in the name of the Lord our God!

Whatever you are praying for trust that it is yours in the name of the Lord. It doesn't have to make sense, it doesn't have to look natural. You have a supernatural God whose blessings often make no sense, whose power is indescribable, and who makes the impossible possible. Miracles are effortless to Him. Trust in Him, not in others' strength.

Trust in God's power through you. You already know that you can do all things through Him. The Bible tells us: "Those who trust in themselves are fools." (Proverbs 28:26) Trust in Him! God is working for you and through you. Whatever you are facing today, your highest goal, greatest challenge, and even your most tedious task, all of it can and will be done through Him. Trust in Him.

Trust in His name. Believe in His power. Understand His love for you. Trust His word. Depend on His strength. You can do all things through Him. God loves you and will never cease to amaze you. Trust Him!

My Prayer for You Today:
Father, we trust in you. We often don't understand circumstances, but we stand strong and tall in our trust in you. We thank you for past and future miracles. Be with us today as we face our daily lives. We can do all things through you. Fill us with your love and your strength. We love you, Father. We praise you. Amen.

BLESS THEM

"Don't repay evil for evil. Don't retaliate with insults when people insult you. Instead, pay them back with a blessing. That is what God has called you to do, and he will bless you for it." 1 Peter 3:9

It is too easy to get angry with those who insult, hurt, betray, and humiliate you. You are called to love them anyway. Rather than insulting them in return, pay them back with a blessing.

Today, pray for those who hurt you. Send a blessing to those at work talking about you. Ask God to open the floodgates of heaven upon your enemies' lives. Bless those who curse you. Love those who hate you. Serve those who mistreat you. In doing so, you will be the light in their dark world. In doing so, they will experience God's grace through you.

Friend, when you live for God, people will insult you. They will judge and hurt you. They did it to Jesus and will do it to you. But your test is to stand still, and love them despite their actions. You are to bless them even though they deserve your curse.

God will bless you for your patience and love. God knows how you've been mistreated and will bless you. Your blessing comes from Him. Let people talk while God blesses you.

Keep silence and be blessed!

My Prayer for You Today:
Father, thank you for the patience and control of keeping silence while others hurt us, talk about us, and betray us. Thank you that you see all things and know all things and that you will bless us despite our enemies' curses. We surrender all to you, Father. Fight for us. Speak on our behalf. We love you and trust only in you. Amen.

NEW STRENGTH

"Those who trust in the Lord will find new strength. They will soar high on wings like eagles. They will run and not grow weary. They will walk and not faint." Isaiah 40:31

Today may you find new strength in God. May you trust Him enough to push through and persevere. May you reach new heights.

Friend, your ability to push through despite disappointments relies on your trust in God. Do you trust Him enough to try again? Do you trust Him enough to take another step, to dream another dream, to attempt another project? Do you trust God enough to start over when your world seems to have crumbled and you are back to square one?

Renew your strength in Him. You cannot start over alone, but with Him who strengthens you, a new start is possible. When you lose hope and feel lost in the dark, remember that He is your light. Your strength comes from God. You can do all things through Him. Renew your strength, trust in Him and His promises, take another step, breathe, and try again.

What you are going through is all part of the process. Trust Him. Everything is exactly as it should be. Find strength in Him.

My Prayer for You Today:
Father, we look to you for new strength today. Fill us with your strength, your courage in order for us to persevere, to keep going enthusiastically. We cannot do it alone Father. We need you. Be with us, fill us, Lord. We surrender all to you, trusting in your divine love and your insurmountable power. We love you. Amen.

TOP NEVER BOTTOM

"The Lord will make you the head, not the tail… you will always be at the top, never at the bottom." Deuteronomy 28:13

Your victory has been declared long before you were born. It is written. You are the head, not the tail, at the top, never at the bottom!

Change your mind today! Nothing happening in your life is placing you at the bottom. Contrary to your belief, you are not a victim but a victor, not a loser but a winner, not cursed but blessed, not forgotten but forever saved and loved. No matter what your situation looks like today, your destiny is at the top. Believe it!

God will make you the head, not the tail. He has amazing things in store for you. He will use you to save others, to bring hope and love to those in need, to serve and bless those around you. He chose you because you know what it's like to feel low, yet you persevere. He chose you because, despite your struggles, you didn't give up. Your destiny is at the top because you once felt at the bottom and turned to Him.

Friend, God loves you so much that He declared you the head and placed you at the top. Do not waste your position. Serve, love, and be blessed!

My Prayer for You Today:
Father, today we embrace life with the attitude of being the head, not the tail. We face our day knowing that we are at the top because you placed us there. Thank you for loving us so much. We surrender our day to you. Use us to bless others. Let everything we touch prosper, and may everyone we encounter find hope. We love you, Lord. Amen.

LOVE DEEPLY

"Above all, love each other deeply because love covers over a multitude of sins." 1 Peter 4:8

The older you get, the more you realize that life is a school and the lesson is love. Every experience teaches you about love. You are called to love because love covers a multitude of sins and because God is love.

You are called to love deeply, truthfully, and unconditionally. Despite your sins, God loves you. Why is it so difficult for you to do the same for others? Why is your sin okay to be forgiven but your neighbor's sin is too much to overlook? You lie, cheat, mislead, and manipulate, and you are still deserving of love. Your neighbor corrupts, deceives, and divides, yet she is not deserving of love? If you deserve love despite your sins, we all do. God loves the just and the unjust, the saint and the sinner. You are called to do the same.

Love covers over a multitude of sins. Today, look at the individuals in your life and love them regardless of their actions. Be of service to them despite their character flaws. Love them deeply like you want to be loved. Today, love deeply.

Love deeply and overlook wrongs. Forgive. Reconnect. Forget. Lend a hand. Pick up the phone and call to mend a broken relationship. Be vulnerable. Love despite the pain. Love to find peace. Just love!

The depth of His love has brought you this far, now it's your turn to love deeply!

My Prayers for You Today:
Father, words cannot describe the depth of your love. Thank you that your love saves. Thank you that you love us so much that nothing we do can ever separate us from you. Thank you, Father, for the opportunity to love deeply in your name. Be with us, help us to swallow our pride and to love deeply. We surrender all to you, Father. Amen.

GOD DELIGHTS IN YOU

"The Lord delights in his people; he crowns the humble with victory."
Psalm 149:4

Where you are right now, what you are doing with your life right now, however big or small, delights God greatly. He is so proud of you and loves you beyond words.

God delights in you. He sees your heart. He knows your intentions. He knows how far you have come. He understands your shortcomings and you still bring Him great pride and joy. He crowns you with victory, wraps you in His love, smothers you with His grace, and pours infinite blessings upon your life. Rejoice!

Today, relax in His love. You cannot do anything to change His love for you. You cannot mess it up. God will never stop loving you. You cannot lie too much, you cannot cheat too much, you cannot fornicate so much that He will stop loving you. Nothing you do will change His love for you. You cannot deceive, destroy, nor divide to the point of ending His love for you. He loves you perfectly right now. His blessings and love are based on Him, not your behavior. For this, you should celebrate.

God loves you no matter what and delights in you. Let His love change your attitude, mind, and behavior.

The victory is already yours. You are a child of God!

My Prayer for You Today:
Father, thank you that, despite our failures and mistakes, you love us perfectly and delight in us. We choose to change our attitudes, minds and behaviors because of your love for us. Help us. Be with us today. We love you for your greatness, we thank you for your grace. In Jesus's precious name we pray. Amen.

THE SOURCE

"A man can receive nothing unless it has been given to him from heaven."
John 3:27

God is your source. Everything comes from Him.

Today, be grateful to those who help and support you while remembering that everything is from God. He is your source. He provides. He protects. He loves and supports. God often uses people to bless us. He used the friend to help you obtain the job. He used the doctor to help with your care. God used the unexpected stranger to help you when you were in need. Though it is important to be grateful to people, do not lose sight of God. He is the ultimate source!

God has great things in store for you. Trust Him. He has already declared you victorious. He has given you His unconditional love, which saves. Everything comes from Him. Today, don't look to the world to supply, look to Him. Do not seek your joy in someone else. True happiness, joy, and peace can only be found in Him. Do not chase people for breakthroughs; let God use others to bless you. Seek God!

Wherever you are today, God is your source. He is your source of love, peace, joy, financial abundance, health and bliss. Seek Him!

My Prayer for You Today:
Father, today we realize that you are our source. With you, we can never be depleted and no need will go unmet. Thank you, Father. Help us to seek you in everything and not the world. Be with us as we search for love, peace, acceptance, and abundance. Fill every need. Thank you that it is already done. We praise you. We love you. Amen.

GOD IS GREATER

"You are from God...greater is He who is in you than he who is in the world." 1 John 4:4

God is greater than what you are facing! Whatever the circumstance, He is greater; believe that. Greater is He who is in you than he who is in the world.

This is your reminder: God is greater! The issue you are facing does not surpass His power. The pain you are experiencing is not greater than Him. The mountain you face is not taller than Him. He is greater!

Friend, the amazing fact remains that we are from God. We are His creation, His children, born from His image. That alone should remind you that you too are great. You are a conqueror. You are a child of the almighty. God lives in you. You can do all things through Him. The enemy can't touch you. Disease can't break you. Pain and anxiety cannot suffocate you. You are too blessed!

Today, look within. Greater is He who is in you than he who is in the world. God is greater than what you are facing. With God, you are greater than your neighbor. No one has the upper hand on you. You remain higher in your Father's hand! Relax. Pray. Trust. Believe.

God is greater!

My Prayer for You Today:
Father, today we know and trust that you are greater than everything we could ever face. Thank you that we rest in your palms. Thank you that with you we can face anything. We surrender our troubles to you, thank you for deliverance and miracles. We praise you and love you. Amen.

ACCORDING TO YOUR FAITH

"According to your faith, let it be done to you." Matthew 9:29

Friend, God continues to amaze me! In Matthew 9:29 we are reminded of how important our faith is and the role it plays in our blessings. Faith determines our miracles! When a blind man approached Jesus, he was healed because he had faith that Jesus would heal him.

Do you have faith that God can heal your situation today? Do you have faith that He can answer your prayers? Do you believe? Do you truly believe?

According to your faith, let it be done to you! How big is your faith today? Are you praying over your situation but have doubt that God will change it? Do you believe your fears over your faith? Is it possible that your doubt is delaying your miracle? Have faith in the words you utter over your life. Have faith in God trusting that He will change your life. Have faith that God is able and will heal any situation. Have faith in your prayers, assured that they will all be answered.

According to your faith, let it be done to you! According to your faith, may you have joy, peace, success, love, abundance, bliss, rest, and happiness beyond measure. According to your faith, may all your prayers be answered and may God bless you beyond your wildest dreams. Believe that He is with you and for you. Believe that nothing is impossible for Him. Believe that He can and believe that He will. Believe.

Today, grow your faith in His word. Believe and receive His blessings.

My Prayer for You Today:
Lord, you amaze us. Thank you that our faith predicts outcomes. We choose to grow our faith in you today. We know what an awesome God you are, and we trust in your ability to do the impossible, to hear the unuttered words of our soul, and to meet every need. We love you, Father, and we lift up all prayers to you expecting and thankful for your answer. In Jesus's precious and holy name we pray. Amen

FAITH NOT SIGHT

"We walk by faith, not by sight." 2 Corinthians 5:7

Your life is an expression of your faith in God. At any given moment, you can decide to live in fear of the unknown or to walk by faith.

The Bible tells us: "Hope that is seen is no hope at all. Who hopes for what they already have?"(Romans 8:24) It is easy to talk faith until faith is all you have. It is easy to speak of God's love and grace until you are in a situation where you need Him. Faith is being certain that God has your back. He is in control, though it may often look otherwise.

Friend, no matter what your life looks like today, have faith that God hears you and is working on your situation. Do not let your situation shake your faith. The bigger your faith, the bigger your miracle! Walk in faith.

Walk in faith knowing that what God has for you, no one can take. Walk in faith believing that you can do all things through Him. Walk in faith assured that your life is in His hands and He has great plans for you. Walk in faith confident that nothing is impossible for God and your situation is minute compared to His greatness. Walk in faith trusting His word over your life and believing that when you knock it will be open. When you ask it will be given. And when you seek you shall find.

Faith, not sight: Faith in God, His promises, and His love.

My Prayer for You Today:
Father, we do not understand our circumstances, but we know you. We know the powerful and loving God that you are and we trust in your Word and in your love. Be with us today as we continue to walk in faith. Fill us with your courage and your grace. We need you, Lord. Thank you that it is already done. We love you. Amen.

ARMOR

"Be strong in the Lord and in the strength of His might. Put on the full armor of God, so that you will be able to stand firm." Ephesians 6:11

Everyday has its challenges, but you are a conqueror. Have confidence, as you stand strong in the Lord, nothing will move you, put on His full armor. Stand firm in God!

Another day, another set of issues! Jesus warned us that in this world we would have trouble. (John 16:33) But there is nothing you cannot overcome with God. Put on His full armor as you head to work, hold hard conversations, handle stress, recover from a health scare, start something new, deal with fear and anxiety. There is nothing you cannot handle with His strength. Be strong!

Today, stand in the strength of His might. Whatever comes your way is temporary, but God is eternal. Be confident. You can do all things through Him. Stand firm in your faith; your Father is the Alpha and Omega. He will never leave you nor forsake you. Put your faith in Him. He's proven to you over and over how much He loves you. Stand firm!

Be fruitful in Him!

My Prayer for you today:
Father, in you is our strength and today we pray that you fill us with confidence as we put on your armor and embrace whatever comes our way. We lift up our day to you and ask that you use us to bless others. Show us how to live according to your purpose. Be with us, Lord. We love you. We need you. In Jesus's precious and holy name we pray. Amen.

LIVE OUT LOUD

"I came so you may have life and have it abundantly." John 10:10

Live out loud!!!

Friend, abundantly life is your right, claim it! Do not limit "abundance" to material things, to a sum in your bank account, to the size of your house, or the maker of your car. Today, take abundant living out of the box. Live abundantly out loud. Sing. Dance. Laugh. Do not wait to be received, approved, or accepted. Live! Imagine if birds only sang when they felt heard, or lions only roared when they felt received.

Matthew 6:1 warns us about doing things "to be seen by men." God sees your heart. He knows you and that's all that matters. Live abundantly out loud for Him. Give praise. Serve. Laugh. Enjoy.

Today, wherever life finds you, be intentional on living out loud. Speak your mind. Sing at the top of your lungs. Savor ever spoonful of ice cream. Do the things you love. Be passionate. Enjoy a sunset. Breathe fresh air. Laugh with a friend. Swim with dolphins. Color a picture with a child. Be silly. Be fun. Be you.

Jesus came so you could live out loud. He came so you may enjoy life fully and abundantly. Don't waste another day. Live!

My Prayer for You Today:
Father, thank you that it brings you great joy to see us live abundantly and out loud. Thank you, Father, that right now we all have access to an abundant life full of amazing experiences. Be with us today as we live out loud in you and through you. We love you and thank you for this amazing journey called life. Amen.

KNOWLEDGE AND DISCERNMENT

"I, wisdom, live together with good judgment. I know where to discover knowledge and discernment." Proverbs 8:12

Knowledge and discernment come from God. Seek Him and you will be wise.

Do not consult Google for answers, or your friends for guidance; in Him you will find all the help and guidance you need. Our judgment is often skewed by our emotions and the advice of others. Take time to be still. Let God speak before you open your mouth. Consult Him before you take action.

Friend, make it your practice to seek Him first in every situation. Knowledge and discernment are found in Him. You will know your next step when you consult God first. You will experience a deep sense of peace and wisdom knowing that He is leading you and that everything is in control. Pray first, act second!

Today, discover knowledge and discernment in Him.

My Prayer for You Today:
Lord, today we seek wisdom, knowledge, and discernment in you. Lead us and guide us, Lord, in every situation, under every circumstance. We need you. Help us to be still enough to hear your voice. We thank you for answers. We thank you for guidance. We thank you for your love. We surrender all to you in Jesus's precious and holy name. Amen.

GOD IS ABLE

"...Him who is able to do far more abundantly beyond all that we ask or think, according to the power that works within us." Ephesians 3:20

We serve a God who is able to do the impossible. Whatever you ask or think of, God is able to do far more. Amazing, right?

Dare to pray for your wildest dream! Dare to think your highest thought! Too often we pray small and think small because we are blinded by realistic expectations and limited by earthly circumstances. God is not regulated by natural and realistic perimeters. He is a supernatural God, capable to doing supernatural, amazing, and impossible things.

Today, pray, ask, and think according to His power. Expect deliverance, blessings and guidance according to His authority. You have a big God. Pray, think and ask big things, I dare you! God will amaze you. Every prayer will be answered beyond what you could imagine. Every situation will be blessed beyond your vision.

God is able!

My Prayer for You Today:
Father, today we turn our highest prayers and thoughts to you knowing that even those are smaller than your thoughts and your plans for us. We surrender all to you, Father, knowing that you are able to turn our lives into our ministries, our pain into joy, our weakness into strength. We are so amazed by you, your power, and your love for us. We thank you for everything and trust you with everything. In Jesus's name we pray. Amen.

LOVE

"Whoever does not love does not know God, because God is love." 1 John 4:8

Commit to loving people. As you love, you will experience divine power and bliss because God is love.

It's easy to love nice people. Everyone loves those who are helpful and sweet but your biggest challenge will be to love the unlovable. How do you love those who hurt you? How do we love those who are annoying, frustrating, difficult, rude, mean, and just plain evil? You are called to love people despite their flaws because God loves you despite your flaws.

Let it be your spiritual practice to love people. They do not have to be perfect, but you have to be loving. Commit to loving them despite their actions. The Bible reminds us to love our neighbors (Mark 12:31) and our enemies and to do good to them. (Luke 6:35)

How should you love people today? By following what the Word says: "Love is patient, love is kind. It does not envy, it does not boast, it is not proud. It does not dishonor others, it is not self-seeking, it is not easily angered, it keeps no record of wrongs. Love does not delight in evil but rejoices with truth. It always protects, always trusts, always hopes, always perseveres." 1 Corinthians 13:4-7

Today, love!

My Prayer for You Today:
Father, today help us to see others as you see us and help us to be loving in our thoughts and in our actions. Thank you that you loved us first and that you are love. Help us to follow your example today as we come across difficult people to love. We thank you for your love and your grace. We lift our lives to you knowing that you love us. We praise you. We love you. Amen.

NEW THINGS

"Behold, I am making all things new." Revelations 21:4

Friend, take heart, God is making all things new in your life.

You haven't seen your best days. God is renewing every detail of your life. He is getting ready to bless you with new relationships, new successes, new health, new wealth, and new hope. Leave your old ways and old thoughts in the past. God is making all things new.

Whatever you are going through today, know that a change is coming. Do not look to your past to predict your future, break free from your history. Your destiny does not depend on where you come from. God has blessings for you that you could never have fathomed. No one in your family has seen such blessings and breakthroughs. Trust Him to make all things new.

Today, thank God already for making all things new. His love is being poured on your life and will bless every aspect of it. Trust Him. All the changes you are experiencing are for the best. Trust Him. The challenges and pain are part of the birthing process of your new life. Trust Him.

God loves you so much that He is making all things new in your life. Smile.

My Prayer for You Today:
Father, thank you for making all things new in our lives. We trust you and are excited about a future better than we could pray for. Let your love pour into our lives and renew every aspect of our physical, emotional, and spiritual being. We are so humbled and thankful for your love. Renew us, Father. Bless us and continue to love us unconditionally. We love you. We praise you. Amen.

GIVE THANKS

"Give thanks in all circumstances; for this is the will of God for you." 1 Thessalonians 5:18

When life throws you a curve ball it can be difficult to be thankful, but give thanks anyway. Give thanks in all circumstances!

None of us enjoy the sour moments of life and though we run to God for deliverance, we forget to thank Him for these moments. As you face challenging times today remember to thank Him no matter what. Because you trust God and you do not lean unto your own understanding, you are able to thank Him for challenging times. When your plans do not turn out the way you had hoped, thank Him; broken heart, thank Him; financial difficulties, thank Him; stressed at work, thank Him; frustrated, hopeless, sad, bitter, angry, thank Him. In all circumstances thank Him.

Friend, all things work together for the good of those who love the Lord and are called according to his purpose. (Romans 8:28) For that reason, you, a child of God, are able to give thanks even when you do not understand. You are able to praise Him in the midst of darkness and despair.

Today, give thanks! Thank Him in all circumstances. Thank Him because He is great. Give thanks because of who He is and trust in His love, which delivers, heals, and saves.

God loves you. Thank Him!

My Prayer for You Today:
Lord, thank you for everything. Thank you for the hard times and the good times. Thank you for the failures and the successes. Lord, thank you for always placing the right person at the right time in our lives. Though we do not understand, Father, today we thank you for everything and surrender our lives to you. We trust your time, we need your grace and we are thankful for your love. We love you, Lord. Amen.

JESUS IN YOUR BOAT

"Hush, be still." Mark 4:39

Jesus is in your boat! Stop over-thinking and over-analyzing; be still.

"Hush, be still," are Jesus's famous words when Him and His disciples faced a windstorm while crossing the Sea of Galilee. Jesus was perfectly asleep while His disciples were panicking, overthinking, overanalyzing, and worried. They awakened Jesus in a frantic and asked him, "Don't you care that we are perishing?" (Matthew 4:38)

Does this story sound familiar to your story? When financial storms, health storms, family storms are present in your life, do you panic? Do you scream out to God, wondering why He's letting you perish? When your relationship failed, did you suddenly panic thinking that God forsook you? Today, remember: Jesus is in your boat!

Just as He did for His disciples, He will do for you, He hushed the storm. When the King of kings is with you, be certain that you can weather any storm. When Jesus is in your boat—your life, your heart, your mind—you can cross the Sea of Galilee, the sea of disappointments, the sea of heartaches, the sea of setbacks and challenges, and come out victorious. Today, just as He asked His disciples, Jesus is asking you: "Why are you so afraid? Do you still have no faith?" (Matthew 4:39)

So today, "Be still and know that He is God." (Psalm 46:10) Do not be afraid. Jesus is in your boat!!!! Relax. Chill. Be still!

My Prayer for You Today:
Father, today we seek your peace as you weather through different storms. Thank you that you are in our boat. Thank you that we can trust you to hush any storm. Today have your way in our lives. We love you and praise you. Amen.

WORK

"Faith without works is dead." James 2:17

This is your call to action. Faith without works is dead.

Too often as believers we have faith that God will change our situations and we sit and wait on Him. The doctor warned that you are borderline diabetic, you believe God for healing while devouring ice cream and cake. You have faith that God will bless you with a new business and you fail to develop a business plan. Faith without works is dead. Do your part. Live your faith through actions. Take a step. Do it!

"I will show you my faith by my works." (James 2:18) Moses struck the rock in faith. He could have believed that God would give him water and sat around waiting, yet he accompanied his faith with work by striking the rock. And for Moses "water gushed out." (Numbers 20:11) Friend, if God did it with Moses, He will do it with you. Take the first step in faith and watch your blessings "gush out."

Today, don't just let go and let God. Get going and trust God!

My Prayers for You Today:
Father, today we lift up our first steps toward our goals and dreams. Help us, encourage us, be with us as we move in faith. Lord, thank you that you are faithful and as we get going and trust you, you will reward our efforts. We love you and praise you. Amen.

UNDERSTANDING

"Lean not unto your own understanding, in all your ways acknowledge Him and He will direct your path." Proverbs 3:5-6

Your understanding is limited to your perspective. Relying on your understanding may leave you frustrated, confused, and even hopeless. Acknowledge God in all you do for direction and guidance rather than leaning on your own understanding.

Friend, your understanding is based on your history. Your lens is influenced by your experiences and upbringing. Too often you see things the way your parents saw them. You understand life based on what you observed. You set goals based on what you have been exposed to. Today I want you to know that you haven't seen much, you understand very little, and God has so much more in store for you!

The Bible says that His thoughts are higher than your thoughts. (Isaiah 55:9) Rely on Him who is higher than us. Let us rely on the One who knows the beginning from the end, the Alpha and Omega. Lean on Him rather than your own understanding. Today, stop trying to figure things out, stop making up stories, stop assuming. Acknowledge Him and He will direct your path. Turn it all to God because He knows and you don't. Trust Him to direct you.

Lean not unto your understanding, lean on God!

My Prayer for You Today:
Father, we surrender all to you. Today we choose to live by faith, not understanding much but trusting you completely and fully. We don't know what the future holds, but we know that you hold the future. We trust you with our lives, we trust you with our families. We lift everything to you and thank you for always working things out in our favor. We praise you, Father. We love you. Amen.

STAND ON THE ROCK

"You are to stand on the rock." Exodus 33:21

Whatever is happening in your life today, you are called to stand on the rock!

Life has a way of shaking us and forcing us to take a stand. Too often stand on our profession, our physical looks, our titles and family history. Unfortunately, we tend to stand on what society tells us. In the midst of the storm, stand on the rock. *Stand in Faith.* Stand on His Word. Stand on God.

Psalm 18:2 reminds: "the Lord is my rock, my fortress and my deliverer; my God is my rock, in whom I take refuge, my shield and the horn of my salvation, my stronghold." Take refuge in Him. Stand on His truth and His word. In God you will have your deliverance. Do not be moved. Do not be anxious. Do not let the world shake you. Stand on solid ground. Stand on the rock!

Today, in the midst of the storm, know that God still loves you. Remember that He has you in the palms of His hands. Obey Him today. Listen to His voice. Seek Him. In the midst of emotional turmoil, remember that God is still in control of your life. His plans are greater than yours. In the midst of stress, disappointment and failure, know that God will never leave you or forsake you.

Stand on the rock. Stand on God.

My Prayer for You Today:
Father, today we are deciding boldly and faithfully to stand on you. We stand on your word, and we stand on your love. In the midst of chaos, Lord, we call out to you knowing that you hear us. Be with us. Calm us and guide us. We need you. We pray all this in Jesus's precious and holy name. Amen.

HOPE AND ENCOURAGEMENT

"Such things were written in Scriptures long ago to teach us. And the Scriptures give us hope and encouragement as we wait patiently for God's promises to be fulfilled." Romans 15:4

Where do your hope and encouragement come from?

Friend, if you depend on your spouse to be encouraged, unfortunately you will soon be disappointed. If your source of encouragement is your friend or your job or the economy, sooner or later you will find yourself standing on sinking sand. We have all looked in the wrong places for hope and encouragement. If you are anything like me, you sought hope and encouragement from people, from relationships, from financial success, from your career, and eventually you realize that nothing can bring you the certainty and assurance that God promises.

Open your Bible! Your hope is found in His Word. Read scriptures to reassure you. Lean on Isaiah 41:10: "Do not be afraid, I am with you… I will strengthen you and uphold you." Rely on Deuteronomy 31:6: "I will never leave you nor forsake you." Understand Romans 8:38: "Nothing can separate us from God's love." Remember Luke 7:48: "Your sins are forgiven." Memorize Romans 3:22: "You are the righteousness of God through Christ."

Today, seek His Word as you wait on His promises. Know your worth in Him. Don't burden your neighbor with the responsibility of giving you hope and encouragement. Your essential needs can only be met in Him and through Him. Seek God today. Whatever you are looking for today will be found in Him.

Be blessed!

My Prayer for You Today:
Father, today we come to you to be filled and encouraged, to find hope and meaning, to be renewed and empowered. Be with us. Thank you for your promises. Today we pray for patience as we wait on your promises. We pray for the courage to serve and the strength to be your disciples. We love you and praise you. Amen.

HE KNOWS

"Before they call I will answer; while they are yet speaking I will hear."
Isaiah 65:24

God will answer your cry before you utter a word. He hears you and knows you without you having to speak. Isn't that amazing?

Find peace today in knowing that God knows everything about you. Sit in silence trusting His love. If you never utter another prayer, God will continue to take care of you. If you never share another sigh, He will already understand you. God, your Father, your Creator, knows you and provides according to His riches.

Today, trust God. He knows the beginning from the end. He hears you before you call. He provides before you are ever in need. Trust Him. Drop all fears, anxiety, and worry and embrace His love, grace, and peace. He knows your situation and has already answered.

Before you even speak, God answers!

My Prayer for You Today:
Lord, thank you that you know us and love us so much that even before we ask, you answer. Thank you Father that you are that amazing. Thank you that you work things out in our favor. We surrender all to you in silence today. You know the deepest part of our beings and love us beyond our shortcomings. Thank you. We love you and praise you with all our being. Amen.

RELIABLE

"An unreliable messenger stumbles into trouble, but a reliable messenger brings healing." Proverbs 13:17

Be reliable!

Can others count on you? Is your yes a yes? Is your no a no? Is your word reliable? Can God rely on you to be obedient? Can He trust you to serve? Can He rely on you to love His children? It is written: an unreliable messenger stumbles into trouble. Could it be that you are the reason why your life is in trouble? Could it be that your unreliability and irresponsibility cause you to stumble?

God is the perfect example of reliability. The Bible assures us that He is the same yesterday, today, and forever. (Hebrews 13:8) You can rely on God. His promises are always "yes" in Christ. (2 Corinthians 1:20) He doesn't change His mind about you. He is 100% reliable. You can trust Him all the time, everyday.

Today, be reliable! Keep your word. Follow His Word. Bring healing to others and yourself by being a reliable messenger—a messenger of truth, of love, of forgiveness, and of grace.

My Prayer for You Today:
Father, thank you that you are the perfect example of reliability. Thank you that we can trust you to keep your word. Thank you, Lord that you are the same yesterday, today, and forever. Today we lift up our needs and wants to you, knowing that we can count on you. Be with us today as we aim to be reliable messengers of your Word. We love you and praise you. Amen.

FOR HE IS YOUR GOD

"**So do not fear, for I am with you; do not be dismayed, for I am your God. I will strengthen you and help you; I will uphold you with my righteous right hand.**" Isaiah 41:10

God wants you to know today that whatever you have been worried and stressed about is already taken care of. Do not fear. God is with you.

Whatever it is you are going through today, God will help you and strengthen you. His word tells you not to fear, for He is your God. Choose to do what the Word says. Every time you feel yourself getting scared, remind yourself, "I will not be dismayed, for you are my God."

Circumstances do not change God. Your family issues, career, business, health, exams, school—none of these things change God. He is with you and upholds you. God hasn't changed His mind about you. He loves you fully and completely. Today, remember His word every time you feel fear. Trust Him. Rely on Him to uphold you. Do not fear.

Today, choose not to fear nor be dismayed, for He is your God.

My prayer for You Today:
Father, today we choose to rely on you. Whenever we feel fear, Lord, fill us with your love and your confidence. Be with us and answer our deepest prayers. We need you today. Lord, we surrender all to you in Jesus's precious and holy name. Amen.

THE EYE

"The eye is the lamp of the body. If your eyes are healthy, your whole body will be full of light." Matthew 6:22

What are you choosing to see today? Are your eyes healthy? Are your eyes full of hope and love? The eye is the lamp of the body. What you choose to see colors your life.

Friend, you have a choice to see life as working for you or against you. Your perception is your reality. Let your eyes light your life. Choose to see God in everything and everyone. Choose to see the blessings and not the inconveniences. See your destiny, not your history.

As you focus on Him your entire life, body, and soul will be enlighten. See things as though they are. (Romans 4:17) See God. See beauty. See love. See opportunity. See God's hands working things in your favor. See beautiful coincidences. See the divine unfolding of your life. See light. See hope and joy. See divine peace and bliss.

Today, see God!

My Prayer for You Today:
Father, thank you that with you there is no darkness. Today we choose to see you in everything we do and everyone we encounter. Fill us with your light. Wrap us in your grace and empower us with your love. We thank you that it's already done, in Jesus's name we pray. Amen.

AMBASSADORS

"We are Christ ambassadors; God is making his appeal through us." 2 Corinthians 5:20

Ambassadors are sent to foreign countries as a country's official representative. We are Christ ambassadors. We are sent to this world to represent Him.

Let the world be your foreign country today. You are not of this world. (John 15:17) God wants you to spread love. He chose you to be the light. God chose you to display goodness on His behalf. Today you may disguise your ambassadorship in the role of an attorney, doctor, teacher, or stay-at-home mom, but you are Christ's ambassador. Spread His love.

Today, remember that you represent God and all His goodness. Let His love be evident in your actions and words. Build others, love them, serve them, forgive them, and speak life to them. Accordingly, know who you are. Do not look to the world to define you. You are God's ambassador!!!!

How will you represent God today?

My Prayer for You Today:
Lord, thank you that you chose us to be your ambassadors. Thank you that you love us enough to give us such title. Help us today to represent you in everything we do and say. Let your words come out of our mouths. As we serve you, Lord, fill us with your courage, strength, and love to face a world that is often unkind. We surrender all to you in Jesus's precious name. Amen.

MORE HIM, LESS YOU

"He must increase; I must decrease." John 3:30

Here's the secret to a more joyful life: more God, less you!

Friend, our tendency to be selfish and self-centered causes great pain. We tend to take things personal. We want things for ourselves. We manipulate. We scheme. As a result we find ourselves unhappy, unhealthy, and frustrated. We must change our view from us to Him.

Today, increase God and decrease ego. Increase God and decrease yourself. Increase harmony and decrease differences. Increase unity and decrease division. Increase gratitude and decrease complaints. Increase positive and decrease negative. Focus on Him. It's not all about you. There is a bigger plan at work. Look to Him. Take care of yourself through Him. Spend time praying. Meditate. Thank Him. Increase trust and decrease worry.

God is a god of increase. He loves you fully and completely and as you increase Him in your life, He will bless you with increased joy, peace, love, and whatever your heart desires. Whatever you touch will increase. Invite Him in your life today. Increase time with Him and He will bless you beyond your wildest dreams.

Today, more God, less you!

My Prayer for You Today:
Father, today we make the conscious choice to increase You in our lives. We want more of your presence, more of your love, more of you. Help us to focus on you rather than ourselves. We thank you in advance that as we increase you, you will increase all the blessings and miracles in our lives. We thank you. We love you. Amen.

ACKNOWLEDGE HIM

"In all your ways acknowledge him and he will direct your path."
Proverbs 3:6

When you involve God in all the details of your life, He will direct your path. Do that today!

When God is in every nook and cranny of your life, you will not have to think twice about your decisions, and your direction. Relationships will evolve effortlessly. Doors will open unexpectedly. Challenges will disappear suddenly. Every investment will be fruitful. Acknowledge Him!

Too often we contain God in the Sunday-morning-box of going to church, or the big decisions-and-trouble-box. Why do we only seek Him on Sundays and when we're in trouble? Are you the kind of friend who only wants to be acknowledged on a certain day and when others are in trouble? Are you solely a rescue friend? No, and neither is God! God is a God of details. Involve Him in every decision, every day, minute after minute. Be in constant communication with Him. Acknowledge Him. Share your dreams, hopes, fears, challenges with Him and He will direct your path.

Acknowledge Him!

My Prayer for You Today:
Father, today we pray that we may acknowledge you in all our ways. We pray that you direct our path and that you bless us unconditionally. Be in every detail of our lives and let your hand be evident in the realization of our dreams, our answered prayers, and our experience of divine peace and love. We pray all this in Jesus's precious name. Amen.

TRUST

"Do not let your hearts be troubled. Trust in God." John 14:1

When you trust God, your world can be falling apart and you will not be moved. You will be neither worried nor anxious, because you know that God is in control.

At the sight of trouble, do not let your hearts be troubled. Look for the blessing in every situation. When your relationship fails, trust God. When your job seems unbearable, trust God. When your family seems like the most dysfunctional family on earth, trust God. When the health report looks scary, trust God. When what you hoped for is different than what you received, trust God.

Whatever you are going through today, choose to trust God. Trusting God is a moment-by-moment decision to seek Him, to pray rather than panic, to believe rather than quit. Trusting God requires you to believe the Word, not the world. Trusting God means to call on Him first, not the contacts on your phone.

Today, choose to believe in His love and grace. He loves you unconditionally. Choose to see the blessing among the inconvenience. Nothing is an inconvenience. Nothing is out of order. When you trust God, there is no such thing as bad luck. There is, however, endless opportunities, infinite blessings, and countless miracles. Surrender. Trust God.

My Prayer for You Today:
Father, today we choose to trust you in everything. We know that your hand is orchestrating everything in our lives and we trust you even when we don't understand. Thank you, Father. Lord, help us to continue to be bold and faithful at the sight of inconveniences. We love you, Lord. We adore you. Everything is in your hands. Amen.

THANK AND PRAISE

"Stand every morning to thank and praise the Lord… do the same in the evening." 1 Chronicles 23:30

Plain and simple: praise the Lord morning and evening!

When you start your day with a grateful heart, God blesses you with more opportunities to be grateful. Begin your day with a positive attitude. Start off with a prayer. Say a simple "thank you." Stand in gratitude. Stand in hope. Stand every morning in peace and in love.

Today, take time to thank and praise God morning and evening. Remember how far you've come and thank Him. Praise Him for every smile and every tear. Thank Him for another day. Praise Him for miracles. Thank Him for accomplishing another goal. Give thanks and praise Him. He is an amazing God.

Stand every morning to thank and praise the Lord!

My Prayer for You Today:
Father, today we stand to thank and praise you for your goodness, your love, your grace, and your favor. Thank you, Lord, that everything you do is good. Thank you, Father, for unconditional blessings and opportunities. Fill our hearts with your love, which allows us to be of service to others. Thank you, Lord, for everything. Amen.

TIME

"With the Lord one day is as a thousand years, and a thousand years as one day." 2 Peter 3:8

Friend, with God life is everlasting. Scripture tells us that with Him a day is like a thousand years and a thousand years is like one day.

Take hear today. You have been praying for deliverance for a week. You have prayed for your marriage for years. You have prayed for your children for a lifetime. God has not forgotten. Take heart. Do not let your faith fall in the face of time.

Enjoy your life moment by moment without the limitations of calendars. When you live your life with God first, everything is timeless. Take time to enjoy each breath, each smile, and each simple act of kindness. Do not measure your life in dates, but in moments. Live a great life through Him.

Today, take time to be in the moment. Enjoy every interaction and every conversation. Smile. Laugh. Love. God is found in the beauty of timeless moments.

Spread a thousand years worth of love today.

My Prayer for You Today:
Lord, today we thank you for timelessness. Thank you for your love that allows us to enjoy every moment. We surrender our day to you. Let it be timeless in your name. We love you. We adore you, in Jesus's name. Amen.

BE FRUITFUL

"Take no part in unfruitful works of darkness." Ephesians 5:11

If what you are doing is not bringing you fruits, stop doing it. Take no part in unfruitful works of darkness.

Today consider darkness anything and anyone that dims your light. Darkness is anything that diminishes your joy and takes away your peace of mind. Works of darkness may be individuals, circumstances, your state of mind and your way of thinking. Take no part in such things. If it doesn't grow you, take no part of it.

God is a God of fruitfulness. He continually grows us. God blesses us with more and adds more to our lives. Similarly, He expects for us to be fruitful in all our ways. God wants us to grow and prosper, to feel more joy, to be more at peace, to grow in our relationship with Him and others, to laugh more, to love more and to live more fully.

If your life is not fruitful, it is time for a change. Don't settle. God has fruitful blessings in store for you. Receive them!

My Prayer for You Today:
Father, thank you that you continually bless us with more. Today, help us to be clear with our intentions and our actions and cut off anything or anyone that doesn't add fruit to our lives. Give us courage to make changes necessary in order to experience more of your love and divine peace. We surrender all to you, Lord. In Jesus's precious name we pray. Amen.

GOD KNOWS YOU

"He counts the number of stars; He gives names to all of them." Psalm 147:4

Wow! God knows the number of stars and names them all. Amazing!

There are approximately 10 billion galaxies. Within each galaxy, there is an estimated 100 billion stars. Imagine a God big enough not only to create galaxies and stars, but to also name them. If God can create something so splendid, is there anything He cannot do? Is your problem really too big for Him to handle?

"He counts the number of stars; He gives names to all of them." The depth of this verse brings peace. God is big enough to be trusted. Trust Him. God knows you. He knows you! You are no stranger to Him. He knows your name. He knows your strengths and weaknesses. He knows your circumstances. If He knows the number of stars, He also knows the magnitude your needs. He even knows the number of hairs on your head. (Luke 12:7) He also knows the number of dreams in your heart.

Today, remember that God knows you. Your spouse will never know you as well as God knows you. Your friends and family do not know you as completely as Him. You don't know yourself better than He knows you. God knows you. He loves you. Trust Him today. He knows the details of your life. He knows your needs. He knows your dreams. He will leave nothing untouched, nothing unanswered, nothing unblessed.

God knows you!

My Prayer for You Today:
Father, today we seek to understand the depth of your love for us and the depth of your knowledge. You amaze us, Lord. You know our end from our beginning, you understand our situation, you know us better than we know ourselves and for that we thank you and honor you. We surrender our lives to you and trust in your knowing. Bless us today. Leave nothing untouched, no prayer unanswered in Jesus's name. Amen.

GUIDANCE

"Shouldn't people ask God for guidance?" Isaiah 8:19

Seek guidance from God. Ask Him.

If your source of guidance is not God, you are settling for limited guidance. The Prophet Isaiah commented on consulting mediums and the dead. Why ask for guidance from anyone else other than God?

Whatever you are going through today, big or small, mundane or extraordinary, seek God's guidance. He knows best and He knows all. Your family can only provide you with a limited perspective. Your friends may unintentionally misguide you. God knows the way. He lights the way and He is the way. Seek Him.

Today, take time to quiet your mind and seek His guidance. Invite Him in all the little details of your life. He works wonders. Proverbs 3:6 reminds: "Acknowledge Him in all our ways and He will make our paths straight." Is that not what you want? Don't you want to be guided and led in the abundant, fulfilling straight path?

Ask God for guidance, and receive it!

My Prayer for You Today:
Lord, you know what each of us is going through in our spiritual lives, professional and personal lives, relationships, etc. You know it all, Father and today we seek your guidance above all. Lead us, speak to us, guide us, Lord. We can only rely on you, the All Knowing, All Loving God of the universe. Guide us, Father, right now. Give us clues. Speak! In Jesus's precious and holy name we pray for and receive your guidance. Amen.

CLOTHE YOURSELF

"Clothe yourselves with compassion, kindness, humility, gentleness, and patience." Colossians 3:12

This verse says it all and says it so beautifully. Today, clothe yourselves with compassion, kindness, humility, gentleness, and patience.

Your day will be so much more light and enjoyable if you follow what the scripture prescribes. Be compassionate toward others. Treat others with kindness. Be gentle. Show patience. Find it in your heart to be compassionate with your neighbor and with yourself.

Kindness heals. Today, heal those around you and yourself with kindness and gentleness. Rather than boasting about your accomplishments, boast about your God. Be humble. You've made it this far because of His grace. Practice the art of patience with those around you and with God. The Bible tells us to wait patiently on the Lord. (Psalm 37:7) God is at work in your life. Be patient.

When you clothe yourself with compassion, kindness, humility, gentleness, and patience, you embody Christ. Clothe yourself with Christ-like characters.

Clothe yourself with God.

My Prayer for You Today:
Lord, thank you for your word. Thank you that your word feeds us and leads us to living a life that honors you. Help us on our journey to develop and practice compassion, kindness, humility, gentleness, and patience. Be with us today and use us to bless others. We love you, Lord. We owe it all to you, in Jesus's holy name. Amen.

GOD'S ARMOR

"Put on all of God's armor so that you will be able to stand first against all strategies of the devil." Ephesians 6:11

Friend, the truth is that the devil is after you. The devil is ready to destroy and divide. Thankfully God is stronger than all strategies of the devil. Today, put on God's armor.

Let God's armor shield you from negative people. Let His arm keep you safe from confusion, lies, manipulation, and laziness. Put on His armor—the belt of truth and divine peace, the shield of faith and salvation—in order to stand against all schemes of destruction. Let God shield you from your everyday stress. Let Him keep you away from frustration. His armor will protect you from worries and fear and guard you from your own self-destructive thoughts. His armor allows you to stand firm.

Today, when your day seems unbearable, seek Him. Clothe yourself with His truth and His love. He is your ultimate protector. He is the diffuser of conflict, the father of peace, and the author of your life. God loves you so much that He will shield you from all things that jeopardize your perfect peace and abundant bliss.

Shield yourself in Him. Wrap yourself in His love.

My Prayer for You Today:
Father, shield us. Be with us today as we face our daily responsibilities with faith and hope. Fill us with your spirit, wrap us in your grace and love. We need you. Bless us, lead us to everything that is beautiful and grand. We surrender all to you. Amen.

PRAYER PARTNER

"If two of you agree here on earth concerning anything you ask, my Father in heaven will do it for you. Where two or three have gathered together in my name, I am there in their midst." Matthew 18:19-20

Life is too fragile to go through it alone. We don't think twice about seeking business partners or workout partners, yet we are reluctant to seek prayer partners. If you can find someone to go to the club with, to travel with, yet you can't find anyone to pray with, you are doing yourself a great disservice.

God wants you to fellowship. He wants you to gather in His name. God wants you to pray with others, to agree with and pray for one another. When your faith is faint, and your valley is low, find someone to stand with you in prayer and to believe for you.

Today, ask God to bless you with a prayer partner. Meanwhile, ask someone how you can pray for them. Be intentional in seeking a prayer partner. God's Word doesn't lie. If two of you agree on anything and ask God, He will do it! Test it out! Agree and pray with someone today. You will be amazed at how God will answer your corporate prayer.

Pray with someone today.

My Prayer for You Today:
Father, thank you that where two or three are gathered in your name, there you are. Father, today I stand in prayer with my friends, asking for your healing hands on all aspects of our lives. I pray for prosperity in our health and finances, for peace and joy in our relationships and with our families. We lift up every need, Father, and thank you that you have already answered. We praise you and love you, Lord. Amen.

MIRACLES

"God did extraordinary miracles by the hands of Paul." Acts 19:11

Friend, miracles happen! God performs miracles through people. He did extraordinary miracles through Paul and will do so through you. Are you available?

Miracles are made out of need. We all dream of miracles but despise being in a need for a miracle. If you were not broken you would not need the miracle of wholeness. If you were not sick you would not need the miracle of healing. If you were not lost and confused you would not need the miracle of finding yourself in Him.

Today, know that God performs miracles. He uses people. Be available for His use. Sometimes His miracles do not look like what we expect, be open to those helping you. God has a miracle in store for you. Receive it!

My Prayer for You Today:
Father, today we open ourselves to miracles. Thank you for using us to do your work and to perform your miracles. You are so good. We ask for miracles in our families, our relationships, our finances, our dreams, our health, and our careers. We love you, Lord. Amen.

AS THOUGH THEY WERE

"Call those things which be not as though they were." Romans 4:17

Friend, your biggest dream, your deepest desire, your fondest wish—speak of it! Speak of them in the present tense, as if they are. The way you speak reflects your faith. Call those things that are not as though they are.

Live on the basis of what you desire, not what you see. Speak of the person you are becoming, not who you were. Celebrate the job you desire before you even get the job! Speak of the spouse that you are before even having the ring. It does not matter that you have not seen the house yet, nor met the husband; speak as though you have!

Words have creative power. Speak things into existence. God has already answered your prayers in the spiritual realm. Let them manifest in the physical. Have faith. Speak with expectation. Speak with confidence. All your desires will manifest. Believe it. Speak it.

Today, speak of those things which be not as though they were!

My Prayer for You Today:
Father, today we speak of our victory, breakthroughs, desires knowing that you have already answered our prayers. Thank you, Lord. We celebrate your greatness today. We praise you for your love, thank you for blessing us. Fill us today with faith and confidence to speak of those things that are not as though they were. We do so in your name. Amen.

GOD MULTIPLIES

"We only have five loaves of bread and two fish,"... "Bring them here to me," said Jesus... They all ate and were satisfied and... picked up twelve basketfuls of left over..." (Matthew 14:13-21)

The story of Jesus feeding a crowd of over 5000 is so inspiring. It is exciting to know that God can do so much with so little. Five loaves of bread and two fish doesn't naturally feed 5000 people. It just doesn't add up. But God is not a natural God! In His supernatural goodness, five loaves of bread and two fish not only satisfies, but it overfeeds, leaving baskets of leftovers. Wow! God is amazing.

Jesus is telling you to bring the little bits that you have to him. Whatever it is, bring it to Him. If you have little joy, little hope, little health, little money, little faith, bring it all to Him and He will do more with it than you can ever fathom. He will give you more than enough to satisfy you. He will give you baskets of leftovers.

God will not only feed you with the little you have. He also wants to use you with the little you have. Today whether you consider yourself of little talents or little gifts, bring them all to God to be used to serve others. Don't shortchange yourself. God wants your little gift of music, your little gift of encouragement, your little skills of advocacy, your little gifts of friendship, your little skills in wellness, your limited writing talents; He wants them all to serve more than 5000. Bring them all to Him.

Today remember that God multiplies. Addition is too minute for His grandeur. He multiplies! Whatever it is today, bring it to Him; He will amaze you.

Your God multiplies!!!!

My Prayer for You Today:
Father, you are so amazing. You are a God who multiplies. Lord, today we bring the bits and pieces that we have and thank you already for doing more than we could fathom. We love you, Lord. You amaze us. Today we declare multiplicity in our health, wealth, peace, and joy. We declare abundance in all areas of our lives in Jesus's name. Amen.

CHILDREN OF GOD

"In Christ Jesus you are all children of God through faith…" Galatians 3:26

You are a child of God!

God has no grandchildren. Isn't that an amazing thought? God has no grandchildren, no stepchildren, no distant relatives. God only has children. Thankfully, we are all children of God, all heir of His Kingdom, all loved unconditionally by him. The thought that your worst enemy is just as much of a child of God as you are is both annoying and comforting. Annoying because—well, that's your enemy, no one should like them . . . and comforting because it speaks of God's character and how amazing He truly is.

"We are God's children!" (Romans 8:16) We belong to Him. He is our Father, our creator. We belong to Him. For those of us blessed to be earthly parents, we understand the depth of our love for our children, the willingness to sacrifice everything for them, and how quick we are to give up our lives on their behalf. How much more do you think God would do for you?

Today remember that God has no grandchildren. We are all children of God. Breathe that in and be encouraged. Be empowered that the King of Kings and Lord of Lord is on your side. You can call on Him at all times. He will always defend you and always takes care of you. He loves you always. You are His child.

Relax. Breathe. You are a child of God!

My Prayer for You Today:
Father, your love amazes us. Today we are so humbled to be called your children. This brings us a great sense of peace. Thank you, Father, that you will always love us, always take care of us. Thank you. We are so grateful. We praise you. We love you. Amen.

ASK

"You don't have what you want because you don't ask God for it." James 4:2

You will never get what you do not have the courage to ask. If you walk into a restaurant and you do not order a meal, you will not eat. Likewise, when you don't ask God for what you want, you will not receive. Today, dare to ask.

God is not offended by your demands. God is not afraid of your requests. He is not intimidated by your desires. He is able to grant you everything you ask for. Dare to ask! He is able to do exceedingly more than you ask. (Ephesians 3:20) He is able to accomplish more than you can imagine. Ask.

Ask and you shall receive. Be bold today and ask God for what you want. Don't let your limited thinking stop you. Don't let your perceived reality fool you. Ask for exactly what you want. Nothing is too big. Ask. Nothing is impossible. Ask. God is a God of impossibilities. With Him all things are possible. (Matthew 19:26)

Ask!

My Prayer for You Today:
Lord, here I am, on behalf of my sisters and brothers, asking for dreams to come true. Today I ask for new businesses, for breakthroughs, for transformations, for miraculous healing, for repaired relationships, for new relationships, for marriages and weddings, for school completion and graduations, for financial abundance, for promotions, for health, for wealth, for happiness, and for peace, Lord. Lord, bless each and every one of us, and forgive us for limiting you through our small thinking. We choose today to believe in you for the impossible, for the miraculous. We are so thankful that you can do infinitely more than we think. Thank you, Father. We surrender our lives to you, change us from the inside out; change our thinking and prepare us to receive your blessings. Thank you, Father. We love you. Amen.

DELIGHT YOURSELF

"Delight yourself in the Lord and he will give you the desires of your heart." Psalm 37:4

The verb "delight" means to "please greatly" or to "find great pleasure." You may reword this scripture by saying, "Please yourself greatly in the Lord and he will give you the desires of your heart." Do not misunderstand this scripture by thinking you need to please God in order for Him to give you the desires of your heart.

Please yourself in the Lord.

How do you please yourself in the Lord? Pleasing yourself requires you to be authentic and to do what you love. Do what excites you. Follow your passion. Be yourself. How does a rabbit delight in the Lord? By being a rabbit, by doing what rabbits do. Thus, you too delight in the Lord by being yourself. Do what makes your soul smile.

God is loving and graceful. Why then would he require his beloved children to be miserable in order to please him? God smiles when He sees you living life abundantly. God rejoices at the sound of your laughter. God loves to see you happy.

Today, please God by doing what you love. Praise God by doing what brings light to your eyes. Delight in Him by doing what opens your spirit. Bring honor and glory to God by living authentically.

Bask in His love. Delight yourself in God.

My Prayer for You Today:
Lord, thank you today that you already love us wholly and completely. Thank you that we don't have to do anything to earn that love, because Jesus did it all on the cross already. Thank you, Father, that your perfect love allows us to be authentic and to enjoy our lives and to do what brings us pleasure. Thank you, Father, that as we delight in life, in all the blessings you've given us, we are delighting in you and bringing glory to your name. Renew our minds, Lord, by allowing us to enjoy life without feeling guilty. Thank you, Lord, for everything. We surrender all to you in Jesus's name. Amen.

FRUIT OF THE SPIRIT

"**The fruit of the Spirit is love, joy, peace, patience, goodness, faithfulness, gentleness, and self-control. Against such things there is no law.**" Galatians 5:22-23

Jesus came to fulfill the law. The Law of Moses in the Old Testament seemed harsh and portrayed a vengeful God. A law that required bloodshed sacrifices, a law that didn't include grace. Thankfully, Jesus fulfilled the law and shed His blood. (Matthew 5:17)

There is no law against the fruit of the spirit. You can accomplish so much more with joy, peace, goodness, faithfulness, gentleness, and self-control than you could ever do with rules, regulations, and law. You can do so much more today by being patient. You can touch so many people with kindness and you can change your life with self-control.

"By their fruit you will recognize them." (Matthew 7:16) Those were Jesus' wise words in teaching His disciples how to decipher from true and false prophets. Do people know you by your fruit? Do your fruits display the person you want to be? Do you call yourself a Christian or a spiritual person or a loving person, yet you're impatient, rude, and cold? Others will recognize you by your fruit. They will encounter God through you by your fruit. What have you displayed?

Today, let others recognize you by your fruits. Display the fruits of the spirit: love, joy, peace, patience, goodness, faithfulness, gentleness, and self-control!

My Prayer for You Today:
Father, thank you that your grace is sufficient. Lord, today we invite you in our hearts and soul. Lord, thank you that as you reside in us; we will bear much fruit and we will embody the fruits of the spirit. Be with us today. Fill us, Lord. We love you and need you. Amen.

CONFIDENCE

"Cultivate God confidence." 1 Corinthians 10:12

Your confidence comes from God.

Remember when you were in college and you studied for an exam, and all of a sudden your worries went away and you knew you would do well? Or when you interviewed for the job that the CEO recommended you for, and you were confident that you already had it? How about when you were bullied and your big brother stuck up for you? These are just elementary examples of confidence, yet they can teach us so much about being confident in God. When you know Him, it's difficult not to be confident.

There's a confidence that comes from knowing God is for you. The Creator of the universe is on your side! The Alpha and Omega, who raises people from the dead, who created billions of stars, who fathomed human beings, is sticking up for you right now. How can you not be confident? When God orders your steps, your next step is always your best step. When you know God, you are confident in your future. You trust that life always works out for your good. When you know God, you have confidence in His promises.

Today, rather than focusing on self-confidence, cultivate God-confidence. To know Him is to be confident in Him and in His love. You already know God; you know what He's done for you before. He loves you. Be confident in His love. The same God who took care of you then will continue to take care of you. Today, keep your head up, stand up tall and reach higher. Breathe. Relax. God has your back.

My Prayer for You Today:
Lord, today we surrender our lives to you. We are confident that you are moving mountains for us and guiding us. Remind us today to have confidence in you rather than in ourselves. Whatever it is, we can't do it alone, Lord. It's all in your hands. We lift our needs to you knowing that you hear us. We praise you, Father. Amen.

KINDNESS AND GRACE

"The Lord is merciful and compassionate… filled with unfailing love." Psalm 145:8 **"He is rich in kindness and grace."** Ephesians 1:7

What if your idea of God is incorrect? What if your idea that God is a being outside of yourself, sitting on a throne judging your every move, is completely wrong?

Today I want to introduce you to a God who is rich in kindness and grace. Embrace a God who works things out in your favor. Open your heart to a God who is gentle and soft. Open your heart to a God who is loving and giving. Open your heart to His love, which is unfailing. God is compassionate and merciful always.

How will your life be different today, knowing that God's love is unfailing? What will you do today, knowing that He loves you and is working things out for you, regardless of how things look?

Today, embrace His kindness and Grace. Live in His love. Remember that nothing you do can separate you from God. Bask in His love. Receive His grace. Accept it. Use it to step out in faith and live abundantly.

My Prayer for you today:
Father, thank you for your love, compassion, kindness, and grace. Thank you today that you are working things out in our lives and answering prayers. Remind us, Lord, that despite our circumstances and our missteps you still love us completely and wholly. Thank you that your love never fails. We surrender our day to you, Father. Help us to live in your kindness today as we face our daily chores, challenges, and blessings. Be with us today. We love you. We adore you. Amen.

BE NOT DISCOURAGED

"This is my command—be strong and courageous! Do not be afraid or discouraged." Joshua 1:9

Today, God wants you to keep praying, keep hoping, keep believing, and do not be discouraged.

If you're anything like me, you prayed for something specific two years ago and didn't receive it; you prayed for it again the next year and still didn't get your answer. Time has a way of getting us discouraged. You've been waiting for the mate, waiting for the breakthrough, waiting for healing, waiting for answers, waiting for better days, yet you feel like God is answering everyone else's prayers except yours. If that's you today, you are not alone. Take heart.

All of God's promises are *yes* and *amen* through Christ. (2 Corinthians 1:20) God always keeps His promises; take heart, have enough courage to keep praying, enough courage to keep believing, enough courage to celebrate others' blessings while you wait for your answer. Friends, in the waiting period God is cleansing your heart, God is changing your mind and God is pruning your life.

Today, take heart. Be courageous. Keep believing. Don't let time plant seeds of doubt in your heart. God has already answered your prayers, He said yes! Yes for better, yes for more, yes for your mate, yes to your success; today say yes to praising Him, yes to believing Him, yes to bringing glory to Him while you wait.

Be blessed!

My Prayer for You Today:
Father, today you know our hearts. Forgive us, Lord, as our impatience brings doubt and discouragement. Today we hold on to your word, Father, which is always true. Father, thank you that you have already answered our prayers. Thank you, Lord, that as we wait on you, you are making us more like you. We praise you, Lord, and we thank you for everything in Jesus's name. Amen.

THINK GOD

"Think about things that are excellent and worthy of praise." Philippians 4:8

What are you thinking about today? Is your mind filled with thoughts of fear, discouragement, hopelessness, and anxiety or are you thinking about things that are true, excellent, and worthy of praise?

Today, change your thoughts consciously. Every time you think of something that worries you, make the conscious decision to think of things that are excellent instead. Think about your best future. Think about your upcoming birthday. Think about your vacation. Think about beauty. Think about things that make you smile.

God's love for you is something to think about. Think about how much He loves you. Remember that God is pleased with you. His favor follows you. Think about His grace that gives you chances after chances. Think about Him. Think about the fact that "it is written."(Matthew 4:4) Your victory is written! Your success is written!

You may not be where you want to be today, but rather than focusing on your circumstances, think about your vision and destination. Your thoughts are your transportation to your destiny. "Fix your thoughts on what is true, and honorable, and right and pure, and lovely and admirable." (Philippians 4:8) And friend, whenever you fix your thoughts on such things, you fix your thoughts on God!

Today, think God!

My Prayer for You Today:
Lord, thank you that you are changing each and every one of us by changing our thoughts. Thank you, Lord, that you have done so much for us that we cannot stop thinking about your love and your grace and your goodness. Father, speak to us, remind us of your plans for us, remind us of your love for us. Today Lord I pray for healing in our bodies and spirits, I pray for new opportunities, I pray for opened doors, I pray for answered prayers. Lord, you assured us that whatever we ask for in your name we will receive. Today we ask for breakthroughs, we ask for peace, we ask for blessings in every area of our lives. We ask that we fulfill your purpose in our lives. We ask for you to guide us to high places. We ask all of this in Jesus's name and receive it right now. Thank you, Lord. Amen.

BE STILL

"Be still, and know that I am God." Psalm 46:10

This scripture has gotten me through the most difficult times in my life, and though I understood the magnitude and grandeur of God, I struggled with the idea of being still. As I journey through life, I now realize that my lack of faith and understanding of the depth of God's love for me is always the reason why I struggle at being still. Today, are you able to be still despite your circumstances? Are you able to find stillness amidst the storm? Or is your mind running rapid with thoughts of worry, fear, and anxiety?

Stillness requires trust. Stillness requires understanding. Stillness requires faith in His promises. Stillness reminds you that nothing is left to chance. Stillness reminds you that you are where you are supposed to be. Stillness acknowledges that God has planned your days. He knows the number of hairs on your head, so surely He knows your situation right now.

Be still and know that God is working for you and through you. Be still and know that God is loving, loyal, faithful, and compassionate. Be still and know that God has plans for you to prosper and grow. Be still in your victory. He has already declared you victorious. You will fulfill your desires in Him. Be still and know that God answers your prayers even before you ask. Be still and know that God is the One and Only, the Alpha and Omega. Be still and know that with God all things are possible. (Matthew 19:26)

Be still!

My Prayer for You Today:
Lord, thank you for right here right now. Thank you, Father, that nothing is impossible to you. Thank you that miracles are easy and effortless for you. Father, here we are today seeking stillness and peace in you and in your promises for our lives. Help us to shut our minds to worry and fear and to open ourselves to your love and your grace. Let your love shine upon us today, Father. You know the storms of our lives, Lord, we thank you for the stillness amidst the storms. Thank you that you are building us for something bigger and better. We trust you, Lord. We trust you! Renew us today. Fill us with your courage and strength. We pray all of this in Jesus's holy name. Amen.

ASK, SEEK, KNOCK

"Ask and it will be given to you; seek and you will find; knock and the door will be opened to you." Matthew 7:7

Today, this verse is calling you to action through faith and persistence. Too often we cling to the idea of "waiting upon the Lord," which may be very appropriate in some circumstances, but today, take action. Ask. Seek. And knock. Are you faithful and persistent in asking God for exactly what you want? Are you seeking that which you wish to find? Are you knocking persistently at the door of your destiny?

Doubt and fear are the enemies of your faith. They paralyze you with lies like "it will never happen," "that's too big for you to ask for," "that's impossible." The scripture didn't say "ask and it might be given to you; seek and you might find; knock and the door might be opened to you." The scripture said it *will* happen. The word "will" in the scripture is the 100% guarantee clause of God's promises. You will be given. You will find. And it will be opened to you. Guaranteed! Today, be bold, faithful, and persistent: ask for exactly what you want, nothing less. Seek that which you desire. Knock at the door you want open.

"You don't have what you want because you don't ask God for it." (James 4:2) Today, trust His word and His promises. Ask faithfully. Expect to receive. Seek exactly what you want. You will find it. Knock, knock, and knock again until the floodgates of blessings open upon your life.

Ask, seek, and knock!

My Prayer for You Today:
Father, today empower us to ask for exactly what we want. Thank you, Lord, that you always give us what we faithfully ask. Thank you, Father, that as we seek you, your wisdom, your grace, and your courage, we will find you. Thank you for opening the door to new opportunities, promotions, increases, renewed health, new relationships, miracles, new businesses, new adventures. Thank you, Father, that it brings you great pleasure to answer our prayers. Thank you, Lord, that as we ask, seek, and knock you will bless us by giving, bringing us to find, and opening doors to our deepest desires. We surrender our lives to you. We love you. Amen.

EVERY DESIRE

"You open your hand and satisfy the desire of every living thing." Psalm 145:16

God is capable of meeting your every need and more importantly, He has the ability to meet everyone's need. Today, stop believing the lie that God is blessing someone else at your expense. He is God, why would He do that? Our human mind has been trained to believe in the idea of limited resources; we only have so much time, so much energy, so much money, and we are limited by those ideas and believe that God is the same way. God is limitless. He has inexhaustible resources, blessings, and provisions.

Whatever you desire today, God is able to grant it! Don't waste energy worrying about other individuals. Their needs will be met as well as yours. Don't be troubled by someone's promotion. Yours has already been declared. Don't lose sleep over missed opportunities. God will open a door. Don't frown over someone else's success. You were born victorious.

Praise and thank God for satisfying your desires and the desire of every living thing. Rejoice and celebrate the blessings of a friend. God has blessings in store for you as well. He is abundant and infinite and so are His blessings. Receive them.

Today, let Him know your every desire and be ready to receive. He is going to bless you beyond what you can fathom. I'm excited for you!!!!

My Prayer for You Today:
Lord, today I rejoice in the blessings of my brothers and sisters. How amazing are you, Lord, that you are able to meet the desire of every living thing! Thank you, Father, that you are abundant in blessings, in grace, and in love. We rest in your abilities. We depend on you to fulfill our every need. Thank you, Father, for reminding us today that in due time you answer every prayer. Thank you for the evidence of your love in every area of our lives. Today, we rebuke all spirits of fear, doubt, jealousy, and worry and we surrender to your love and grace. Thank you, Lord, for answered prayers. Thank you for miracles. Thank you for provisions. Thank you, Father, for blessings. Be with us today as we celebrate you. We pray all in this in Jesus's precious and holy name, amen.

COMMIT TO THE LORD

"Commit to the Lord whatever you do, and your plans will succeed."
Proverbs 16:3

Everything is spiritual! The work you do today, your career, your home, your relationships, raising children, going to school, in between jobs, at your dream job, all of it is God's work. Today let God dwell in every detail of your life.

Whatever you do today, dedicate it to God. Your pledge is not to the new weight loss program or the new president of the company or the new business idea—let your commitment be to the One who never changes. Commit to the One who works things out for your good. Commit the One who directs your steps.

It is far easier to commit to God, who never changes, than to commit to a changing world. It is far greater to commit to the One who loves you unconditionally than to men who love you today and reject you tomorrow. Commit to solid ground. Commit to the Rock. When you do so, you are able to stand firm. Commit all your ways to Him and you will surely succeed.

Today, whether you are working on Wall Street or at the local McDonalds, commit your work to God. Whatever you do, do it for Him and through Him. Put God in charge of your work. Commit to Him.

My Prayer for You Today:
Lord, today we commit all our ways and work to you. We invite you to dwell in the smallest details of our lives. Remind us today that everything we do is for you and through you, Father. Thank you, Lord, for the opportunity to serve you in the most ordinary ways. Be with us today and let your light shine through us so that others may know that you reside in us. Today, we declare ourselves rooted and established in you. We pray all this in Jesus's name. Amen.

FORGET AND REACH

"Forgetting those things which are behind, and reaching forth unto those things which are before" Philippians 3:13

Are you stuck in the past? Good or bad, are you spending time and energy discussing, reliving, and reminiscing about the past instead of thinking about your future? Your destiny is not in the past, if it were, you would be there. Today is the day you reach ahead and forget those things—people, events, hearthaches, successes—that are behind.

Fix your eyes on the goal. Focus on the finish line. Reach for your vision. Move toward your destiny. Let your past be your starting point, not your focus point. Your past was necessary to shape and mold you in preparation for your future. Use it as a stepping stone rather than a crutch.

Today, what are you holding on to from your past that is keeping you from receiving God's blessings? What must you forget in order to surrender to His promises? Decide right now to leave behind the divorce, leave behind the lies, leave behind the failures, leave behind the disappointments and press toward your destiny. Your future far outweighs your past. Your destiny will outshine your past!

Today, forget those things that are behind and reach for His love, His grace, His promises, His plans, His blessings, His increase!

My Prayer for You Today:
Father, today we thank you for our past, as it prepared us for our destiny. Thank you, Lord, that you use all things together for our good. Thank you for using our past trials and tribulations to build us and prepare us for increase. Today we declare in your name the forgetting of our past and the reaching for your blessings upon our lives. Today we declare increase in every area of our lives. We declare blessings of health, wealth, happiness, peace, and prosperity. Thank you, God, that it is so! Amen.

SOLID ROCK

"Anyone who listens to my teaching and follows it is wise, like a person who builds a house on solid rock." Matthew 7:24

God's Word is solid rock.

Anyone who listens to His Word builds his life on solid rock. What are you building your life on? Are you building your house on family traditions? Do you follow society's recommendations to build your life? Is your marriage based on His Word? Are you raising your children based on God's guidance? Friend, when things crumble around you, will your foundation withstand you?

Today, be wise. Build your life on solid rock. Build it on the One who never changes. Build your character on the One who will prevail. Stand on the One who will outlast all others. Build yourself on His truth. Let His Word be your foundation. "The grass withers and the flowers fall, but the word of our God endures forever." (Isaiah 40:8)

Decide today to stand on solid rock. Decide today to stand on love. Be rooted and established in love. (Ephesians 3:17) God is love.

Today, build on solid rock. Build on love. Build on God!

My Prayer for You Today:
Lord, today we come to you tired, depleted, and in need of you. Help us, Lord, renew us, fill us with your energy, your courage, your love to endure life and to seek you no matter what. Lord, you know the temptations of this world, you know the challenges we face, be with us today as we seek to build our lives on you and yet continue to be tempted by this world. Help us to decipher the truth. Lead us to places and people that are of you and from you. Be with us today, Father. We declare you our solid rock, so it is! Amen.

NO VARIATION

"Every good gift and every perfect gift is from above, and comes down from the Father of Lights, with whom there is no variation or shadow of turning." James 1:17

In God there is no deviation. He is not one way today and totally different tomorrow. He is perfect and the same today and everyday.

We live in a world of constant change. We are used to people who love us today and hate us tomorrow. Some applaud us today and crucify us tomorrow. Thankfully, God is not like that. There is nothing two-faced about God, nothing fickle. There is no variation in God. He never changes. He is the same yesterday, today and forever. (Hebrews 13:8) God is love right now, today, and forever.

You can count on the Father of Lights. In Him there is no darkness, no shadows. Everything He does is good. Change your perspective on your circumstances and realize that God is good all the time. You can count on Him. He has not changed His mind about you. He has not changed His mind about blessing you. He still wants to fulfill His promises in your life.

His gifts and His calling are without repentance. You didn't drink so much that He changed His mind. You didn't smoke so much that He changed his mind. You didn't fornicate so much that He changed His mind. Regardless of your past, God has blessed you with perfect gifts, and will fulfill His promises in your life.

Today, find peace in knowing that He never changes. He loves you perfectly and wholly. Rest in His promises for your life. Be encouraged.

My Prayer for You Today:
Lord, thank you that you never change. Thank you that in a world of constant change we can anchor our lives to you, assured that you will never turn your back on us. Thank you, Father, that all gifts are from you. Teach us today how to utilize our gifts to bless others. Father, we surrender our lives to you. Give us the faith and confidence to know that nothing we've done can take away your love for us. Thank you, Father, for being loyal and true. Father, today we rebuke all feelings of regret, of inferiority, of self-doubt, of pity, and we surrender to your love and your grace to carry us to our purpose and destiny. We pray all of this in Jesus's precious and holy name. Amen.

STAND FIRM

"Believe in the Lord your God, and you will be able to stand firm." 2 Chronicles 20:20

Today, despite what you are going through, you are able to stand firm, keep your calm, and prevail. Regardless of what you may think, you are capable of withstanding due to your faith and your confidence in God. Stand in faith. You can stand firm a little longer. You can take another step. You can withstand another punch. You can survive another disappointment.

Like a deeply rooted tree still standing, enduring seasons of drought and rain, you too, deeply rooted in God, will stand firm through the seasons of your life. Anchored to the One who strengthens you, you may be inconvenienced by life's circumstances but you will never be uprooted. Stand firm through the seasons of life. Like the Apostle Paul, you will learn how to be content with whatever you have, how to live on almost nothing or with everything. You will learn the secret of living in every situation, whether it is with a full or empty stomach, with plenty or little, for you can do all things through Him who strengthens you. (Philippians 4: 11-13)

Today, stand firm! Stand firm knowing that this too shall pass. Stand firm knowing that nothing under His control is ever out of control. Stand firm assured that God is at work in your life. Stand firm assured that He is always with you. Stand firm. Stand in faith.

My Prayer for You Today:
Lord, today I pray for your strength as we stand through the different seasons of our lives. I pray, Lord, that you be with us and remind us of your love despite our circumstances. Lord, thank you that our circumstances will never uproot us, for we are anchored to you and to your promises. Thank you that you will never leave us or forsake us. Today, Lord, we thank you for the hard times as you are preparing us for harvest. Thank you for challenging circumstances as they are building our dependence on you. Thank you, Father, for teaching us to be patient, to trust in you, and to stand firm. Be with us today, as we stand faithfully in your promises. We surrender all to you. We love you. We adore you. We pray all of this in Jesus's name. Amen.

AUTHOR OF PEACE

"God is not the author of confusion, but of Peace." 1 Corinthians 14:33

A version of this scripture uses the word "disorder" rather than confusion. "God is not a God of disorder, but of peace." (NLT) In our need for control and clarity, we ask too many questions only to find ourselves confused, worried, and anxious.

Confusion implies disorder and chaos. Those are not characteristics of God. God does everything in a fitting and orderly way. (1 Corinthians 14:40) He is a God of order and peace. Our peace lies in knowing the character of God. God has left nothing to chance, nothing just happens!

Today, rather than questioning every detail of your life, surrender to peace in knowing that God makes all things work together for the good of those who love Him. (Romans 8:28) There is a bigger process at work in your lives. There is a deeper meaning to things that require you to remain calm. Be at peace and trust Him despite your misunderstanding and lack of clarity. Whenever you find yourself worried and confused, shift your attention to God.

Today, find peace in Him. Instead of trying to figure things out, surrender them to Him. Today, let your confusion, disorder, and chaos be dissolved in your trust in Him who loves you and will never forsake you.

My Prayer for You Today:
Lord, today we are taking a break from worry, fear, anxiety, and confusion. We surrender all to you, knowing that you are more than able to bless us, more than able to work things out in our lives. Thank you, Lord, that you are up to something great and marvelous on our behalf. We open ourselves to your blessings and your peace. Thank you that you are the author of peace, and the author of our lives. Today, Lord, we rest in your love, grace, and peace. Thank you, Father. We pray all this in Jesus's name. Amen.

CORNERSTONE

"The stone the builders rejected has become the cornerstone." Psalm 118:22

In the engineering world, a cornerstone is a capstone that joins two walls and in which all other stones are set in reference. Similarly, Jesus was referred to as the "chief cornerstone," (Ephesians 2:20) joining two worlds, the spiritual and the earthly; joining us to God.

Despite being the "chief cornerstone" and the "Rock", Jesus was rejected, discarded, and isolated. Today, remember that Jesus was rejected and that you too will be rejected. Do not be surprised when it happens. God will use your rejection to place you as the cornerstone.

In your rejection you will find your direction. When people walk away from you, let them walk! Don't talk another person into staying in your life, into loving you or calling you. Your destiny is not tied to anyone. The job you didn't get is directing you to the one you are meant to have. The lover who left you freed you for your destined spiritual partner. The friend who betrayed you led you to God as your most loyal and true companion. Today, take heart and rejoice in your rejection. Thank God for your rejection!

Decide today not to shed another tear over your rejection because "The one who trusts in Him will never be put to shame." (1 Peter 2:6)

My Prayer for You Today:
Lord, thank you that through our rejection you are directing us to our destiny. Thank you, Father, that you have declared us cornerstones! Thank you, Lord, that the very things that hurt us will be the foundation for our victory and our joy. We trust you, Lord. In our sorrows, we trust you. In our rejection, we trust you. In our confusion, we trust you. We are so excited to see the miracles you have in store for us, Father. We thank you already, for it is written. We praise you, Lord, we adore you and we pray all this in Jesus, the Chief Cornerstone's, name. Amen.

GET UP

"... He said, "Young man, I say to you, get up!"... (Luke 7:14)

In the gospel of Luke, Jesus resurrects a young man in the midst of a funeral. With His touch, and His word, Jesus brought life and light to the man's circumstances and blessed his mourning mother. This story ought to bring you hope today and make you shout. In the midst of your battle, in the midst of your struggle, God can restore your life! Today, God is telling you to "get up!" Don't lay down in defeat. Don't coward in fear. Get up!

Prior to Jesus performing this miracle, He saw the crying mother and said, "Don't cry." (Luke 7:13) This message is for you: don't cry. God is getting ready to perform the miracle you didn't even know you needed. He is getting ready to bless you in ways you can not fathom. What you thought was a dead-end situation will be resurrected. Where you saw no hope, God will bring light. Don't cry and get up!

Today, get up! Get up and put on the armor of God. Get up and pray! Get up and speak life! Get up and believe! Get up and try again! Get up and keep going! Get up and thank God! Get up and have faith! Today, get up!

My Prayer for You Today:
Father, today we trust you more than ever. We can't see the light at the end of the tunnel, but we are so thankful that you are the light. Father, today we turn to you to restore our lives, to bless our relationships, to repair our finances, and to renew our health. We turn to you, Lord, knowing that you are able. We thank you for miracles. We are humbled by your love. We praise you and love you in Jesus's precious and holy name. Amen.

SET APART

"I knew you before I formed you in your mother's womb. Before you were born I set you apart and appointed you..." Jeremiah 1:5

For all the times you felt different, weird, and thought you didn't fit in, I want to tell you there's a reason for that! God set you apart from the rest. He didn't create you to fit in with the crowd. God formed you for a specific purpose, with your specific talents and gifts.

God knew you, set you apart, and appointed you before you were born. That alone should give you chills. He knew you before you were born. For all the days you felt alone, unappreciated, unnoticed, He knew you before you were born. He knew your function, your purpose, and your gifts before He formed you in your mother's womb. Relax. He left nothing to chance. Relax. He knew you before you were born and knows you now. Relax!

Don't copy the behavior and customs of this world. (Romans 12:2) Don't spend another day trying to fit in. Stop trying to be like other people. Your identity is in God. He set you apart. Find Him to find your individuality. Seek Him to discover your gifts. Know Him to know yourself.

Today, relax in Him and be you!

My Prayer for You Today:
Lord, thank you that you are not in the robot-making business. Thank you that you made each one of us with individual gifts and talents; thank you, Lord, that you know us fully and completely. Father, today we are inspired by your love and creativity. Thank you, Father, that we don't fit into the world, we fit into you. Be with us today as we discover and move from your purpose. Lord, guide us, lead our steps. We trust you, Father, and find peace in knowing that you know us. We surrender all to you and pray this in Jesus's holy name. Amen.

GOD VS. THEM

"If God is for us, who can ever be against us?" Romans 8:31

As you journey through life, you may feel like the world is against you. The friends in whom you trusted betrayed you. Life seems to be against you. Every new endeavor fails and leaves you feeling defeated. Contrary to your feelings, though you feel depleted and defeated, your victory has already been declared. God is on your side.

Though you may lose a battle, the war is yours to win. You may lose an argument, but God has the final word. Victory is yours no matter what. Stop focusing on how things look and know that nothing can work against you. Nothing can harm you or take your opportunity. God is on your side. You have an advantage in every situation. You have a leg up in every conversation and every challenge. The One who will always prevail is on your side.

"In all these things we are more than conquerors through him." (Romans 8:37) God is with you. He will fight for you and give you victory. (Deuteronomy 20:4) Your blessings won't make sense to you, nor to the world, just be thankful. The breaks you'll get, despite all the lies and schemes against you, won't make sense, just be thankful. The success you will experience won't make sense because of all the roadblocks, just be thankful.

The world will look at your success and say you got lucky, but the truth is, God was on your side all along! You were not limited to the world. You don't live under the law but rather "under the freedom of God's grace." (Romans 6:14)

Today, remember that you have already won. It's you and God against the world, no one can beat that!

My Prayer for You Today:
Lord, thank you that with you we cannot be defeated. Thank you, Lord, that you are always by our side. Thank you that you have the final word in our situation. Remind us today to keep heart, to persevere despite feeling attacked, betrayed, and depleted by the world. Thank you, Father, for being with us and fighting for us. Thank you that we are functioning under your grace and your love. We surrender all to you and trust our lives in your hand. Thank you, Lord. Amen.

RIGHTEOUS TROUBLES

"The righteous person may have many troubles, but the Lord delivers him from them all." Psalm 34:19

When trouble comes your way, God will deliver you.

When trouble comes, too often we start to believe it is because we have done something wrong. Your troubles are not an indication of wrongdoing. You have been made righteous! Stop believing the lies that you're unlucky, cursed, or being punished. God loves you too much for that!

Jesus reminds that in this world you will have tribulations. (John 16:33) Today, take heart. Trouble comes to strengthen you, to grow your faith, to humble you, and to ensure your dependence on God. Trouble comes to reveal your character, to disclose your persistence, to prepare you for His plans. Trouble comes for a purpose, not a punishment. Trouble comes to the righteous, not the wicked. Trouble comes to build, not to destroy. Trouble comes so that you may discover His love, His peace, His loyalty. Trouble comes so that you may seek and find Him.

Today, remember that troubles come "but the Lord delivers" you from them all. Stand firm! The rollercoaster ride will soon stop. Hold on tight through the shield of faith, the belt of truth, and His peace. (Ephesians 6:14-18) God keeps His promises and you have been promised deliverance. Today, hold on to His promises. You have been made righteous through Christ. You have been set free through Him and by Him.

Today, take heart and trust Him!

My Prayer for You Today:
Lord, thank you that you will deliver us from troubles and heartaches. Thank you, Father, that our troubles are not an indication that you forgot about us or are punishing us. Lord, thank you that everything is happening according to your plans. Thank you, Lord, that you have great plans for us, plans to prosper us and give us hope. Lord, today we hope in you. We trust in you and we seek comfort in you. Be with us today, Lord, as we stand firm despite wanting to break down, as we move on despite wanting to hide and cry. Comfort us, Lord, we cry out to you. Thank you that you always listen and that you are always there. We surrender all to you. We rest in you, Father. Thank you. Amen.

HIS BLESSINGS WILL OVERTAKE YOU

"All these blessings will come upon you and overtake you." Deuteronomy 28:2

The Bible is filled with God's promises for your lives. One of them is listed in Deuteronomy 28:2. If you listen to His voice, His blessings will overtake you.

His blessings will overtake you. They will fill your life. They will be poured out onto you. God will open the floodgates of Heaven and pour out blessings you will not have enough room to store. (Malachi 3:10) Today, trust His promise. His blessings will overtake you. Imagine the waves of the ocean, how they overtake the shores. His blessings will overtake you in the same way. They will rush on your life like the waves of the ocean.

Today, keep doing your best. Keep praying. Keep believing. Keep obeying and watch God's faithfulness. All of His promises are *yes* and *amen*. (2 Corinthians 1:20) His blessings will overtake you. God has blessings in store for you that you cannot even imagine. They will complicate your life in a good way. Get excited! Be thankful. You have a God who loves you and it brings Him great joy to bless you.

My Prayer for You Today:
Father, thank you that you have blessings in store for us that will overtake us, that will fill us in ways only you can. Your faithfulness amazes us, Lord, and it humbles us that you love us so much. Thank you, Father, for your love. Thank you for your mercy. Today we open our hearts and lives to obey you, to hear and listen to your voice. Your will is our will, Father. We praise you and love you. Amen.

PLEASED

"God is pleased with me." Psalm 18:19

We are all too familiar with the social epidemic of people-pleasing. We have all been hurt, betrayed, and fooled by trying to please others and we ourselves have hurt, betrayed, and fooled those trying to please us. Today, stop the madness! Rather than seeking to please people, know that God is pleased with you.

God is infinitely delighted with you. He loves you despite the lies you tell and the people you hurt. He is pleased with where you are right now. God sees your destiny. He knows where you are going and is happy with you.

Don't spend another day feeling guilty and believing that God is mad at you. He knows your limitations and loves you. He knows your past and loves you despite it. He is pleased with you right now, today. God's love and acceptance is not based on who you are and what you do, it's based on who He is.

Today, move through your day in God's peace knowing that He is smiling at you. He loves you and is proud of who you are becoming. Every breath you take pleases Him. Every smile and every heartbeat pleases Him. He loves you. Today, be encouraged. Wherever you are, He is there and He is pleased!

My Prayer for You Today:
Lord, thank you that you are pleased with us today. Thank you, Lord that your love allows you to look beyond our shortcomings. We are so grateful for your love and your grace and your salvation. We surrender our day to you, Lord. Let us be empowered and inspired by your love and by knowing that you're pleased with us. Today we rebuke all fear and guilt and we open ourselves to your love and grace. We pray all this in Jesus's precious name. Amen.

INFINITELY MORE

"Now all glory to God, who is able, through his mighty power at work within us, to accomplish infinitely more than we might ask or think."
Ephesians 3:20

God is able, with his mighty power within us, to accomplish infinitely more. This verse is a call for you to align yourself with His power in every endeavor and achieve more. No task is too big. God is able!

God is infinitely more! He is infinitely more loving than you think, infinitely more loyal, infinitely more graceful, infinitely more powerful, infinitely more forgiving, infinitely more caring, infinitely more able, infinitely more willing, infinitely more knowing… He is infinitely more!

Allow Him today to accomplish "infinitely more" in every area of your life—more joy, more peace, more love, more success, more blessings, more money. God is not looking at your situation and scratching His head wondering what to do. He is able to bless you infinitely more than you ask or think.

Today, dare to ask for more. Dare to think more of yourself. Dare to seek more for your life. And watch God bless you infinitely more and beyond your wildest dreams. Think big. Ask big. And be ready to receive infinitely bigger, better, and more. Today, ask for an inch and He will bless you with a mile! Get excited to receive more blessings, more love, more peace, more success, more money, more joy, more God!!!

Today, dare to ask and dream BIG and receive infinitely more!

My Prayer for you today:
Lord, thank you that you are able to do more than we can imagine and more than we can ask for. Thank you, Lord, that you are able. Thank you, Father, for working within us. Lord, today we ask that you bless us beyond our wildest dreams, that you bless us with more joy, more love, more success, more grace. Today we declare abundance in every area of our lives, Father. Thank you that whatever we ask, we receive. We praise you, Lord. We surrender our lives to you. We open our hearts and mind to your blessings. Today, in Jesus's name, we dare to ask for infinitely more blessings, Lord. Surprise us with blessings. Overwhelm us with your love. We love you. Amen.

NEVER LEAVE NOR FORSAKE

"I will never leave you nor forsake you" Joshua 1:5

For all the times you feel alone, confused, and depleted, this is your reminder. God has promised to be with you. He will never fail you nor abandon you. Be reminded that God keeps his promises. Friends may leave you, family may betray you, but God is and always will be there.

Stop giving so much attention to the problems in your life. Focus on the power in your life. God is power. Seek Him. Turn your attention to Him. Whenever you feel alone and forgotten, remember that He knew you before you were in your mother's womb. (Jeremiah 1:5) He knows the number of hairs on your head. (Luke 12:7) And God promises to strengthen you, help you, and uphold you. (Isaiah 41:10) You have never been alone. He will never leave.

Today, know that God is working as the great puppeteer in your life. You are not alone. God didn't forsake you despite your troubles. He is here. He is with you. God loves you too much to leave you. You are worth too much to Him to be forsaken. He cares too much. He is too big to leave, too forgiving to forget you, too powerful to fail you. I assure you that God is here right now, preparing you, comforting you, putting the right people in your life, opening doors for you, strengthening you, and loving you. He will never leave you, not now, not ever.

Today, at the core of your being, know that God is with you.

My Prayer for You Today:
Lord, thank you that you will never leave us nor forsake us. Father, help us to focus on you rather than our situation. We need you, Lord. We feel burdened and depleted and tired. Help! Come to our rescue, Father. Be with us today. Help us to feel your presence and know that we are not alone. We surrender all to you, Father. We can't make it without you. Be with us as we walk new territories, as we have difficult conversations, as we encounter challenging situations. Thank you that everything that happens today is part of your plan for our lives. We trust you with everything. Thank you, Lord, for being with us. We love you and pray all this in Jesus's name. Amen.

INTEGRITY

"The Lord detest people with crooked hearts, but he delights in those with integrity." Proverbs 11:20

God honors integrity!

Integrity means doing what is right regardless of what others have done to you. Integrity means you are the same person at work, at home, at church, and at the club. Integrity means you fight for what you believe with the same passion whether it concerns your son or a stranger. Be a person of integrity. Stand up for something. Someone with integrity has the same moral compass when addressing his friend and his enemy. Someone with integrity is authentic and honest under all circumstances. Someone with integrity greets the Pope and the janitor with the same respect. Today, be someone with integrity.

God honors integrity because God is the same yesterday, today, and forever. (Hebrews 13:8) God doesn't say one thing and do another. He doesn't love you today and hate you tomorrow. He is a God of integrity. He honors integrity because that is who He is: loyal, honest, and true. He blesses the just and the unjust, "and sends rain on the righteous and the unrighteous." (Matthew 5:45)

Today, be a person of integrity. Treat people based on who you are, not who they are. Do what is right. Stand for something. Be honest. Be authentic. Tell the truth. Be a person of integrity. God honors integrity.

My Prayer for You Today:
Lord, thank you that you have given us the perfect example of someone with integrity in Jesus. Father, help us today to live our lives with integrity. Lord, change our hearts and our minds and help us to honor you by being authentic and telling the truth. We need you today as we face a world full of lies. Today we stand on your truth. We love you and praise you. Amen.

COWARDS

"Why are you such cowards? Don't you have any faith at all?" Mark 4:40

Jesus referred to His disciples as cowards and questioned their faith when they were paralyzed by fear at the sight of a windstorm.

Today, ask yourself the same questions: why are you such a coward when faced with the storms in your life? Why are you such a coward when it comes to your dreams? Don't you have any faith at all? Don't you know who your God is? Don't you know how much He loves you? Don't you know the plans He has for you? Don't you believe His promises? Don't you know that with Him nothing is impossible? (Luke 1:37)

A coward lacks courage and is consumed with fear. God has not given us a spirit of fear, but of power, love, and self-discipline. (2 Timothy 1:7) Experiencing fear is normal, but being paralyzed by fear is faithless. Stop being a coward. Let your faith move you beyond your fear. Be empowered by God. Don't let the storms of life scare you. In an instant God is able to quiet your storms. Move beyond fear and into your destiny.

Today remember that God is with you through the storms of life. He will lead you into new territory. Have faith. Faith is for the place where sight fails. Today, walk by faith, not by sight. (2 Corinthians 5:7)

Today, don't be a coward, have faith!

My Prayer for You Today:
Father, today we walk by faith not by sight. We declare ourselves courageous and strong in the midst of adversity and the storms in our lives. Thank you, Lord, that you are with us. We need you, Father, to overcome and move beyond our fears. Be with us today as we step out in faith unto new territory. Order our steps and guide us, Lord. We cry out to you, you are all we know and we need for comfort, guidance, and peace. Today, bless us with your love, your peace, and your grace as we move faithfully through storms and into our destiny. We pray all of this in Jesus's precious name. Amen.

PRAISE HIM

"Let everything that has breath praise the Lord." Psalm 150:6

God deserves your praise. God deserves all the praise. For His goodness, His grace, and His love God deserves your praise. For His creative abilities and His genius capabilities evident when He designed the galaxies, the earth, and the vast number of grains of sand, He deserves your praise. For His indescribable, immeasurable, incomprehensible awesomeness He deserves all the praise.

How then do we praise the Lord? Is it a Sunday morning routine with shouts and raised hands? Is it a ritual with specific words? How does a bird praise the Lord? The verse calls for everything that has breath to praise Him, which would surely include birds, dogs, dolphins, and other animals. A bird praises the Lord by flying. A bird praises the Lord by singing. A dog praises the Lord by barking and wagging its' tail, and a dolphin praises the Lord by enjoying the sea.

Similarly, for you, praise the Lord by being fully yourself. Praise Him by following our passion. Praise Him by living the life of your dreams and by being happy. Praise Him by following His Word. Today, let your life praise the Lord. Indulge in every experience. Be present in every moment. Be thankful for every breath. Praise Him through every smile. Praise Him through your obedience. Praise Him through your love.

Today, simply by being you, praise the Lord!

My Prayer for You Today:
Lord, today let every breath we take praise you. We are so amazed by you, Lord. Wow! You amaze us! We thank you that we are fearfully and wonderfully made. Thank you for blessings beyond measures. We praise you for everything you've done, all the doors you've opened for us, all the answered prayers. We know that if it wasn't for your grace and your love, we wouldn't have made it this far. Thank you, Father, for being with us always. We surrender our lives to you and declare every aspect of our lives praise to you. We love you. Amen.

CONFIDENT OF HIS WORK

"Being confident of this, that He who began a good work in you will carry it on to completion..." Philippians 1:6

God will finish what He started. Know that! He will complete the good work He started in you. He will bring it to a flourishing finish. Be confident of it! You may feel stuck today, but where you are right now is not where you will stay. He has more for you, there's no doubt about it!

God is not done with you yet. You haven't seen your best days. Stay the course. Keep faith. He has great plans for you. This is your time of preparation. He will answer your prayers and bless you abundantly. Stand firm in His promises. Be confident. He will finish what He started in you.

The nights you spent in tears were not in vain. The hopelessness you felt was not in vain. He is preparing you for something great. Through trials and pain, God is building your character, "so do not throw away your confidence, it will be richly rewarded." (Hebrews 10:35)

Be confident in God! Be confident when you are talking about your life. Be confident and declare God's promises in your life. God is a God of abundance and miracles. Be confident in proclaiming miracles in your life. Speak it! Don't shy away. Do not doubt His promises. He showed you over and over His love and His power. Be confident that God will finish what He started in your life. He will bless you more than you think. He will deliver you from all trouble and will use your life as a blessing to others.

Today, be confident!

My Prayer for You Today:
Lord, thank you that you are a wholesome God, a God of completion, and that you will complete the good work in us. Thank you, Father. Forgive us for doubting you by living in fear and worry. Today we declare your blessings of completion in the different areas of our lives. We declare them over our relationships, our careers, our finances, our children, our plans, our dreams, and our goals. Complete the good work in us, Lord. Guide our steps. Be with us. We surrender our lives to you and are confident that you will bless us abundantly. We thank you that it's already done. In Jesus's precious and holy name we pray. Amen.

FISHERS OF MEN

"Come and follow me and I will make you fishers of men." Matthew 4:19

Jesus asked Simon and Andrew to follow Him and he would teach them how to serve and catch men. God uses relationships to mold us. He uses people to build us and shape us. Are you fishers of men or chasers of earthly success? Do you care more about your relationships than your possessions?

Life is meant to be shared. Fishers of men get along with people. They value fellowship. Fishers of men are friends. They give. They celebrate others. They inspire. They teach. Fishers of men serve. Fishers of men know that God blesses us through connections and relationships. Fishers of men understand that God uses people to materialize the miracle. You are called to be a fisher of men, through your presence, your smile, and your care; you are called to be a fisher of men in your relationship with your spouse, your friends, your children, your co-workers, and your neighbors.

Today, be a fisher of men in all your relationships. Crucify your feelings and get along with people. Speak the truth in love. (Ephesians 4:15) When God dwells in you as a fisher of men, you become loving, caring, giving, and forgiving, because those are His characteristics.

Today, let the light of God shine through you as you build authentic relationships. Today, make meaningful connections with those whose path you cross. Today, be a fisher of men. Serve Him by serving men!

My Prayer for You Today:
Lord, thank you that you chose us to be fishers of men. Thank you that you trust us enough to bless us with relationships and fellowship with others. Let your light shine through us today as we interact with your children. Let your light be evident in our lives as we learn to love, to give, and to forgive. Be with us today as we speak our truth in love and remain authentic in who you made us to be. Thank you for the opportunity to grow in relationships. We surrender all to you, Father. Thank you for all those who have crossed our path, thank you for those you chose to be life companions to us. We are so thankful. We love you and praise you. Amen.

WATCH AND THANK

"Devote yourself to prayer, being watchful and thankful" Colossians 4:2

Today, keep your eyes on the blessing and be thankful! Being watchful and thankful calls for you to be alert to the miracle and to say thank you! Too often we see the struggles and the challenges and ignore the blessings. Today, watch and thank!

You may not be where you want to be, but you are not where you use to be—thank Him! You may not have what you want, but you have what you need—thank Him! You may not have the support of family and friends, but you have His love and loyalty—thank Him! Your situation may look dire, but He didn't bring you this far to leave you—thank Him!

Today be watchful, assured that miracles and blessings surround you!

The scripture also calls for you to commit and devote yourself to prayer. Have you prayed about it more than you talked about it? Have you taken it to God or to your friends? Do you vent to men or to God? Paul reminds: "Do not be anxious about anything, but in every situation, by prayer and petition, with thanksgiving, present your requests to God." (Philippians 4:6)

Today, pray, be watchful and thank Him!

My Prayer for You Today:
Father, today we have our eyes on you. We thank you, Lord, that you have brought us this far. We thank you that you have blessed us beyond measures and forgive us for forgetting to thank you enough for that. Lord, we surrender our lives to you. Thank you that through prayer we are able to communicate with you and find peace, strength, and wisdom. Thank you, Father, for blessings to come. We love you. We adore you. Amen.

SOW GOD

"Be not deceived, whatsoever a man sow, he will reap." Galatians 6:7

What seeds are you planting?

Beware of the seeds you sow. You will reap what you sow. A gardener who plants corn seeds never expects to reap tomatoes. Likewise, you can't plant cucumber seeds and expect to reap roses. In the spiritual world, like the physical, you will reap what you sow. You cannot sow negative thoughts and expect a positive life. You cannot sow worry and fear and expect peace and joy. You cannot sow gossip and expect unity. You cannot sow anger and expect love. Sow that which you want to reap.

Every thought is a seed. Beware of your thoughts. Every prayer is a seed. Every action is a seed. Sow wisely. Today, decide to sow abundantly those seeds you wish to reap. Sow seeds of love, hope, patience, kindness, faith, and self-discipline. Sow seeds of friendship and acceptance. Sow towards your destiny and your purpose. What is it that you want to collect on harvest day? Sow it now!

Don't waste your time on seeds you don't want. Don't waste another minute sowing that which you don't desire. Don't sow crumbs if you desire loafs. Don't sow mediocrity if you desire greatness. Don't sow laziness if you desire success. Today, sow that which you want to reap!

"Those who live to please the Spirit will harvest everlasting life from the Spirit. So let's not get tired of doing what is good. At just the right time, we will reap a harvest of blessing if we don't give up." (Galatians 6:8-10)

Today, sow love and reap God!

My Prayer for You Today:
Lord, today we sow love, peace, wisdom, faith, acceptance, friendship, and self-discipline. Father, we surrender our week to you and sow that which we wish to harvest. Be with us as we embark on this journey. We need you. We can't do it alone. We thank you for blessing us and preparing us for great things. We surrender our lives to you. We love you. Amen.

BLESS AND BREAK

"...then looking up to heaven, he blessed them and broke them..." Luke 9:16

We are all familiar with the story of Jesus feeding 5000 with five loaves and two fish. The faith in the story is often lost in the results. Today, I want to bring your attention to the process Jesus went through and the faith Jesus displayed and inspire you to do the same in your life.

Jesus looked up to heaven, then blessed and broke what wasn't enough! How many times have you looked to God, thanked, blessed and shared what seemed insufficient? Have you thanked Him for your gifts and shared them with the world, or are you thinking you're not gifted enough, not knowledgeable enough, not special enough? Have you thanked, blessed, and shared or are you too busy focusing on lack?

Until you can be thankful for something that is not enough, it cannot be multiplied to what is more than enough. Let this inspire you to trust Him when you don't have enough. Trust Him to multiply your lack and to bless you with more than enough. Look to Him. Be thankful for your lack of joy, lack of money, lack of health, lack of love, lack of direction, lack of clarity, because He will bless you abundantly with overflowing blessings in all areas of your life. Just like the story where there were leftover loaves and fish, you will have overflowing, leftover blessings. Trust Him!

Remember, He blessed them and broke them; the blessing is in the breaking! It is the breaking of life that produces the blessing of life. Today, trust Him in your brokenness. Take heart! God is getting ready to multiply and magnify your life to give you more than enough, to bless you beyond your imagination. Trust Him! Your brokenness will be used to bless you. It is a process. Take heart. Have faith. Trust Him.

God will bless your brokenness. Trust Him.

My Prayer for You Today:
Lord, in our brokenness we seek you. Thank you for reminding us today, Father, that you are a God who multiplies. Thank you, Lord, that you always provide. Father, today we take heart and trust you in every area of our lives. Thank you, Lord, for overflowing blessings and provisions. We look to you today. Be with us as we walk faithfully in your blessings. We praise you, we adore you. In Jesus's precious name we pray. Amen.

FEAST AND OVERFLOW

"He prepares a feast in front of my enemies... My cup overflows with blessings." Psalm 23:5

If you haven't experienced God's sense of humor, let this verse remind you that He has one! In front of your enemies, He displays your feast. God will give you the last laugh. He is a God of overflow, of more than enough, of abundance. Your cup will overflow with blessings!

For all those who doubt you, put you down, and crucify you; your success will be your testimony. God will bless you despite them and in front of them. His blessings will be your evidence. In due time, they will witness your feast. They will witness your success. They will be blinded by your victory.

Your cup will overflow with blessings. Dare to ask big. Dream big and receive big. God will bless you beyond your imagination. When you ask for crumbs, He will bless you with loafs. When you ask for one, He will bless you with a thousand. Trust Him for more than enough! Thank Him for your overflow.

Regardless of your situation today, do not be afraid, you will not be ashamed or disgraced. (Isaiah 54:4) God will pour out blessings so great that you will not have room for them. (Malachi 3:10)

Today, declare overflow!

My Prayer for You Today:
Lord, today we declare overflow blessings in every area of our lives. Thank you, Lord, that you are a God of abundance. Lord, in your name, we declare our blessings, our successes, our victories as our testimonies. Thank you, Father, for answered prayers. Thank you for overflow blessings of health and peace within our families, for overflow blessings of increase for our businesses and in our careers, for overflow blessings of grace, love, joy, clarity, and guidance. Open the floodgates of blessings on our lives. We thank you that it's already done! Amen.

MUSTARD SEED

"If you have faith as small as a mustard seed...nothing will be impossible for you." Matthew 17:20

You don't need a lot of faith today, just a little bit, as small as a mustard seed! With a little bit of faith, nothing will be impossible for you. God loves us so much that He is will reward faith as small as a mustard seed with the impossible. Wow!

Hang on to faith as small as a mustard seed to believe that your situation will change. With a mustard seed of faith, believe that you haven't seen your best days. With a mustard seed of faith remember that He hears you and knows your needs. Hang on to a mustard seed of faith for the assurance of things hoped for and the evidence of things not seen. (Hebrews 11:1)

When 99.99% of the odds are against you, 0.01% is your mustard seed! You feel like giving up, but faith as small as a mustard seed tells you to hold on and that God is loyal. You don't have a job, you're depressed, deflated, and down; faith as small as a mustard seed reminds you that this too shall pass. Hold on to your mustard seed!

Today, think of your impossible. What is your deepest desire? What is your biggest aspiration? What is your greatest hope? With faith as small as a mustard seed, be reminded that nothing is impossible for you. Nothing! Your wildest dream will come to pass, just have faith as small as a mustard seed. Your deepest desire will concretize, just lean on faith as small as a mustard seed. Whatever it is, hang on to it and believe in it with faith as small as a mustard seed. Today, know that you don't need a lot of faith, just a little, the size of a mustard seed!

Take heart, be empowered, because with faith the size of a mustard seed, nothing is impossible!

My Prayer for You Today:
Wow, Father, today we believe! We have faith as small as a mustard seed, Lord, and we believe in the impossible. Today, Lord, we believe in answered prayers, in open doors, in new breakthroughs, in new opportunities, in dreams come true, today we believe in miracles. Thank you, Lord, for rewarding our small faith with the impossible. You are an awesome God. We love you and praise you all the days of our lives. Amen.

HIS TIME

"My times are in your hands." Psalm 31:15

The better you know God, the more you realize that His timing is always perfect. Your times are in His hands. Trusting Him includes trusting His timing.

Everything in your life is right on time. Everything is happening the way it should. Your times are in His hands. Trust Him. Your blessings unfold according to His plans and His time. You are always under His watch, filled with His love, and wrapped in His grace. You will come to realize that God has always been and is always on time.

Had you walked out the door one second earlier, you would not have gotten your break. Had you not gone through the challenges, you would not have been ready for the blessings. Had you not taken that phone call, that trip, that route, you would not be where you are. Today, be assured that the blessings are right on time. The people you meet walk into your life at the right time. The miracles happen just when you need them.

Look back today and be grateful for all that has brought you to this day. Shout thank you for every experience that has shaped you. Today, know that delays are not denials. Trust His timing. Everything your heart desires will come to pass in due time. Trust Him.

Your times are in His hands.

My Prayer for You Today:
Father, we trust your timing. Thank you that your time is always the right time and thank you that right now we can experience your love, your grace, your abundance, and your loyalty. We declare today, Lord, that this is our season, our time! We declare that this is our time for deliverance, our time for abundance, our time for peace, our time for health, our time for joy. Thank you that it's already done! Thank you, Father, for your blessings. We thank you for your loyalty and for your love. We trust you and we trust your timing. We praise you for your goodness, Lord. Thank you. You are great! We love you. Amen.

LAUGH

"He will once again fill your mouth with laughter and your lips with shouts of joy." Job 8:21

Life has a way of stealing your joy, dulling your smile and silencing your laugh. No matter what you've been through, God will once again fill your mouth with laughter and your lips with shouts of joy.

Laughter is the best blessing! Allow yourself to receive that blessing for the silliest things—a joke, a tease, with others or by yourself. It doesn't have to make sense, it doesn't have to be a comedy show, simply allow yourself a great laugh today. There is a time for everything, a time to weep and a time to laugh; a time to mourn and a time to dance. (Ecclesiastes 3:4) Today is your day to laugh!

His joy and love are expressed in your laughter. God will let you laugh again. Go ahead and enjoy yourself. Laugh. Have fun. Relax. He is in control. God is pleased with you. (1 Peter 2:19) It brings Him great joy to see you laugh. Take time to laugh. Laugh like a child. Laugh at your mistakes. Laugh at your missteps. Laugh at your misunderstandings. Laugh until your stomach hurts. Let Him fill your mouth with laughter.

Today, laugh!

My Prayer for You Today:
Lord, today we thank you for laughter. We thank you for the many ways you bless us with laughter and friendship and fun and peace. Thank you, Lord, that it brings you great joy to see us happy. Today we declare happiness and laughter in our lives. Despite our challenges, Lord, we put our worries aside and commit to laughing today. We thank you for your blessings. We surrender our lives to you. Thank you for all you've done and all you plan on doing. We pray in Jesus's holy name. Amen.

NEW HEIGHT

"I will make you ride on the heights of the earth." Isaiah 58:14

Our God is a God of heights, higher than all others and above all. And God wants to take you to great heights, higher dimensions, with greater blessings. He promises to make us ride on the heights of the earth.

God is taking you higher. The petty arguments that usually upset you will no longer phase you. Small work will no longer challenge you. Your ways will change from mediocrity to greatness. You will no longer be pleased with the superficial, but you will be empowered by the authentic. God will make you ride to your highest potential. He will take you to new heights in your career and in your relationships. He will bless you with higher experiences, greater joy, and deeper peace.

As you experience new heights, you will begin to understand how wide, how long, how high and how deep His love is for you. (Ephesians 3:18) His love will shelter you while He takes you to higher dimensions. Though you may be paralyzed with fear, He will comfort you with His grace. (1 Peter 5:10) Though you may be uncertain and feel lost, you will walk by faith, not by sight. (2 Corinthians 5:7) Though you may stumble, you will not fall; He will make your step firm. (Psalm 37:23) You will rise above all.

God is great, higher than the heavens, higher than the farthest stars (Job 22:12) and He will take you to new heights. Be open to higher experiences in every aspect of your life. Move to higher ground and deeper peace. Ride on the heights of the earth!

Today, let God take you higher!

My Prayer for You Today:
Lord, thank you that you are higher than all. Thank you, Lord, that you will take us to higher grounds, to greater relationships and bigger experiences. Lord, we surrender our lives to you. Though we may experience fear, we trust you, Father. Be with us as we deepen our relationships with those around us, as we move to higher experiences, with great love and peace. We thank you that you are a God of heights. We thank you that your ways are higher than ours. We surrender all to you, in Jesus's precious name we pray, Amen.

GOD HEARS

"Father, thank you for hearing me." John 11:41

Today, you may feel discouraged, hopeless, and tired but remember that God hears you. Leave your worries to Him and thank Him for always hearing you. Thank Him right here, right now!

God hears your prayers. He hears your cries and knows your needs. God knows your needs before you ask Him. (Matthew 6:8). He knows when you sit, and when you rise. He knows your thoughts. (Psalm 139:2) He hears your prayers. (Psalm 65:2) His ears are open to our cries. (Psalm 34:15) Today, thank Him for hearing you.

Spend time thanking Him rather than begging Him. Thank Him for his blessings upon your life. Thank Him for dreams come true. Thank Him for you are wonderfully and fearfully made. Thank Him for meeting your every need. Thank him for right here, right now.

Today, take heart, be encouraged, find hope and ambition in knowing that He hears you. Wherever you are today, at your job or at the unemployment line, at school, at home, in abundance or in need, happy or sad, commit to doing your best. Remember that God knows your situation. He hears you. Surrender all to Him. He is more than able, more than willing, and more than powerful. God hears you.

He already knows, just thank Him!

My Prayer for You Today:
Lord, thank you that you hear us. Thank you, Lord, that even before we think, ask, and do, you already know. Thank you, Father, that you are guiding our steps. Lord, help us to be inspired and encouraged by you knowing that you hear us. Today we don't ask for anything, Lord, but we thank you for everything. Thank you for blessing us. Thank you for taking care of us, thank you for hearing us, Father. We surrender all to you. We love you, Lord. We adore you. In Jesus's name we pray. Amen.

QUIET LOVE

"He will quiet you with his love." Zephaniah 3:17

God will calm you in the midst of your storms. His love is enough to comfort you. God's love will quiet you and uphold you. In quietness and trust is your strength. (Isaiah 30:15)

You no longer have to fight your own battles. You don't have to speak up for your own defense. Nor do you have to convince others of your righteousness. Keep quiet and let God do the work. Like a mother who soothes her newborn, God will soothe you. His love will calm you. His tenderness will keep you still and safe.

Today, find your strength in His love. God loves you so much. You are safe in His arms. He is moving mountains for you. God is making circumstances work in your favor. He is opening new doors and new opportunities for you. Bask in His love. Relax in His everlasting arms. Find rest in His tenderness.

God's love is unconditional. His perfect love is with you. He loves you perfectly and wholly. Today find peace in His love. Let His love strengthen you. Find stillness in His everlasting arms.

Today, let God quiet you with His love.

My Prayer for You Today:
Lord, today I pray that you quiet us with your love. When we tend to worry and fear, remind us of how much you love us and are working for us. Thank you, Lord, for your unconditional love. Father, today we rest in your love. We find our strength in you. Be with us today as we radiate your love. Direct our steps. We surrender all to you. Amen.

IRON

"Iron sharpens iron." Proverbs 27:17

This is your call to surround yourself with people who love you. Spend time with those who support you. Be in company of those who help you grow. You may have to find new friends; you may have to stop answering certain phone calls. If you are going to head toward your destiny you need to surround yourself with those who will enhance your faith. You need sharpening from those who give you hope. You need individuals who make you believe, not doubt, people who celebrate you, not just tolerate you. Remember: iron sharpens iron.

This verse calls you to fellowship. Challenge, support, and grow others. "For we know, where two or more are gathered in His name, He is in the midst of us." (Matthew 18:20) There is power in numbers. Jesus shared that if two or three agree on something and ask for it, it will be done. (Matthew 18:19) Find fellowship. Sharpen someone and get sharpened.

Today, inventorize your life. Survey those around you. Are they building you up? Are they loving you? Supporting you? Sharpening you? And are you doing the same for them? Iron sharpens iron. Sharpen those around you with your gifts and talents. Sharpen them with your love, your attention, your creativity, and your presence. Sharpen them with your God given gifts. And let others sharpen you with their gifts.

God will sharpen you as He dwells in you and in the depth of your soul.

My Prayer for You Today:
Lord, today we surround ourselves with those who love you and want to serve you as they sharpen our lives and help us grow spiritually and closer to you. Help us to be a blessing to others as we thank you for using others to bless us. Lord, be with us today, sharpen us, make us brighter, stronger, more in tuned with you. Open the gates of Heaven on our lives. Help us to move toward our destiny, to do what we were made to do. You know our purpose, Lord, lead us, show us the way. We trust our lives in your hands. We surrender all to you, Lord. Amen.

HIS HANDS

"...God who holds in his hand your life and all your ways." Daniel 5:23

Your life is in His hands. Your life is in His hands. Your life is in His hands. What do you have to worry about? God gives you breath and holds you in His hands.

The One who created Heaven and Earth holds you in His hands. The Almighty, the Alpha and Omega has you in the palms of His hands. You are safe. You are loved. Your life is guaranteed to be a success, a blessing, and a testimony. You are in His hand.

In His hands is the life of every creature and breath of all mankind. (Job 12:10) In His hands are the depths of the earth. (Psalm 95:4) You are the work of His hands. (Isaiah 64:8) God holds you in His hands. He holds your life. He holds all your ways. He holds your dreams. God holds your destiny. He holds your fondest desires. He holds your deepest needs. God holds your greatest accomplishments. Every fiber of your being, all of you, is in His hands.

Though you do not know what the future holds, today rest in knowing who holds the future. The God of all gods holds your future. The God of all gods holds you. You have nothing to worry about. Everything will be just fine. He holds you in His hands.

God is holding you in His hands.

My Prayer for You Today:
Lord, today we let go and rest in your hands. Thank you, Lord, that you hold us in your hands. Thank you that all our ways, our destiny, everything is in your hands. Today we rebuke the spirit of fear and limitation and surrender to your love to feel safe in your hands. Direct us, Lord. Guide us today. Be with us as we journey through life as your servants and as your children. Let our lives be testimonies of your love. We love you. We praise you. Amen.

PAY ATTENTION

"My son, pay attention to what I say; listen closely to my words."
Proverbs 4:20

The same God who spoke to Moses in the desert is also speaking to you. Pay attention.

There are no coincidences. God speaks to you all the time through the people you meet, and through the circumstances you face. God speaks through the random book you pick to read. He speaks through the ideas that suddenly pop in your head. God speaks through your instincts and intuition. Pay attention to what God is saying. He is speaking. Pay attention.

God's Word tells us that we are his children, his workmanship, that he loves us and has great plans for us, that we are forgiven, that you are no longer slaves, but sons (Galatians 4:6). God speaks to His children. He is speaking to you. Listen. Pay attention.

Are you listening to God or to the voices in your head? Are you paying attention to His words or to your friends' ideas? Pay attention to Him. Listen to Him. His words will enlighten you. God will guide you. God will reveal the truth to you and empower you. His words are a lamp at your feet and a light unto your path. (Psalm 119:105)

God speaks your language. He is always speaking to you. Today, pay attention.

My Prayer for You Today:
Lord, speak to us today. Let us pay attention with an open heart and a sharp mind. Speak to us, Lord. Reveal your plans to us. Answer our prayers in ways that we will not doubt your voice. Speak, Lord! Today, Father let us all hear your voice and witness your love and power upon our lives. We surrender! Amen.

RISEN

"He is risen!" Matthew 28:6

The miracle of the resurrection displays the infinite power of God. It is a demonstration of His magnificence and His unconditional love. Jesus was crucified, died, and on the third day rose again. Wow!

Friend, the same God who raised Jesus from the dead is living in you. The same powerful, infinitely gracious and immeasurably loving God lives in you. (Take that in for a second. Breathe.) That Omniscient, powerful being lives in you. All of that grace, all of that love, all of it, resides in you. Wow!

Death could not limit Him and neither will your circumstances. God loves you so much that He is willing to perform the miracle of resurrection in your life. God will raise you from your current situation. He will answer your prayers. God will resurrect your dreams. Death did not stop Him from fulfilling His purpose through Jesus and your challenges and limitations will not stop Him from completing His work in you.

Celebrate the resurrection of Christ. Declare yourself risen to new heights. You have been risen to new opportunities and risen to blessings beyond measure.

He is risen!

My Prayer for you today:
Lord, wow! You amaze us! We thank you for the greatest gift of love. We are amazed by your power. Lord, today we pray for the same miracle in our lives, in every aspect of our lives and being. Raise us from dead circumstances, dead relationships, dead-end jobs and bring us to new heights in Jesus's name. We praise you, Lord. We thank you for Jesus's sacrifice and your miracle. Thank you! Thank you! Thank you, Lord. Amen.

KEEP PRAYING

"Be patient in trouble and keep on praying." Romans 12:12

Pray, pray, and pray some more!

Whatever you are going through today, be patient and keep on praying. Do not be discouraged. Keep praying! While you wait for the answer, keep praying. While you set another goal, keep praying. Be patient as you wait for the miracle and keep praying. Do not lose sight of your vision. Do not lose faith. Keep praying.

Pray while it hurts. Pray while you are down. Pray though you do not understand. Still pray while you disagree. Pray while you are angry with God. Continue to pray although you want to quit. Pray though it seems like God is not listening. Whatever it is, just keep on praying. The Bible reminds us to "Pray without ceasing," (1 Thessalonians 7:17) "Devote yourself to prayer," (Colossians 1:4) and to "Pray on all occasions." (Ephesians 6:18) Jesus told His disciples they should always pray and not give up. (Luke 18:1) And not to be "anxious about anything but with prayer and petition present your requests to God." (Philippians 4:6)

Friend, today you may feel overwhelmed, tired, and ready to quit, but at just the right time, your patience will be rewarded. The promise is worth the journey. The vision merits the struggle. The pain makes us appreciate the miracle. Today, keep praying!

My Prayer for You Today:
Father, today we choose to be patient and keep on praying. Though we're hurt, confused, tired, and ready to quit, we pray. We need you, Lord. Today we pray for healing, we pray for mending of hearts, we pray for broken relationships, we pray for peace, love, courage, we pray for blessings, we pray for answers, for guidance, for clarity. We need you. Answer us in Jesus's name. Amen.

SPEAK LIFE

"Whoever restrains his words has knowledge... even a fool who keeps silent is considered wise; when he closes his lips, he is deemed intelligent."
Proverbs 17:27-28

Today, restrain your words. Keep silent. And be wise.

People do not need to know your deepest thoughts. They do not need to share in your complaints. Your frustration and anger do not need to be vocalized. Be quiet. Vent to God. Speak to the One who can help, the True Counselor, the One who is able to handle anything.

"The prudent hold their tongues." (Proverbs 10:19) "The tongue has the power of life and death." (Proverbs 18:21) Be prudent. Be quiet. Choose your words wisely.

Today, commit to using your tongue to build. Be selective with your speech. Speak words of life. Hold your words of anger and frustration. Refrain from complaining and comparing. "What you say flows from what is in your heart." (Luke 6:45) Let your heart be full of love, peace, and understanding so that your words may color your life and the lives of those around you.

Speak life!

My Prayer for You Today:
Father, today help us to keep our lips shut from negativity. Let everything we say honor you and bring light to those around us. Father, speak through us. Speak words of love and peace. Lord, we need you to tame our tongues. Take over. We surrender all to you in Jesus's precious name. Amen.

OPEN GATE

"The gate… it opened for them of its own accord…" Acts 12:10

The story of Peter and his rescue is fascinating. Step by step, God led. Moment by moment, God delivered. This ought to bring you great hope and encourage you to trust Him!

Be encouraged. God will open doors for you. Things will workout on their own accord. Trust His timing. You don't have to know the entire way, God will lead you one step at a time. You don't have to understand how. God will open gates and break shackles. Trust Him!

God promises that He will deliver you. (Psalm 50:15) Call on Him and He will answer. (Jeremiah 33:3) Trust Him to open doors. Trust Him to line up divine appointments. Trust Him with the desires of your heart. Trust Him with your family, your children, your spouse, and all the details of your circumstances. He is faithful! He will open doors for you!

Today, find hope. If God did it for Peter, He will do it for you. Gates will open. Opportunities will arise. Shackles will be broken and blessings will be poured! He loves you that much! Trust Him!

My Prayer for You Today:
Father, thank you that you are faithful. Thank you, Lord, that you will open gates and pour out blessings. Father, today we anchor our hope in you. We thank you for blessings we couldn't have imagined. We thank you for divine appointments and perfect timing. Thank you, Lord, that you love us so much. Today we bask in your love and in your faithfulness, as we trust your perfect timing. Thank you, Father. Amen.

HEARING

"Faith comes from hearing the word of God." Romans 10:17

Let God's word build your faith. Faith comes from the word that never changes. Faith comes from the ultimate truth. Faith comes from hearing the Word of God.

Friend, you spend too much time hearing and listening to the world. The world tells you the economy is bad, the acts of violence are an epidemic, the foods you eat are causing cancer, and the books you read are filled with lies. Over and over you hear stories that fill you with fear, doubt, and worries. Those words are not of God.

God's Word brings hope and empowers. It reminds you that all things are possible with God. (Matthew 19:26) His Word builds your faith, and reminds you that no matter your circumstances, God will provide. God's Word gives you hope and a future. It assures you that in this world you will have tribulations but that you are never alone and God will never forsake us. (Deuteronomy 31:8)

Today, pay attention to what you are hearing and listening. If the words you listen to bring you fear and doubt; they are not from God. Build your faith by hearing the Word of God, which always brings light and hope.

Today, don't let the world fool you; let His Word feed you!

My Prayer for You Today:
Father, today we choose to believe and hear your word. Thank you, Lord, that your word brings hope and light. Thank you, Father, that your word empowers us and reminds us of your unconditional love. Help us, Lord, to focus on your word rather than others. We love you, Father. We surrender all to you knowing that you are the Alpha and Omega, the miracle-maker, the blessing-giver, and the ultimate lover. We love you, Lord. Amen.

GOD SAVES

"But everyone who calls on the name of the Lord will be saved." Acts 2:21

One call saves. One call delivers. One call restores. One call frees. Make the call to the One who saves. Today, call on God!

Friend, everyone who calls on the name of the Lord will be saved. Call on His name in times of desperation. Call on His name in time of despair. Call on Him in time of hopelessness, worry and fear. When your life is falling apart, call on Him and He will save you. When your troubles seem bigger than your faith, call on God. When things seem unjust and unclear, call on Him who saves!

Call on His name. He hears you and will save you. God is your comforter. He is your provider. God is your rock and your refuge. He hears your cries. Rather than calling your friends, call your God. He will save you from your fears. He will save you from those who persecute you. He will save you from your challenges. He will save you from wrong thinking and dark thoughts. Call on His name. Speak to Him, seek Him, turn to Him, vent to Him. God saves!

Everyone who calls on Him will be saved. When you call on God, you will be heard—never a busy signal, never an ignored call, always His saving grace and His unfailing love. Today, when you feel hopeless and have nowhere else to turn, call on Him and you will be saved.

Call on God!

My Prayer for You Today:
Lord, today we call on you to save us. Save us from wrong thinking, from our worries and fears, save us from those who persecute us and those who speak ill of us, save us, Lord, from our challenging situations and raise us to new heights in your name. Remind us today, Lord, to always call on you in all situations. Thank you that you always hear us and always save us. We lean on only you, Father. Thank you for your saving grace and your love. We pray in Jesus's precious name. Amen.

NO CONDEMNATION

"I do not condemn you… Go…" John 8:11

There is no condemnation for those who are in Christ Jesus. (Romans 8:1) None! Zero! Nada! No condemnation!

Your slate has been wiped clean. Stop beating yourself up. Stop reliving the past. No more drowning in regrets. So what if you lied? So what if you cheated? Yes you were hurtful, and yes you betrayed others, but what you did then is not a reflection of who you are now. If God doesn't condemn you, who are you to condemn yourself?

Friend, the minute you repent and confess, He is faithful to forgive you. (1 John 1:9) He automatically forgets your wrongdoing. He looks at you through the lenses of Jesus. He has made you righteous through Him. Stop replaying regrets and punishing yourself for something you have already been forgiven for. It's like making monthly payments to a credit card with a zero balance. Nonsense!

Today, go on with your day free of guilt, free of regrets, free of self-condemnation, because your Creator, who loves you unconditionally, has set you free indeed. (John 8:36) He has declared you righteous. "You are not in the realm of the flesh but are in the realm of the spirit." (Romans 8:9)

Smile!

My Prayer for You Today:
Father, thank you that you do not condemn us. Lord, you know our past; you know our shortcomings, yet you love us anyway. You amaze us! Your love humbles us. Thank you for a clean slate, thank you for freedom, thank you for forgiveness. Today we step out in faith, leaving behind the burden of guilt and shame. We surrender all to you in Jesus's precious name. Amen.

HEART

"God knows your heart." Luke 16:15

God knows your heart. He knows your intentions, your desires, sees beyond your circumstances, and knows you at the core of your being.

God doesn't see things the way you see them. People judge by outward appearance, but the Lord looks at the heart. (1 Samuel 16:7) The One who never changes looks at your heart and sees beyond flesh. God sees your intentions and your desires. He looks at your heart. And He loves what He sees.

God knows your intentions. He knows your heart, and more importantly, loves you regardless of others' judgments. Friend, don't fall for the trap of pleasing others and adhering to their opinions. It is between you and God! Don't let others' criticism and shaming cloud your vision. God knows your heart. And despite your missteps and poor actions, your heart remains pure and good as you seek God.

At the core of your being, God knows you. You do not need words to describe your desires to Him. You do not have to explain your intentions, nor defend your actions. He knows your heart. Your actions and intentions do not surprise Him but instead they allow Him to fill you with His love and grace.

He knows you. God knows your heart!

My Prayer for You Today:
Father, thank you that you see our hearts. Thank you, Lord, that you know our hearts are pure, and only seek to please you and serve you. Today, help us, Lord, to focus on you rather than to be pressured by others' opinion of us. We surrender our lives to you. Be with us, lead us. We pray all this in Jesus's name. Amen.

AGENT OF GRACE

"The word became flesh...full of grace and truth." John 1:14

Jesus is the ultimate Agent of Grace.

Grace allows you to enjoy things you do not deserve. We often celebrate the benefits of grace until grace is given to someone we dislike. The coworker who is lazy suddenly gets a promotion; the family who can already afford a vacation just won another giveaway; the not-so-cute gal just got engaged. Meanwhile, you have been waiting for your breakthrough, bitter and angry that others are receiving what they do not deserve.

His grace is sufficient. (2 Corinthians 12:9) We certainly do not deserve it, yet God's nature allows us to benefit from things we don't deserve. His grace allows us to enjoy things we didn't work for, and He lets us bask in His love and peace while we are still dysfunctional. He promises that He will give us houses we did not build, (Deuteronomy 6:11) vineyards we do not plant, (Joshua 24:13) and underserving forgiveness of sins and righteousness through Jesus. That's grace!

Today, be an Agent of Grace. Give people a break. Cut them some slack. Treat them well even if they don't deserve it. Smile and love them even if they betray you. Be kind even if they are rude. Jesus himself said: "it's not the healthy who need a doctor, but the sick." (Mark 2:17) Thus, those in need of your grace may be the most difficult individuals you encounter. They may be rude and mean. They may be negative. Give them grace anyway.

Today, be an Agent of Grace!

My Prayer for You Today:
Father, we are so underserving of your grace yet we reap the benefits. Thank you that you do not treat us based on what we deserve, but based on who you are. Today, Father, we are committing to being Agents of Grace in your name. Help us to be patient and kind, to be loving and forgiving. We love you, Lord and give you all the praise in Jesus's name. Amen.

GUARD YOUR HEART

"Above all else, guard your heart, for it is the wellspring of life." Proverbs 4:23

Life is a matter of the heart. Guard your heart, for it determines the course of your life. Today, be selective, be cautious, and let God reside in the depth of your heart.

Whatever comes out of your mouth comes from the heart. (Matthew 15:18) Those things either build or break your life. Caution! Guard your heart from anything that doesn't add value to you. Guard your heart from negative emotions. Guard your heart from negative people and hopeless circumstances.

Your heart is the wellspring of your life. It determines your actions. Your heart affects your journey. It influences your determination and determines the trajectory of your life. King Solomon advised followers to guard their hearts, as he understood the powerful effects the heart has on shaping one's life. Today, take his advice and guard your heart as it leads every area of your life.

Friend, God resides in the depth of your heart. Let Him determine the course of your life. God seeks to be the wellspring of your life. Keep Him in your heart. Put Him first in all areas of your life. Place God first in your relationships, your endeavors, your dreams, hopes and aspirations. Today, fill your heart with God and watch your life blossom.

My Prayer for You Today:
Lord, thank you for today. Thank you, Father, for guarding our hearts and for residing in the depth of our being. Be with us today as we live from an honest and pure heart and serve you. We surrender all to you. Fill us with your love and grace. We love you, Father. Amen.

SPEAK, BELIEVE AND BE RENEWED

"Having the same spirit of faith, according to what is written, 'I believed, therefore I spoke'... therefore we do not lose heart... though our outer man is decaying, our inner man is being renewed day by day..." 2 Corinthians 4: 13-15

The spirit of faith that lives in you is renewing you day by day!

Friend, words are like hammers, they can be used to build or to break. Today, choose to speak words that build. Speak that which you believe. Speak based on your faith, not your fears. Speak from the powerful Spirit within and not from the careless worries of the world. Believe and speak!

Today, do not lose heart. Speak! Do not get discouraged. Believe! God will complete the work He started in you. He will fulfill His promises in you. It doesn't matter how dire the circumstances may look, you have a God who is capable, a God who is willing and a God who loves you. There is nothing impossible with God. (Matthew 19:26)

Keep the spirit of faith. Believe. Speak. Be renewed!

My Prayer for You Today:
Lord, today, like the Apostle Paul, we will speak based on our faith in you. We will proclaim our healing, our deliverance, our success based on you and your loyalty. Father, thank you that you are faithful. Thank you for your unconditional love. Today we surrender our worries and cares to you and bask in your amazing grace and never-ending love. We love you and praise you. Amen.

MUCH FRUIT

"If a man remains in me and I in him, he will bear much fruit; apart from me you can do nothing." John 15:5

Let this be the recipe for your life. If you wish to be fruitful in all areas of your life, you must be rooted and established in God. It's that simple!

Apart from God you can do nothing. The life you worked hard to build on lies, fame, deceit, and corruption will eventually crumble. The relationships you built on control, fear, and jealousy will dissolve. Success without Him is short lived. Build your life on solid ground. Develop yourself through Him. He is the vine, we are the branches. (John 15:5)

Friend, the solution is simple: focus on God. Pray your heart out. Follow His lead. Put Him first in every situation. Don't let others deter you. Nothing is too small for His involvement—such as the pair of socks you want to buy—and nothing is too big for His control—such as your health, your finances, your purpose in life. Let God dwell in all the details of your life, let Him in every little nook and cranny.

Choose to bear much fruit in your relationships, your finances, your career, your health, and your success. Remain in God and be fruitful in love, peace, courage, and joy. Find abundance in Him. With God you can do all things. (Philippians 4:13)

Today, remain in Him and bear much fruit!

My Prayer for You Today:
Lord, today we choose to remain in you. We invite you to dwell in every little nook and cranny of our lives. We need you, Father. Thank you that we can do all things with you. Thank you, Father, that you have declared us fruitful in all areas of our lives. We thank you for your goodness and we thank you for your love. Be with us today. Let everything we touch grow. In Jesus's name we pray. Amen.

WEALTH

"Honor the Lord with your wealth." Proverbs 3:9

Too many of us have been turned off by the religious who condemn based on finances. We have all encountered those who preach against financial wealth, limiting the Most High to dollars.

Your wealth is not limited to your finances. You are far wealthier than your bank account can measure. Your wealth includes your gifts and talents, your presence and personality. Your wealth encompasses your entire being. If God blessed you with creativity, honor Him with it. If He blessed you with the ability to motivate and encourage people, use that wealth to honor Him. Whether you cook, clean, teach, preach, write, sing, or practice medicine, wherever lies your gift, lies your wealth and you should honor God with it.

Today, do not be fooled, we all know about tithing and honoring God with our finances, but God wants so much more than your money. He wants your gifts and talents. God wants your dreams and aspirations. He wants your heart. Honor Him with your wealth.

If you did not know you were wealthy, now you know. You are wealthy in love and in peace. You are wealthy in kindness, goodness, and grace. You are wealthy in brilliance and beauty. You are wealthy.

Go out and honor God with your wealth!

My Prayer for You Today:
Father, today we thank you for the privilege of honoring you with our wealth. We thank you for the gifts that you have given us, the gifts of personality and grace, the gifts of talent and passion, and today we give them all back to you in honor and glory. You continue to amaze us, Lord. We are so humbled by your love. We love you and praise you. Amen.

BEAUTY FOR ASHES

"The Lord will give you beauty for ashes, the oil of joy for mourning and the garment of praise for the spirit of heaviness." Isaiah 61:3

Your mourning, your ashes, your struggle will be rewarded. The blessings are the rewards! God will give you beauty for ashes!

Let this verse bring you hope. Today, trust that your prayers are being answered and your cries are being heard. Don't judge what's in you by what is around you. You may be suffering right now, but you have kings and nations in you. (1 Peter 2:9) You may be broke right now, but you have the Almighty in you. Your circumstances do not define you, God does!

Don't settle! Don't settle for less than God's best. God will give you joy for your mourning. Don't become satisfied with something that should only encourage you. Trust God to answer your prayers beyond your wildest dreams. Don't settle for good enough. God will grant your heart's wishes.

Today, know that your struggle is not in vain. Trust God as He prepares you for the mountaintop! Soon enough God will give you beauty for ashes! Take heart. Don't settle. Trust Him.

My Prayer For You:
Lord, thank you that you have great plans for us. Thank you, Father, that the blessings are the rewards. We hunger for you, Father. We are excited to see the rewards you have in store for us. Thank you, Lord. We surrender our lives to you, knowing that you have great plans for us and that you are always working for our good. We love you, Lord. We praise you. Amen.

DO NOT GIVE UP

"As for you, be strong and do not give up, for your work will be rewarded."
2 Chronicles 15:7

Keep up the good work!

Whatever you are facing today, take heart and keep pushing through. Whether you are trying to reach a fitness goal or a financial goal, every step counts. Whether you are building a home or building a business, keep up and do not give up. Slow progress is still progress. Do not give up. Your hard work and dedication will be rewarded. Your commitment makes a difference.

Today, be strong and do not give up. God sees every detail. He knows every effort. He will reward every sweat. He will compensate for every tear. Keep doing your best! Today, walk in to work with your head high. Lace your shoes with a strong spirit. Make another attempt with confidence. God will reward your work.

Your reward comes from Him. Stay focused. Stay encouraged. Be strong and do not give up!

My Prayer for You Today:
Father, today we seek encouragement and motivation from you. Thank you that our reward comes from you. Thank you that you see every tough decision and you know the depth of our struggle. We surrender all to you and keep our eyes on you as we press forward giving you all the glory, and giving you all the praise in Jesus's name. Amen.

GOD WORDS

"Gracious words are a honeycomb, sweet to the soul and healing to the bones." Proverbs 16:24

Be aware of your words. Let your words heal, build, support, and show love. Let them be sweet to the soul and healing to the bones.

Friend, words are powerful. Use them to speak life and abundance and peace into your life and to others. Use words to build, not break; to love, not hate; to support, not offend; to applaud, not criticize. Let your words to yourself and others reflect God's love for and loyalty to you.

Today, speak words of love, peace, support, admiration, and celebration. Speak those words to yourself and to others. Remind yourself of how amazing you are and how far you've come, regardless of your challenges. Love yourself with words and do the same to someone else today. Be your own cheerleader. Encourage. Build and love yourself by speaking His word into your life.

Speak His word!

My Prayer For You Today:
Lord, thank you that your Word builds. We surrender our lives and our speaking to you today. Let every word we say be of you and from you. Thank you, Father that you speak life, love, and abundance. Open the floodgates of blessings upon our lives. We thank you that it's already done. We praise you and adore you. Amen.

GOD EXAMPLE

"Don't let anyone look down on you because you are young, but set an example for the believers in speech, in conduct, in love, in faith, and in purity." 1 Timothy 4:12

Friend, people will look down on you for one reason or another. They may think you are too young or too old, inexperienced or outdated. They may judge your past, your dreams, your decisions—whatever it is, don't let the opinions of others affect you.

Let your life be a testament of God's love. Be an example of His love. Let your faith in Him be evident. While others may judge you because of your past, God knows your destiny. He understands your shortcomings and loves you despite it all. You are an example of God's work. You are an example of His unfailing love. You have experienced His loyalty. Your words reflect Him.

Today, set an example for others in speech, in conduct, in love, in faith, and in purity. (1 Timothy 4:12) Let others see God in everything you do. Speak His word. Love others. Be faithful and full of hope and integrity.

Be an example of God!

My Prayer For You Today:
Lord, show us how to be an example of you here on earth. Be with us today as we live in love, in integrity, and in faith. Use us, Lord, to bring hope to others. Use us to bless others. We surrender our lives to you and ask that you be in every detail of our lives. We trust you, Father, to open doors and answer prayers. Thank you that it's already done. We praise you. Amen.

GIVE MUCH

"From everyone who has been given much, much will be demanded; and from the one who has been entrusted with much, much more will be asked…" Luke 12:48

To whom much is given, much is required. God has been too good to you for you to settle for mediocrity. Let your greatness be your "thank you" to God for all his blessings. Today, God is asking more of you because He's given so much to you.

Friend, God is asking a lot of you, because there's a lot in you. Don't be flustered. You got this! Flow with it. God has gifted you and entrusted you with much. You are fully loaded and equipped through Him to live a great life. Let greatness seep out of your pores.

Your current situation, dysfunctional family, demanding job, stressful finances, diminishing health, challenging relationships have all been entrusted to you. God knows you can handle all of it and that you can change them all. God trusts you to move from your situation to your destiny. Greatness is in you! Use every circumstance, every situation and every challenge to serve Him, to reflect His love, and to thank Him for trusting you.

Today, respond to God's demand of you. Give more. Do more. Love more. Be more!

My Prayer For You Today:
Lord, thank you for trusting us and demanding more of us. Today we are surrendering to your demands and open our lives to serve you in more ways. We thank you for trusting us so much, we thank you for giving us opportunities to love you and love our neighbor. Fill us with your love and grace as we serve you this week. Be with us, Father. We need you. We love you and praise you. Amen.

FOCUS ON GOD

"Keep me from paying attention to what is worthless, Lord. Give me life through your word. " Psalm 119:37

Friends, let this be your prayer today—that you may focus on those things that are praise worthy and positive in your life and be renewed by His word.

Rather than paying attention to the problems in your life, focus on the power in your life. Too often we know exactly what we don't want but we are uncertain about what we do want. We know exactly the type of marriage we don't want, the type of job we despise, the friends we choose not to have and the financial problems we want to avoid. Those things are worthless. Spend your time praying to God for what you desire!

Another version of this verse specifies, "Turn my eyes from looking at vanity." Anything that fades is vanity! The grass withers and the flowers fade but the Word of God stands forever. (Isaiah 40:8) Today, pay attention to His word. Anchor your life on His promises. Stand on Him. Stand in faith.

Today, focus on the power in your life and leave the worthless behind. There's life in His Word. May you be empowered, rejuvenated, and motivated by God and may all the debris of life fall out of your thinking.

Today, stop paying attention to junk and focus on God!

My Prayer for You Today:
Lord, today keep us focused on you. Keep our minds and hearts on you. Thank you that as we focus on you, you will empower us and guide us. Fill us with your love today. Guide our steps. Lead us into success, happiness, joy, and peace. Thank you that it's already done. Amen.

AROMA OF CHRIST

"For we are the aroma of Christ to God." 2 Corinthians 2:15

When people walk by you, do they smell Christ? Before you open your mouth, people ought to smell God on you. Your life should exude His love and His grace. When you walk in a room, before you introduce yourself others ought to see something different about you. That something is God!

Friend, you are the aroma of Christ. (2 Corinthians 2:15) You are the light of the world. (Matthew 5:14) You are the salt of the earth. (Matthew 5:13) There is something different about you. Your life should display God without you uttering a word.

Today, ask yourself, "Do people see Christ when they see me?" "Do I have the aroma of Christ?" "Does my life smell like love?" When people experience you, do they experience Him? Today, it doesn't matter what you say, your life has an aroma that is obvious long before you come close to someone and that lingers long after you leave. Let that aroma be the aroma of Christ—an aroma of light, love, forgiveness, generosity, positivity, encouragement, and hope.

You are the aroma of Christ!

My Prayer for You Today:
Father, thank you that you value us so much that you declared us the salt of the earth, the light of the world and the aroma of Christ. Lord, what an honor it is for us to hold such titles. Today we ask for your grace and your courage to live as the aroma of Christ. Help us to display Jesus-characters and love and serve others like He did. We surrender all to you, Father. Be with us today. We love you and praise you. Amen.

LOOK WITHIN

"The Kingdom of God is within you." Luke 17:21

This verse is the best-kept secret. Whatever you can imagine about the kingdom of God, the heavens, the beauty, the abundance, the awesomeness, all of it is within you. Wow!

You may have searched for validation from family, friends, relationships, career, academic accomplishment, monetary gains, materialistic attainment only to feel disappointed, dissatisfied, unfulfilled, and seeking more meaning. Let this verse remind you that you already have that which you are seeking. You have the Kingdom of God within you.

Friend, don't look for it outside of yourself. It's all within! Don't waste another minute seeking validation and acceptance from the world. At your core, you have it all! The Kingdom of God is within you!!! His kingdom—the kingdom of our mighty God—is within you. Yes! That's a cause for celebration.

The kingdom of God is righteousness, peace, and joy. (Romans 14:17) All of it is within. All of the joy, love, peace, wisdom, courage, and hope you seek is within you. God is within you!

Today, don't look out. Look within!

My Prayer for You Today:
Lord, thank you that all that you are is within us. Thank you, Father, that you loved us so much that you placed all goodness, all capabilities, all miracles within us and that we don't have to beg and search for them amongst the world. Thank you, Father. Help us today to get connected to you from within. Be with us as we seek and find you in the most intimate way. We thank you that it's already done! In Jesus's precious name we pray. Amen.

NO HARM, NO WORRIES

"The Lord will keep you from all harm….He will watch over your life."
Psalm 121:7

Friend your motto today is "No harm, no worries," because God is watching over your life! God promises to keep you from all harm. And God keeps his promises.

Don't be troubled by trouble. God is watching over your life. Those who attack and criticize you are not harming you. Let them talk. Those who have ill wishes towards you cannot affect you. Let them wish. Your life is in God's hands. No one can change God's mind about you. It is impossible to change His mind. He alone determines your fate. Your miracles come from Him. Your blessings come from God.

God has you in a protective bubble, filled with His love, His grace, and His peace. You are protected. You are loved. No one can harm you. It's between you and God! God is watching over your life. God is opening new doors for you. He is pulling the strings behind the curtains like a great puppeteer. You are safe. Rest in Him.

Speak your truth. No harm, no worries, God is watching over you!

My Prayer for You Today:
Father, thank you that no harm can come our way when you are our keeper and watcher. Thank you, Lord, for protecting us and leading us. Help us today to keep our eyes on you and not be distracted by the noise of the world. Keep us in your peace, Father. Renew us. Fill us with purpose and strength and motivation to do your work. We surrender all to you, Father. We praise you. We love you. Amen.

KEEP SILENCE

"The Lord will fight for you while you keep silent." Exodus 14:14

The battle is not yours. While you remain still and at peace, God will fight for you. Friend, life has a way of getting you agitated and angered. Your role is to keep silent. God's got it!

God will fight for you. No need to plan your revenge. You do not have to think about defending yourself. You do not have to respond. God will let no harm come your way. God Himself will fight for you. God has not let you down yet, and He will not let you down now. God doesn't lose. The battle has already been won!

Keep silent. Don't utter another word against those who offend you. Be still. Don't attempt to speak your mind or defend your position. Be silent. Be still in Him. God is handling everything. Stand in faith. Stand in trust. Stand in God.

Today, let your silence speak!

My Prayer for You Today:
Lord, help us to keep silent as you fight for us. Keep us in your peace, Father. We surrender our trials and tribulations to you. Remind us that you are preparing us for something better. Thank you, Father, for being in control. We trust you. Let no weapon formed against us prosper. We surrender all to you in Jesus's precious name. Amen.

INSTRUMENT

"He is a chosen instrument of mine to carry my name..." Acts 9:15

God chose you as His instrument!

Your life is not your own. You were not born to wonder aimlessly. You were not created just to exist. You are not meant struggle through life. You have much more worth and significance. You were created to be an instrument of God. You were made to carry His name. Your purpose is to shine His light. You are an instrument of His love.

God chose you! He chose you because He knew you could do it. He chose you because He trusts you with His legacy. He chose you because you are the best person for the job. God chose you!

Today, if you didn't already know it, you are a chosen instrument of God. You are empowered by His spirit to love like He loves you, to serve like He serves you, to give like he gives to you, to forgive like He forgives you, to shine like He continues to shine upon you.

You have a responsibility. Take it seriously. You are God's chosen instrument!

My Prayer for You Today:
Father, thank you for choosing us. We are so humbled by your favor. Lord, we certainly do not feel worthy, but today we accept the role of your instrument in this world. Use us, Lord. Use us to bless your children, to love and serve you through your children. Empower us to shine in a world full of darkness. Keep us safe and wrap us in our grace as we serve you. We love you, Lord. Amen.

MOTHERS

"Do not forsake your mother's teaching." Proverbs 6:20

Do not neglect your mother's teaching.

Many mothers have shaped you. One carried you in her womb while others carried you in their hearts. Women have cared for you, given you advice, been an example to you, and loved you. From your biological mother, aunts, family friends, teachers, mentors, God has blessed you immensely with women who have taught you about life. Today, be grateful.

May you be filled with the love of the women in your life. Be reminded that God loves you through them. Savor your mother's teaching. Celebrate her unconditional love.

Today, be grateful for the imprint of your mother on your soul!

My Prayer for You Today:
Lord, today we are so thankful for the women you have placed in our lives. Thank you, Father, for nurturing us through them. Thank you for teaching us through their examples and their words. We uplift them today, Father, and ask that you bless them abundantly. Let their kindness and love be rewarded, Father. We thank you for them today. We love you, Father, we praise you, in Jesus's precious and holy name. Amen.

SHEPHERD

"He had compassion on them because they were like sheep without a shepherd." Mark 6:34

So many of us go through life like sheep without a shepherd. We are lost in our thinking. We lack direction and guidance. We venture alone or associate with the wrong crowd. We fascinate over new doctrines today and reject them tomorrow. We are fooled by a theory today and find a new one next week. Thankfully, Jesus had compassion for the lost and provided guidance for those living like sheep without a shepherd.

"The Lord's people will not be like sheep without a shepherd." (Numbers 27:17) We have a God who is there to guide and provide, to direct and lead. "If any of you lacks wisdom, you should ask God." (James 1:5) Within you lives the Alpha and Omega. The Creator who is all-knowing and all-loving resides in you. You have a Shepherd who never sleeps. You belong to a Shepherd who will never let you venture aimlessly. Follow your Shepherd.

Today, don't act like a sheep without a shepherd. You are a child of God. He has great plans for you. Stop chasing the world and focus on Him. He is more than able to guide you. He is more than willing to lead you. And He will bless you abundantly.

Today, follow your Shepherd!

My Prayer for You Today:
Lord, thank you that we are your children. Thank you that you are our shepherd and you lead us to prosperity and success. Forgive us, Father, for chasing the world, rather than seeking you. Today, help us to keep our eyes on you as we surrender all that we are and all that we will be to you. We love you and praise you. Amen.

HIS THOUGHTS HIS WAYS

"So are My ways higher than your ways and My thoughts than your thoughts." Isaiah 55:9

Friend, your highest thought is God's lowest thought. Your highest accomplishment is His lowest. I pray you understand the magnitude of this scripture and the enormity of God.

His ways and His thoughts are higher than yours. When you are facing a situation and you can't think your way out of it, let God do the thinking. When you can't find your way and you feel lost and misguided, let God lead the way. When things seem uncertain and unclear, let Him be the lamp for your feet and the light on your path. (Psalm 119: 105)

You cannot fathom the way God thinks. The magnitude of His love and grace is unimaginable. The grandeur of His creativity is indescribable. So today, rest in knowing that He is bigger than you can imagine, more powerful than you can comprehend. There are no words to describe Him. Your understanding is too limited to grasp His depth.

Rejoice in your ignorance and celebrate His greatness. Find peace in knowing that there is nothing too big for Him to handle. Magnify His power and not your troubles. Attempt to understand His ways and not the world's. Have faith that His ways are higher than yours and that with Him nothing is impossible.

Today, rest in His thoughts and find peace in His ways.

My Prayer for You Today:
Lord, we cannot fathom your magnitude. You who created the galaxies, the earth, the deep ocean, you *amaze us. Thank you today that your ways are higher than ours, and your thoughts are higher than ours. We thank you that despite your grandeur you care for us and we are a priority to you. Thank you, Father. We surrender all to you. Help us today to understand the depth of your love and to live from a place of peace and faith knowing that nothing is too big for you. Thank you, Father. We praise you today. Amen.*

ENGRAVED

"I have engraved you on the palms of my hands." Isaiah 49:16

Wow, you are engraved on God's hands!

Today, bury the lies once and for all. Get rid of the lies that made you think He abandon you. Forget the ridiculousness that made you feel forsaken and forgotten. Drop the fabrications that made you believe that He doesn't care and doesn't love you. Leave behind the foolishness that made you think He doesn't know you. Bury the lies once and for all.

The truth is: your Creator knows you. He loves you. He delights in you. And He has you engraved on the palms of His hands. He knew you before you were formed. (Jeremiah 1:5) His love for you is without condition. He has removed your transgressions and forgotten and forgiven your shortcomings. When God looks at you, He smiles. He is pleased with you and He is in awe of you.

Today, know that God has engraved you on the palms of His hands. You are loved. You are valued. God loves you. Stand in the freedom of His love. *Stand in faith.* You are forever imprinted in His heart. He loves you. The Creator of the universe delights in you. He thinks you are to die for. He loves you that much. The Almighty God has you engraved on His hands. He loves you. He really, really, really loves you!

You are ENGRAVED!

My Prayer for You Today:
Lord, today we just want to thank you for engraving our names, our souls, our desires, our everything on the palms of your hands. Father, your love continues to amaze us and humble us. You are so amazing! You are so awesome! We thank you for your love. Lord, if we ever forget how valuable we are to you, please remind us. We surrender all to you and praise you today and everyday in Jesus's name. Amen.

ACKNOWLEDGEMENTS

So many people have come into my life and made my journey wonderful. I have so much to be thankful for and many to acknowledge:

I want to first acknowledge the men who have loved me and been by my side throughout this growing process and throughout my journey as an author: my father, Bob, and my brother, Axel. The dream came true because you built it with me. Dad, thank you for the nights at the kitchen counter when I was paralyzed with fear, when you believed in me more than I believed in myself. Ax, words could never express my love and gratitude for you. Thank you for your love, your support, and your sweat. Thank you for motivating me and loving me through it all. This means more to me because I get to share it with you. Thank you to my older brothers Luco and Ibob. Luco, you have been my lifelong cheerleader and for that I am so grateful. Bi, thank you for being my comic relief, my source of drama, and my soul companion. I love you both very much.

To my children, Benie and Dubby, thank you for being patient with me. Thank you for motivating me to dream big while you ate frozen pizzas and listened to my long philosophical theories of life. Benieboo, your ethics and discipline never cease to amaze me. Dubbydoo, your joy for life and infectious laughter warm my soul. "Ma" loves you both more than words could ever convey.

To the many women who have loved me, supported me, and shaped me: thank you. Mom, without you there is no me. I haven't always been the easiest and nicest daughter, but you have always been the most supportive and loving mother. To my grandmothers, Mamie Maud and Mamie Ger, your spirits ignite in me a flame that will never die. I bet you two are up there enjoying the book and bragging about your "Nounou." To my many girlfriends who have colored my life with friendship, laughter, and fun, I thank you from the bottom of my heart: Amy Foote, Marchelle Moten, Natalie Georgeon, Deanna Green, Nathalie Vertus, Amy Kallioinen, Ashley Flowers, Tynisha Meidl, Kenya Hubbard, Vanessa Soukar, Lisa Douyon, Stephania Tassy. I love you, sisters!

To Brian and Carole Weiss, thank you for opening my life to a new dimension. Thank you for teaching me that *Only Love is Real* and reminding me that we are all connected. I am forever humbled by your friendship, love and attention.

To my avid Gilgal Devotionals readers, thank you for your words of encouragement. Thank you for keeping me accountable and emailing me every time the devotionals were late. Thank you for praying for me. Thank you for letting God use me as a vessel in your life to share His love. Thank you for your continued love and support. You mean more to me than I could ever express. From the bottom of my heart, thank you.

CPSIA information can be obtained
at www.ICGtesting.com
Printed in the USA
FFOW02n1936161016
28500FF